STILL ALRIGHT

STILL ALRIGHT

A MEMOIR

KENNY LOGGINS

WITH JASON TURBOW

hachette
BOOKS

NEW YORK

Hachette Books
Hachette Book Group
1290 Avenue of the Americas
New York, NY 10104
HachetteBooks.com
Twitter.com/HachetteBooks
Instagram.com/HachetteBooks

First Edition: June 2022

Published by Hachette Books, an imprint of Perseus Books, LLC, a subsidiary of Hachette Book Group, Inc. The Hachette Books name and logo is a trademark of the Hachette Book Group.

The Hachette Speakers Bureau provides a wide range of authors for speaking events. To find out more, go to www.hachettespeakersbureau.com or call (866) 376-6591.

The publisher is not responsible for websites (or their content) that are not owned by the publisher.

Editorial production by Christine Marra, *Marra*thon Production Services. www.marrathoneditorial.org

Print book interior design by Jane Raese.
Set in 11-point Adobe Caslon

Library of Congress Control Number: 2022932450

ISBNs: 978-0-306-92536-8 (hardcover); 978-0-306-83049-5 (signed edition); 978-0-306-83050-1 (B&N signed edition); 978-0-306-92537-5 (ebook)

Printed in the United States of America

LSC-C

Printing 1, 2022

CONTENTS

INTRODUCTION

THIS STORY DOESN'T START with a disappearing truck, but it certainly fucking feels like it.

In 1989, two things happened at once that would deeply impact my career. The first was that I began recording what would become my *Leap of Faith* album. The second was that Don Ienner became the president of Columbia Records. I'd been with Columbia since the very beginning, through eight Loggins & Messina albums and seven solo ones. I'd sold millions of records and reached the top of the charts—just not that much of late. It had been three years since "Danger Zone" and five years since "Footloose." Given that I hadn't had a top-10 album since 1978, company execs were beginning to wonder if I still had it.

Among Ienner's first orders of business was to figure out the label's obligations, and when he got around to reviewing my contract, he saw that

I was already $500,000 into studio costs (and counting) for *Leap of Faith*, and not a person on his staff had actually heard the music.

From where I sat, though, that half mil was money well spent. So much music was pouring through me that *Leap of Faith* had all but written itself, every word and note falling perfectly into place. Melodic ideas scored my dreams so frequently that I kept a tape recorder next to the bed. For the first time in my life, I could imagine complete songs as if they were playing on my stereo. The arc of the album was following the arc of my life, and I was writing it all as it unfolded before me. I innately understood everything I wanted the music to be.

Columbia had recently been acquired by Sony, and the new boss was busy slashing the slumping label's artist roster, ultimately cutting loose a third of the acts. I had already spent a ton of their money on my new record, and it wasn't even finished yet. I grew nervous. Would I be the next to go?

The West Coast head of A&R for Columbia, a guy named Ron Oberman, certainly thought so. He lobbied Ienner to drop me from the label as part of the overall house-cleaning efforts. Luckily for me, my old friend Bobby Colomby—the founding drummer of Blood, Sweat & Tears—had recently become the senior VP for creative development, not just for Columbia Records but for all of Sony Music. When Ienner called Bobby to get his take on who he might cut from the label, Bobby convinced him I should stay by promising to personally shepherd my new project.

Apparently, Colomby and Oberman had quite the confrontation over it. The urban legend is that Bobby held Ron out of a second-story window until he reassessed his position. I doubt anything like that actually happened, but Bobby's a native New Yorker and I wouldn't put it past him. At the very least, it illustrates the kind of passionate support he gave me.

Before too long, I received word that Don wanted to hear what I'd recorded. He set a meeting for a month out. Trouble was, *Leap of Faith* was still in bits and pieces at that point—I didn't even have any rough mixes ready to show him, let alone all the overdubs I had planned. None of the songs even sounded like a record yet. I had a lot of work ahead of me to make it right, and it was increasingly clear that Donnie's opinion would be the deciding factor when it came to my future with Columbia. Yeah, I was stressed.

As it happened, Ienner's message arrived just as I was packing up my operation for a move from LA to Santa Barbara. By that point, the basic tracks were in place and I wanted to do the overdubs—my vocals, a ton of percussion, and lots of secondary instrumentation—closer to home. Into the truck went our amps, guitars, microphones, stands, and speakers, along with two Mitsubishi 32-track digital recorders and the big eighteen-inch reels containing the master tapes. I had thirty days to get everything ready for my big meeting, and I needed every minute of them.

Then it all went sideways.

It's only a ninety-minute drive from LA to Santa Barbara, an easy hop, but after an all-nighter at the studio, the guitar tech driving the van decided to stop at home for a shower and a quick nap. That's when the truck was stolen.

It was just fucking gone.

Bobby called me at home with the news. I couldn't have cared less about the instruments or the recorders. Those were replaceable. My master tapes, though, were priceless—the sum of twelve months of steady toil put into the album.

I still had the slave reels, though that was small consolation. In the days before unlimited digital tracking, "slaves" were mixed down from master recordings to leave as much space as possible for overdubs, which could then be transferred back to the original, high-quality master. It's unfortunate terminology, but it was industry standard back then. The recording quality on the tapes in my possession was unacceptable for an official release, let alone a career-saving preview for Columbia's new boss. They were good enough for me to take cues from, and not much else.

This is going to sound weird, but when I heard my tapes were missing, I didn't panic. Not even a little. There's no logical explanation for it, but despite every upsetting detail, I knew instinctively that things would turn out okay. Really, I had only one decision to make: I could return to LA and rerecord the basic tracks in a hurry, or I could proceed as if nothing had happened and continue to overdub on my slaves, according to the original plan. If the masters failed to emerge, the quality would be far too low for Ienner to approve. Add to that the expense of rerecording everything, and my time with Columbia would almost certainly be over. *Leap of Faith* would probably never see daylight.

So I took a literal leap of faith.

I knew in my bones that those tapes would return. Not hoped. *Knew.* And not eventually, but in time for my meeting with Ienner. This was the record I'd been waiting all my life to make, coming to me in waves of inspiration like nothing I'd experienced before. How could all this music be flowing through me only to end up lost and abandoned?

The decision was instantaneous for me, obvious almost as soon as Bobby told me what had happened. In fact, I laid out my plan during that very same phone call. Bobby was too despondent to even offer a pretense of reassurance. "I'm so sorry, dude," he said. "This is a disaster, really. What are you going to do?"

Somehow I found myself talking *him* off of the ledge. "It's going to be okay, Bobby," I said. He probably thought I'd lost my mind.

"Are you saying you're going to rerecord the masters?" he asked.

I smiled at what should have been a devastating question. "Nope," I said. "I'm gonna keep going as if nothing happened, then I'll mix it all together when the truck shows up."

Bobby took a long breath. "Can I have some of what you're taking?" he whispered.

I had no idea how any of this would happen, of course, only that it was a certainty. I kept working away on those slaves, adding a one-of-a-kind performance by synth wizard John Barnes, some vocal harmonies by Mavis Staples, and an amazing David Lindley slide-guitar solo while I waited for the good news.

A week went by, then two. No word. I kept working. Three weeks. Now we were counting days.

Five days before the biggest meeting of my career, it happened: my manager, Shep Gordon, called to tell me the truck had been located just a few blocks from where it was stolen. "There were about a dozen tickets on the windshield," he said. "Obviously we were the recipients of some expert sleuthing by our local police department." I'm pretty sure he was joking about that last part. I was thrilled by the news, right up until Shep told me the cargo box had been cleaned out, every instrument gone. Those Mitsubishi recorders were probably already being parted out in Mexico.

Oh shit. What about my master tapes?

I stopped breathing, hoping there was more. There was. The only items left behind, Bobby said, locked up safe in the cab, were my tapes—all four master reels.

The more I thought about it, the more I wondered if somebody connected with the studio, maybe a recording engineer, had been in on the heist. Those instruments were valuable, but the tapes weren't worth much to anybody but me. Whoever did it clearly knew enough about what was going on to secure them up front. So whoever you are, thanks for that . . . I guess.

Within twelve hours, my engineer and co-producer, Terry Nelson, was piecing together songs, dubbing new tracks we'd recently recorded onto the master reels. We worked around the clock for four days straight. Our final task involved cutting a special version for my meeting with Ienner—a digital audio tape with all the instrumentation but none of my lead vocals. Bobby had insisted I perform those live. "It'll be like a personal concert," he said. "You'll blow him away." I'd never heard of anyone doing something like that. It was unorthodox and risky, but hell, so was my album. I agreed. Yeah, the meeting was that important.

On barely any sleep, we wrapped things up with only hours to spare.

The next morning I drove to the Beverly Wilshire Hotel, where Ienner had a cabana in the gardens out back.

First, though, I had a stop to make. Shep was auctioning off a wall from his office for charity. It had been autographed by some of the world's most prominent performers, and he wanted me to add my name before it was removed from the premises. I ended up signing underneath Raquel Welch and Cher, and wrote one thing more, something Geronimo once said to his warriors before sending them into battle: "It is a good day to die." If you were going to war, the theory went, fight as if you were already dead, and you'd have nothing to lose. Given my upcoming meeting, it seemed appropriate.

From there I headed to the Beverly Wilshire, where I found Ienner in his cottage. Colomby was already there. Donnie welcomed me in and plopped down on a couch. "I'm really excited to hear this," he said. Well, so was I.

I put the DAT into the stereo, took a deep breath, and gave my first-ever one-man concert for a two-person audience. As I sang, I kept watching Donnie for clues. He seemed to be enjoying it, but I couldn't be sure. At one point he said, "Only you would rhyme 'exist' with 'precipice.'" I took that as a good sign.

When the final notes of "Too Early for the Sun" faded from the speakers, I held my breath. Donnie didn't make me wait long to let me know what he was thinking. He let out a long sigh, rose from the couch, and actually hugged me. "I don't know if we'll sell only a few records or millions," he said. "I'm just proud to have this one on Columbia."

They probably could have heard my sigh of relief in Santa Barbara.

Ienner backed up his sentiments with Columbia's checkbook. The label not only devoted a considerable budget to advertising and marketing, but gave me extra money to finish the record. *Leap of Faith* ended up spending fifty-eight weeks on the *Billboard* charts. Luckily for me, the adult contemporary radio format was taking off at just that time, and my new stuff was perfect for it. Radio stations played my song "The Real Thing" for so long that my promo guys had to call stations and ask them to stop because it was delaying the release of our next single, "Conviction of the Heart." Then they played *that* song forever. After that, they moved on to "Now or Never."

Through all my years in the industry, I'd never had three singles released from one album.

Thanks to Donnie's belief in the record, *Leap of Faith* had five. It continues to be the favorite piece of work I've ever done.

CHAPTER 1

CALIFORNIA HERE WE COME

SHORTLY BEFORE I was born, my father, making a Christmas promise I'm pretty sure he never expected to keep, told my oldest brother, Bobby, that if I arrived on his birthday he could name me.

Bobby turned seven on January 7, 1948, and I came into the world just a few hours after he blew out his birthday candles. This is how, for a short while, anyway, Dad paid off his promise and I was known as Clark Kent Loggins.

Thankfully, my father considered the potentially harsh reality of saddling a kid with such a name, and convinced Bobby to change things up. So I became Kenneth Clark Loggins. I guess that kinda makes me a singer-songwriter version of Superman.

That my dad sold my brother on changing my name isn't too surprising, since he was a salesman by trade. As far as I know, he had always been a salesman, a real-life Willy Loman, selling whatever he could to get by. He possessed an easy charm and relaxed style, akin to his pop idol, Bing Crosby. He always seemed to have a pipe between his teeth and a porkpie hat atop his head. He seems like a good place to start this story.

Robert George Loggins grew up in Butte, Montana, the fourth of Harry and Stasia's eight children, and in 1940 moved with the family to Seattle. In his twenties, during the Great Depression, when everybody worked the angles in order to survive, my dad and some friends piled into a Star touring car and traveled down the coast, passing themselves off as seminarians working their way through school by selling subscriptions to the *Franciscan Herald*. They'd stop at Catholic parishes and convince the priests to entreat their Sunday parishioners to support this holy cause. None of it was true, of course, except for the part about the subscriptions—and my dad's commission.

What Dad really wanted, I think, was to reach Los Angeles and become a movie star. As soon as his group reached Hollywood, my dad jumped ship and moved in with a friend he knew from back in Montana. Years later, I found a photo taken of him during this time. It looks remarkably like a publicity shot: my dad dressed up in a black smoking jacket, lounging casually like John Barrymore in white bucks, smoke curling up lazily from the cigarette in his hand. I asked my father about it late in his life, and he explained it away as a spur of the moment thing he did as kind of a joke. I don't buy it. I believe the picture tells the story of a young man who was headed to Hollywood all along.

His dream came crashing down when his new wife ran off with his best friend. (Did I mention that he got married? Neither did he. It was a family secret until I was in my thirties. Seems he met a girl in Hollywood and married her—and lost her—within the span of a year.) The breakup left my father so devastated that he developed a nearly fatal case of pneumonia. He couldn't get out of bed, and refused to eat. His sister Rita had to come down from Seattle and drive him back home. Thus ended Robert Loggins's Hollywood dream, at least until I came along.

Returning to Seattle, though, wasn't all bad. That's where he met my mom, Lina Massie, and raised three children, so it worked out okay for him in the end. It certainly did for me.

My dad's most successful business venture was with a small costume jewelry company called Sarah Coventry, for which he traveled all over Washington State hosting in-home parties much like Tupperware sales-people would famously do in the 1950s. He was so successful at moving large quantities of inexpensive bracelets and necklaces that management offered to transfer him to the company's new territory in Southern California.

The plan was for my father to go down ahead of the rest of the family and find us a place to live. I was only six years old, but I vividly remember him asking whether I'd like to join him. I was the only one of us kids he asked along, and boy was I thrilled. Dad had been on the road selling things for most of my young life, and I barely knew him. One rainy Monday morning he pulled me from my first-grade classroom, and we hit the highway. I didn't know it at the time, but that trip would change my life. (I do wonder what my career would have looked like had I grown up as a Seattle musician. Hard to imagine Loggins & Messina as a proto-grunge band.)

Along the way we stayed in the kind of small, neon-lit 1950s motor lodges that US Route 99 was known for. I don't recall visiting a single tourist site, but those motels sure captured my imagination. I'd never seen anything like them. It all felt very grown-up and glamorous.

We sang "California Here I Come" as loud as we could while we crossed the Golden Gate Bridge, shouting the chorus as the wind whipped through our open windows. In Los Angeles, Dad bought me a small motorcycle jacket and cap, like what Brando wore in *The Wild One*. "Welcome to Hollywood," he said as he handed it to me.

Our destination was Alhambra, about fifteen miles east of Hollywood, past Chavez Ravine and through Chinatown, where a bunch of my father's family lived. While Dad looked for a place I stayed with my spinster aunts, Didi and Lizzie, and then later with my Uncle Frank, Aunt Helen, and their three kids, all of whom were older than me. Frank was a pretty religious guy and put me in second grade at the same grammar school, All Souls, that his youngest daughter, Peggy, attended.

Dad eventually found a place for our family to live just a couple of blocks away, and thanked Frank for his hospitality by enrolling all of us kids in local Catholic schools. I stayed on at All Souls, where I was joined by my middle brother, Danny, while the eldest, Bob, went to San Gabriel Mission High School. Up to that moment in our young lives, none of us had any religious training, and it was like being thrown into a tub of ice water. The first time Sister Mary Elizabeth ordered my class to kneel I had no clue what she was talking about—I'd never prayed before. I found myself trapped inside a school full of nuns with an insistence on discipline like nothing I'd seen. Having my knuckles rapped with a ruler during class was old-school schooling, and completely disorienting. For Danny, who didn't take orders well (he was more like James Dean than Saint James the Apostle), it was especially difficult. His relationship with religion got off to a bad start and never really improved.

I, on the other hand, was too young to know any better, and quickly adapted to my new environment. I liked learning and was a pretty good student. It was the best way I found to stay in the nuns' good graces and avoid that ruler.

Music and Catholic school first intersected in seventh grade, when the nuns selected me to be the primary altar boy for their monthly Solemn High Mass. I was beginning to develop an interest in music, and was eager to participate . . . up until they told me the role involved singing. That stopped me in my tracks. Sing? In front of the entire school? No fuckin' way. I turned them down. My music career would have to wait a few more years.

MY DAD'S HOLLYWOOD fascination was rekindled in 1956, when the *Queen for a Day* show made the jump from radio to TV, and he arranged to get Sarah Coventry jewelry featured on it. That was a big deal: the show's models would wear the jewelry and contestants would get a chance to win it. Even as a kid, I could tell he was excited by the prospects.

Unfortunately, the good times didn't last. Seattle had a small-town quality to it back then, and the house-party approach that had worked so well there did not translate to the sprawl of Southern California. LA was also on the vanguard of fashion in a way that Seattle wasn't, and maybe people just weren't as interested in costume jewelry. Even with the TV exposure, Sarah Coventry didn't catch hold, and as the company's fortunes flagged my dad was unexpectedly let go. He soon developed insomnia so severe that he had to nap during the day, which effectively made him unemployable. For reasons I never understood, he became his own worst enemy.

At first, my dad tried starting his own jewelry company, called Cathé, but his salespeople stole his sample cases, which left him with no product and depleted our savings. After that, he picked up whatever sales gigs he could: life insurance, real estate, used cars. He got a job sorting mail at the post office, which I think was mostly to get my mom off of his back, but his insomnia made keeping regular hours impossible. He even tried selling home saunas—anything he could do on his own hours. Nothing stuck. I think his insomnia was at the core of some sort of emotional disintegration that science didn't yet understand. Today they might call it manic-depression and put you on SSRIs.

It was heartbreaking for me to watch this once unstoppable force come apart before my eyes. I found out later that my dad was so ashamed of his failures that he sometimes pretended to go to work in the mornings to a job he didn't have, so his kids wouldn't see anything but the illusion of a working father. I occasionally came home from school to find him asleep on the couch in a coat and tie, having given up early on that day's charade.

By that point, my mother had stepped in to support the family with a sales job at McKay's Drug Store in Alhambra. My father's inability to carry his share of the financial burden became a wedge between them. Neither of them understood why he couldn't sleep or hold a job. Mom came to resent him deeply, even giving up at one point while I was in high school and returning to Seattle for a few months, leaving me and Dad alone in our apartment. I knew he was having a hard time, and I did my best to keep him company through the night, frequently staying up with him to watch the late-late show.

The best solution doctors gave him was a sleeping medication called Miltown. Because it caused drowsiness, they also gave him Dexedrine, the upper of the era, to pop in the mornings. Later, pharmacists mixed them together in a green-and-white capsule called Dexamyl, which is what my dad took in the 1960s. He got hooked, and had to work two or three doctors to accumulate sufficient quantities. In my later teenage years I took to sneaking some of those pills from his sock drawer, especially when I needed to study for finals. I remember my geology teacher looking at me sideways during one field trip in particular, wondering why I'd suddenly become so interested in rock formations.

MY MOTHER WAS more difficult. I loved her dearly, of course, but I never felt as close to her as I think either of us would have liked. She was attentive to the physical needs of us kids, getting up to make breakfast and send us off to school, but our emotional needs were different. She was not a nurturer, and hugs were in short supply. Later in life she told me, "I wasn't the kind of mother who would get down on her knees to play with my children."

Lina Massie (shortened somewhere along the way from Massemiani) was the third of Luigi and Cecilia's four children. They'd made their way from Avezzano, Italy, to Washington State, but their life in the United States didn't seem much easier than it had been in the old world. Neither of her parents ever learned to speak English, and it wasn't long before their lack of prosperity led my grandfather to the bottle. He'd come home in such drunken rages that on many nights the neighbors would sneak his children from the house before he could hurt them. Later on, my mom's mother was so emotionally distant that, even though we all lived near Seattle when I was young, we almost never saw her.

Luigi's abuse could be why my mom ended up having issues with men later in life, particularly the four of us who lived in her house. My mom never hid the fact that she'd desperately wanted a daughter, somebody to offer the type of compassion that seemed to be in short supply with us boys. It left us all constantly trying to prove our love to her, and not understanding why it never seemed to be enough. Now I know that we had no hope of filling her emotional void. I have a specific memory of a Mother's Day in Seattle when I was about five years old. I figured we'd celebrate at dinner, just like we did with birthdays, but midway through the morning my mom blew up, screaming that we were all selfish for not acknowledging her first thing. As an extremely sensitive kid being accused of insensitivity, my mom's anger and tears affected me deeply. It was a formative lesson that doing nothing can upset people just as much as doing the wrong thing.

Incidents like that weren't much fun for a kid like me, but the kind of sensitivity it inspired would become handy as I got older and began to channel it into songs.

ONE BENEFIT OF my father's ongoing joblessness was that it gave him time to spend with his kids, particularly me. I'm not sure why, but of Robert Loggins's three sons, I was the one he poured his energy into. He taught me how to play baseball and golf. When I was nine or ten, my dad and I worked out a bunch of basketball plays and would go two-on-two with Danny and his pals. My dad was my best friend, and it was thrilling for me when we beat the big kids.

I loved sports. Early on I played baseball, even throwing a no-hitter as a fourteen-year-old. (It was covered by the local paper, which called me "lanky," leading to the inevitable nickname "Lanky Loggins.") At San Gabriel Mission High School, I focused on basketball and track. My dad had been a high-hurdler back in Butte in the 1930s, and taught me the craft. He was so good at it that when the Mission High track coach had a stroke during my sophomore year, my dad took over the program. That it was a volunteer job became another bone of contention between him and my mom, but it was good for him and he loved it. Out on that field he became the father I remembered from my childhood. My teammates liked him, too. He was a mellow guy and a great coach. Most of all, I could tell he was happy. That was probably the job he should have been doing all along.

I was a pretty good hurdler myself. Being six feet tall allowed me to step the high hurdles better than most of my teammates. My problem was the spaces between them. My feet flicked out when I ran, which made it kind of like running with flippers on. I managed to win a few races, but ours was a small league and competition wasn't exactly fierce.

The sport I loved most was basketball. Those were the days when a six-footer like me was considered tall enough to play center. (That was true on our team, anyway. I was the shortest center in the league.) My oldest brother, Bob, who'd played at the same high school for the same coach—Coach Crowe—inspired me to go out for the team. Coach Crowe remembered Bob's work ethic, and thought I might bring something similar to the roster. Well, I worked as hard as anybody, but I also had outside interests like music and theater, and Coach Crowe never forgave me for that. He came to think of me as a showboat, which I most definitely was not. Not yet, anyway. Even when I had the game of my life, hitting nearly every shot I put up, Coach found a way to criticize me. My culmination came on a play in which I inadvertently jumped past the basket and still managed to reach backward and tip in a teammate's errant shot. Coach Crowe was so upset with the unorthodoxy of it—basketball was played very differently back then—that even though I was leading the team in scoring, he pulled me from the game. Go figure.

It reminds me of an old joke. This guy, Bill, has everything go wrong for him at once. He loses his job, his car breaks down on the way home, and when he finally gets there he finds that his wife and kids have left him. "Why me?" he cries to the heavens. Just then, the clouds part and a voice booms down from above. "I don't know, Bill," says God. "Something about you just pisses me off."

BOBBY WAS THE first person I knew who tried to write a song. He was fourteen, I was seven. At first, he tried to enlist eleven-year-old Danny to help him, but Dan's attention span got in the way after an hour or two. Bobby was all about tenacity and patience, and took the better part of a week to file the edges and hone his masterpiece—which went something like, "Oh baby, baby, I'm so in love with you . . ." Watching my brothers try to write that tune made an impression on me. Until then I thought songs only came out of the radio. I'd never thought of writing one myself.

Despite that early seminal moment, it was Danny who held the biggest sway over me. Bobby had already left home by the time I reached sixth grade, leaving Danny, three years younger than Bob and four years older than me, as my primary influence precisely when being cool began to matter. While I followed Bob into the Catholic, gender-segregated San Gabriel Mission High, Danny opted for the public high school down the street. It had two primary benefits over Mission High: lots of girls and no nuns.

Dan loved to sing. Back in Seattle, when I was maybe four or five, he taught me the counterpart to the barbershop classic "Down by the Old Mill Stream."

Dan: "Down by the old mill stream . . ."

Me: "Not the river but the stream."

Dan: "Where I first met you . . ."

Me: "Not me but you."

Ours was the comedic version made popular by a fellow named Jerry Colonna in the early 1950s, and it earned me my first-ever applause when we performed it after a business dinner my dad hosted at the house. Before long, it became a family tradition for Dad to trot us out for our little musical numbers whenever company was over. That was my introduction to how much fun performing could be.

I loved to sing with Dan, but more than that I wanted to be just like him. Anything he liked *had* to be cool. Luckily for me, it actually was. By the time Danny was a teenager, he'd become the rock rebel of the family. His love for rock 'n' roll and early R&B turned me on to groups like the Coasters, the Del-Vikings, and Danny & the Juniors. He showed me Fats Domino and Little Richard and Eddie Cochran. We were watching *American Bandstand* together, he and I, when Jerry Lee Lewis stood up and played the piano with his foot. *That* was rock 'n' roll. It was the beginning of my musical awakening, and became a major part of my DNA. It still occasionally shows up in my own music, like the line in "I'm Alright"—"Get it up and get you a job, dip, dip, dip, dip," which is, of course, borrowed from the Silhouettes' "Get a Job."

A couple of years after we moved to California, I discovered Elvis Presley's "Hound Dog" in Danny's record collection. I hadn't yet seen Elvis on TV; for me it was all about the sound. I played that 45 over and over again—an obsession that came with no small amount of risk, since Danny had barred me from his bedroom. That didn't stop me, of course. His record collection was my holy grail, and I had to get to it. My school day ended earlier than his, so I would race home and binge-listen on the little box turntable in his room before he arrived. My worries about getting caught had less to do with Danny walking in than with making sure I put things back exactly how he'd left them. My brother kept his 45s in special binders, in such perfect order that he'd notice if anything was amiss.

One time, he even spotted a disturbance in the dust on the spine of a book. He burst in on me, shouting, "You were in my room!" leaving me to scratch my head and try to figure out how he knew. Clearly, Danny missed his calling; he should have become a detective. Thanks to his unending scrutiny, I could have become a master thief.

I was so taken with all the music Danny fed me that in the fourth grade I tried to start my own rock band. I didn't even play an instrument, and neither did my friends, but that didn't stop us. The only music we could make, of course, was from Danny's portable record player, so we mostly just sat around listening to his 45s. Those kids didn't know any of the songs because they didn't have big brothers like Danny.

The other item I borrowed from Danny was the guitar he'd hung on the wall, an old Kay nylon-string acoustic. It was mostly there as decoration; he never really learned how to play it. I thought that guitar was so beautiful. I didn't know what to do with it, so I'd sneak it down and just hold it. That was the first step toward making my own music. It also led to a full-blown fascination with guitars. I started hanging out at Pedrini's Music in downtown Alhambra, just to ogle the merchandise. Some guys cut out magazine pictures of girls or cars to hang on their bedroom walls. I cut out pictures of guitars.

Noting this, my parents signed me up for guitar lessons at Pedrini's. I had high hopes until I learned that my new teacher didn't know any rock music, or even folk tunes. It turned out he was a guitarist for the Lawrence Welk Orchestra. Lawrence Welk? It was 1960; I wanted to play "If I Had a Hammer," not the "Pennsylvania Polka." Ultimately, it didn't even matter—we never got to the music itself because this fella was all about theory. He kept trying to teach me scales when I wanted only to play and sing. I quit almost immediately, and that pretty much ended the guitar for me until high school, when a guy named Rodney Ruggles showed me a better path.

Rod was twenty-five years old, and the big brother of my friend Marty. He was a struggling professional folksinger who was happy to teach me what he knew—and he knew a lot. The funky back room in his parents' house was his personal folk cave, dimly lit, moody as hell, and home to a half dozen gorgeous acoustic guitars. He collected sheet music and folk-focused magazines like *Sing Out!*, which was the scene's bible back in those days. Rod taught me songs by acts like Gordon Lightfoot, Ian & Sylvia, and Peter, Paul and Mary. The best, though, was Bob Dylan. When I heard "Blowin' in the Wind"—Rod's version, not Dylan's record—I was so moved that I learned to play it that night, straight from the pages of *Sing Out!*. That was only the beginning.

Armed with Danny's guitar and Rod's classic folk songs, I began joining in on local hootenannies—sing-alongs with other wannabe folkies. I worked up an act with a friend from the girls' wing of my high school, Mikele Parisi. She was only about four foot ten, and for the novelty of it I gave her a friend's stand-up bass fiddle to play. It was almost twice as big as her, but so was I. We were both good singers, and our Smothers Brothers–style routine was full of quips and skits. It played well at the frat parties and college halls where most of our gigs took place, though it played less well at the first talent show we entered. I thought our act was solid, but we ended up losing to a guy imitating Bob Dylan—and not even the new electric Dylan, but the older folkie Dylan. I should have taken it as a sign that my repertoire, which consisted entirely of the songs I'd only just learned from Rod, already needed updating.

The loss didn't deter me. Talent shows were kind of a big deal back then, and I kept at it, occasionally with Mikele, but mostly solo. My next one was much bigger, featuring young performers from across the county. I actually had to audition, then make it through several rounds of judging to qualify for the public performance. People had to buy tickets to get in. The competition was serious: amazing bluegrass bands, classical pianists, trained vocalists, and a smattering of pop groups. Somehow, we all lost to a trio of cute high school girls in cellophane grass skirts doing the hula under a black light. Man, the audience went crazy for that. Those girls were oozing with . . . talent. I learned that night that showmanship really does matter. Also that sex sells, and to use black light whenever possible.

In addition to playing with Mikele, I started a group with a couple of guys from the basketball team, Pete Hermes and Mark Stafford, dedicated specifically to old-school folk songs like "If I Had a Hammer" and "Michael Row the Boat Ashore." We called ourselves the Yeomen. We were all still learning how to play our instruments, and our lone live performance (at yet another talent show) ended with an early exit. Our act was outdated, and we didn't look good in grass skirts. I realized then that my material was stuck in a genre that had lost its vibrancy. The times they were a-changin', and boy did I need it. Luckily, change was right around the corner.

What unstuck me was the Beatles.

ONE MORNING NOT LONG AFTER that woebegone Yeomen show, my mother called me into the living room just before leaving for work.

"There's a new band on *Ed Sullivan* tonight that everyone is talking about," she said. "You might want to check them out."

I wasn't used to taking pop-culture cues from my mother, but for some reason I listened to her, and boy was I glad I did.

I'd never heard of the Beatles, but that night I sat on the floor in front of our black-and-white Sylvania, transfixed. Like so many future rockers, the arc of my life changed dramatically over the course of that hour. I stopped playing folk music then and there . . . and so did Dylan. It wasn't long before he released a record with a full band and a bunch of rock songs. As it happened, he also met with the Beatles in their New York City hotel. Talk about my worlds colliding.

Dylan's new electrified rocker was called *Bringing It All Back Home*, and I first encountered it, where else, in Rod Ruggles's back room. I didn't even hear the album—just saw the cover—but the title struck me as poetic. When I learned he didn't actually have a song by that name, I went home that very night and wrote it myself. I didn't even know what the song was about when I started, but it poured out of me, words and music all at once. It was my first glimpse into the hypnotism of songwriting. I never recorded it, but I still remember some of the verses. The main character makes big decisions based on his experiences, and by the end realizes that some of those decisions might not have been the right ones.

I started building pyramids
Just to see how great it was
And suddenly I realized
How little one man does
And it'll only cause me pain
So I'm bringing it all back home

You profit from experience
To be a wiser man
You learn as you travel
As you roam
But it might be just an echo
That you caught inside your hand
And you're bringing it all back home
And I'm bringing it all back home

I was seventeen years old, and with my very first song was already writing introspectively. I had almost no life experience on which to draw, but my imagination filled in the gaps. It came naturally to me to write about imaginary experiences in the first person, as if I'd actually lived them. I'm guessing it's similar to how a novelist invents worlds in a book. One thing that's held true over the years is that my songs communicate to me as if I'm someone other than the guy writing them. Hell, my songs still teach me things to this day. (It took me twenty years to fully understand what 1991's "Conviction of the Heart" was trying to tell me, but that's a story for later.)

I lost all interest in the Yeomen and began gravitating toward other Dylan and Beatles fans at my high school. Before long I'd formed my first rock band, called Five Downing Street. (We were experiencing the first wave of the British Invasion, 10 Downing Street was where the British prime minister lived, and there were five guys in the band. Sometimes you don't need much more than that.) That group was especially fun for me because my brother Danny was in it . . . sort of, sometimes. He was attending Cal State LA by that point, and even though he lived at his fraternity house he still showed up at home often enough to rock with us . . . sort of, sometimes. Every time we practiced, he always seemed to have something else to do.

When Danny did show up for rehearsal it was like the old days. We sang great harmonies together, which wasn't surprising given that we'd been doing it since we were kids. With the Vietnam draft growing hot underneath him, however, Danny decided to place an increased emphasis on schoolwork (the better to maintain deferment) and less on the band he was in with a bunch of high school kids. The rest of the guys grew tired of working up arrangements with his parts missing. I'm not sure Danny even noticed when we broke up.

I quickly formed another band without Danny called the Second Helping. It was my senior year of high school, and that group inspired me to break out the extremely cheap electric six-string with a homemade pickup I'd found at Pedrini's. That thing looked like it was made from a Formica tabletop, felt like it weighed a hundred pounds, and had about thirty-seven switches and dials on it, though the volume knob was the only one that worked. It was a uniquely horrible guitar, but the salesman said it was good for the money, and I believed him. Anyway, it could get loud, and that was enough for me.

I soon upgraded to a slightly better, much lighter guitar, which I set to work customizing. I cut a hole into the bottom edge and sunk in a cowbell that stuck out the back like an exhaust pipe. I secured it with wood putty and pieces from an old Erector set. On stage, I wore a holster with a drumstick in it, and banged on the bell during my bandmates' solos. That guitar lasted until the final show the Second Helping ever played, when I decided to channel Pete Townsend and threw it into the air, mostly so I could hear what it sounded like when it crashed to the floor. The neck broke clean off. It was strangely cathartic. I highly recommend the experience.

The Second Helping was actually a pretty good group: Larry Williams on guitar, Joe Middleton on bass, Mike Vernola on drums, and a keyboard player named Bill Hansen. We covered a bunch of songs by bands like the Byrds and Buffalo Springfield, and of course the Beatles and the Stones, and figured since those guys wrote their own stuff, we should, too. Being the only guy who had ever written a song, I was tagged for the role, and over the course of a year came up with about twenty numbers. That really set us apart from most of the other groups in the area, and we gained a bit of a following.

It was at about that time that a guitarist I sometimes played with, a kid named Scotty, introduced me to pot. My parents would have said we were "experimenting," which I guess was true, though what we were really experimenting with was consciousness. That was when I first understood there were more ways of seeing things than I'd been taught in school, and it opened up a free-flowing creativity for me.

Pot also affected how I heard music. The Beatles—*Sgt. Pepper's* in particular—took on a new degree of importance, and I strove to write songs that accessed a similar kind of awareness. They were doing backwards stuff and looping sounds, creating mind-expanding auditory experiences, and I wanted to try some of that myself. I guess that's why I called one of my compositions "Floating Downstream on an Inflatable Rubber Raft." What can I say? It was the '60s.

The Second Helping played mostly high school and college fraternity dances. Once, we played at a bowling alley, and the owner of the place told me afterward that we should get a new drummer. Everybody had an opinion. What we became known for, however, were battles of the bands. Somebody figured out that if you staged a contest you only had to pay the winner. Soon, that format had cropped up across the southland, with bills filled by volunteer rock 'n' roll wannabes. We must have competed in ten of those things over the course of a year, and I vaguely recall even getting paid a few times.

Before long, we actually got a manager, a local deputy sheriff named Scott Macquarrie, whose dreams of becoming a big-time rock 'n' roll producer seemed to begin with us. He was a stocky guy with a cocky attitude, who was rumored to have once shot a hole in his television with his police-issue Colt .38 because he was annoyed by whatever he'd been watching. His first act as our manager was to accompany us to a high school dance in East LA during the Watts riots. During our first break, a bunch of drunken kids jumped onstage, grabbed our instruments, and tried to take the show into their own hands. I watched from the dance floor, growing very nervous as I tried to figure out what we could do to stop this pending riot of our own. Then Macquarrie calmly walked up to the stage, and from a place that only those assholes could see, opened his jacket and pointed at the pistol on his waist. "He's got a gat!" one of the kids shouted. Those guys spilled off the front of the stage and ran for the door. It left quite an impression on me and the band. Scott had passed the audition.

Scott owned his own reel-to-reel recorder and a half-dozen mics, and very much wanted to get us on tape, hoping to cash in when we hit it big. Because he was an unrepentant old folkie, he had us work up a comedy routine as part of our act, not unlike the groups that headlined local nightclubs. One of the punch lines had to do with a breath mint that was actually a suppository—a rectal joke I barely remember yet is *still* incredibly embarrassing. Then again, Scott was also the guy who booked us at the place where we drew some of our best crowds, a folk haunt in Glendale called the Ice House, where we opened for acts like the Knack, the Dillards, and the Good Time Singers. I guess that kind of shtick was expected in that kind of place. I don't remember anybody booing us off of the stage, anyway.

The Second Helping's big break (if you can call it that) came in July 1966, just after my senior year of high school, when Scott entered us into yet another battle of the bands competition. This one was different, though. It was put on by a Hollywood AM radio station, KFWB, and the grand prize was a Standel amplifier and a recording contract with a local label called Viva Records. Instead of having the acts perform live, KFWB solicited cassettes that they played on the air. The winner was decided by popular vote, which in those days was tallied by postcards people sent in to the station. This is where Scott really paid off for us. He bought a mimeograph machine and printed off postcards by the hundreds. We actually threw postcard-signing parties where friends from high school drank sodas and filled up box after box. Even with that we barely won. Seems some other LA band had a mimeograph machine, too.

Viva Records, the label whose contract we won, was a little outfit on Gower Street in Hollywood that had just been launched by Snuff Garrett, the impresario behind the likes of Bobby Vee, Del Shannon, and Gary Lewis and the Playboys. For us Alhambra kids, this was the big time. As it turned out, the record deal wasn't all we'd thought. We were given only a small window of studio time, just a few hours, that wasn't nearly enough to get anything done. When I didn't like what I was hearing through the monitors, I tried to rearrange things on the fly without any real idea about what I was doing. Snuff made Scott the engineer on the project as part of some side deal, and he mostly just tried to rush us along. I completely buckled under the pressure. The guys in the band weren't digging my direction, and things grew tense. At some point, I mumbled that Scott didn't know what the fuck he was doing. I was smart enough to wait until he left the room to say it, but I meant every word. The guy was into folk music, not the Beatles. Problem was, the studio mics were hot, and Scotty heard my sentiments loud and clear in the control room. All of a sudden, I heard his voice boom over the talk-back speakers: "Oh, really?"

To this day I'm careful about what I say in a studio, because there's always an open mic someplace.

We accomplished so little in the time we'd been given that Viva ended up putting out some homemade recordings we'd done at Scott's place (one of which we'd used to win the battle of the bands). To gussy them up a bit, Snuff turned to a brooding, long-haired keyboardist from Oklahoma he'd recently taken on as a junior partner, which is how Leon Russell gave Larry his fuzz-tone guitar effect for our song "Let Me In." I'd never heard of Leon at that point, but it wasn't long before he was cranking out his own gold records. When we ran into each other years later (something that would eventually happen with regularity), he didn't remember that first encounter, but I sure did.

Even if we had managed to lay down a professional-sounding track or two, I still don't think it would have helped our long-term prospects. I hadn't found my voice yet, and got by mostly by imitating John Lennon and Eric Burdon. It would be a few more years before I found a style of my own.

Nothing really came of that Viva contract, save for the fact that you can now find four Second Helping songs on the internet. What our battle of the bands victory really earned us was a gig as the opening act for the Association at the Pasadena Civic Auditorium. That was a big deal for us. The Association had a No. 1 hit with "Cherish," and although I didn't feel ready for that kind of billing, Scott insisted we were up to the challenge. For the date, Mike the drummer stole a couple of altar-boy cassocks from his Catholic school, which he and I altered to look like *Sgt. Pepper's* coats, complete with epaulets and the like. We wore them as stage costumes.

Upon arriving at the gig, we learned that the Association's management had actually booked them for two nearly simultaneous shows—the one we were playing in Pasadena and another across town, in Hollywood. A few hours before the doors opened, we were given the alarming news that to accommodate their doubleheader, the Association would go on first in Pasadena, and close the Hollywood gig. This meant that instead of us opening for them, the band at the top of the charts would now be opening for *us*. I immediately got nauseous. Like, seriously ill. I began to fear-vomit into whatever trash can I could find, and didn't stop until we took the stage. Thinking back on it, plenty of Association fans must have cleared out once the band they had come to see wrapped up, but in my mind there were still thousands of people in the room when we went on. I was scared stiff, yet when I hit the stage something automatically arose in me that I would come to know well over the years. I felt centered and in the zone. I don't remember much about the show, except, unfortunately, for that horrible comedy routine. Still, the exhilaration that came from performing in front of a large crowd was addictive. I was hooked.

That was the last high-profile show the Second Helping ever played. I'd been at Pasadena City College for about a year by that point, and while we tried to keep the band together for some weekend gigs, it eventually got to be too much, especially after my old Chevy station wagon, which I'd used to haul our PA system around, died. As I recall, there wasn't even an official breakup. We all just went our separate ways.

MY RELATIONSHIP WITH Danny is complicated. He's the guy who taught me about music, the brother I loved to harmonize with. Before long, though, it became a different story. Early on it was mostly a matter of age—what high school freshman wants his ten-year-old brother following him around like a puppy dog? Danny was trying to find his way around his own teenage world, and I consistently seemed to be in his way. I had buck teeth and, according to him, dressed wrong and acted wrong and never said the right things around his friends. I became the butt of their jokes, and couldn't shake the feeling that I was an embarrassment. So I tried to be like him, hoping he might lighten up on me if I got it right. I tried to stand like Danny stood, talk like Danny talked. Sometimes I even wore his shirts, despite them being too big for me. I was constantly asking myself, How do I become more like Danny?

It didn't work—I never became Danny—but the process was instrumental in creating a cooler version of myself. Once girls came into the picture, my motivation became all the more urgent. No matter how groovy I tried to act, I was still tall and skinny, with big ears and very short hair, thanks to Mission High's dress code. Add in my four years at an all-boys school—where I rarely saw girls my age, let alone learned how to talk to them—and I was not exactly Mr. Confidence when it came to the opposite sex.

The guitar came to my rescue. (As did long hair. And my orthodontist.)

The girls' wing of my high school (where boys were *never* allowed) had a competition each year in which each class created and performed a musical. Thanks to my friendship with Mikele, the girls of the senior class asked if I'd help them, and I ended up writing all of the songs in their play. In so doing, I became the first boy to ever participate in that event. Even though I had to hide in the projectionist's booth to watch the performance, it felt like a coup. I was becoming cool.

That was my first step toward using music to meet girls. I soon figured out that bringing my guitar to parties lent me some gravitas, no matter how much I actually possessed. Once I started to sing my own songs, I became more confident in social situations. All it took was a couple of well-picked numbers and the walls came tumblin' down.

DANNY HAD MOVED OUT by the time I was a senior in high school, heading from Cal State LA to Lyndon Johnson's VISTA program— Volunteers in Service to America. It was effectively a domestic Peace Corps, and, importantly to Danny, a viable alternative to the draft. He was sent to Danville, Illinois, where he did tutoring in poor communities, helped build a reading center, and even drove a school bus. He returned after his one-year term, moving back not only to our parents' place in the Villa Roma apartments in Alhambra, but into my bedroom, where I still slept while I attended community college.

One of the reasons Danny came home when he did was that our oldest brother, Bob, was getting married. The week of his arrival was a whirlwind of pre-wedding activity—tuxedo rentals and reunions and parties. As if that wasn't enough of a family-oriented event, about a week later Danny got a phone call from Sheila, a VISTA volunteer he dated in Illinois. She was pregnant. He'd already been considering a move to Berkeley, to be in closer proximity to the Summer of Love, so with that the two of them—soon to be three, with baby Colin—moved up north.

I'm not sure why, but Danny didn't tell me about his impending fatherhood until after he'd gone. He did it via a letter in which he shared his excitement about the situation, and his trepidation over what was to come. What I would give to still have that letter. I remember pretty much exactly what was in it, though, because it moved me to grab an acoustic guitar and write a song. I pulled some of the lyrics directly from Danny's note, like "Pisces, Virgo rising is a very good sign, strong and kind."

I must have done something right, because to this day "Danny's Song" remains one of my most popular tunes, known by the refrain: "Even though we ain't got money / I'm so in love with you, honey." I still lean on it as a trademark number, my quintessential Kenny Loggins folk thing. That song helped me realize that when I wrote about things close to my heart, those songs would matter to other people too. I also write pop tunes, of course, but the ones with lasting impact are the songs with meaning. The songwriters who influenced me most were introspective, like Tim Hardin, Paul Simon, Cat Stevens, and, of course, Lennon and McCartney. For me, James Taylor was America's poet laureate, the most important of the inward-looking songwriters. Their tunes resonate with a deeper kind of seeing that, as a teenager, I was desperate to learn.

That said, I should probably clear up a couple of things about "Danny's Song." It came out directly, with no editing. There are lines I might not have kept later in my career, but at seventeen years old I never expected millions of people to hear my music.

The first part of the song contains some lines about Danny's anticipation for his new child: "He will be like she and me / As free as a dove / Conceived in love / Sun is gonna shine above."

That's not bad English. Danny's wife was (and still is) Sheila, and his nickname for her was "Shi." That's who the baby was going to be like: "Shi and me."

Much, much later—during the process of writing this book, in fact—my old friend Doug Ingoldsby pulled out some notes he'd kept over the years. Doug and I became close shortly after high school, when we would go into the mountains outside of Pasadena to get high and strum guitars. I taught him a bunch of my early songs so we could sing them as duets at parties. This included "Danny's Song," for which I scribbled down the lyrics back in 1968, long before it was ever recorded. Doug kept them folded up in his guitar case, and fished them out years later, after the song became a hit. Back then, I wrote the last part of that same verse with the word "son" instead of "sun": "Son is gonna shine above"—a nifty double-entendre. I can't believe I forgot about that for fifty years.

That was the beginning of an early fertile period. Not many musicians are blessed with such an extensive career, and of those, fewer still get requests for songs they wrote as teenagers. Somehow, I have *two* of those songs. The other one is about a bear.

It came about not long after "Danny's Song," during my final days of high school. One night, instead of studying for finals, I went into my folks' bedroom and wrote a tune about Winnie the Pooh. I was only days away from graduating, and was conscious of the fact that my life was about to change in unknown ways. I was only seventeen, but already feeling nostalgic for a childhood I hadn't yet left. I kept thinking back to A. A. Milne's *The House at Pooh Corner.* That was the first real book I ever read, and it captured my imagination like no other, especially the last chapter where Christopher Robin leaves Winnie-the-Pooh and the Hundred Acre Wood. I simply wrote myself into the story.

That nostalgia, bordering on heartache, comes through in the song without ever being explicitly stated. I think it's a big part of why "House at Pooh Corner" has endured for all these years.

CHAPTER 2

OUT AND ABOUT IN LA

AFTER HIGH SCHOOL I attended Pasadena City College. Really, I didn't have many options. I hadn't taken the SATs because even though my friends all took them, nobody told me I should, too. San Gabriel Mission High didn't have guidance counselors, and my parents—neither of whom went to college themselves—were hardly guardians of that particular flame. That said, I did want to go to college, if only because I needed something to do and I really didn't want to get drafted. With my lack of foresight, Pasadena City College was pretty much my only option.

I figured I would become a music major, but learned that in a department deeply focused on classical, if you didn't play piano you were shit out of luck. I managed to absorb some things about ear training and chordal progressions, but as a long-haired, guitar-picking neo-hippie, I was distinctly *not* the kind of student those professors wanted. It wasn't long before the dean of the department called me into his office and informed me he was on the verge of flunking me, but that if I left the program of my own accord, he'd give me a D. It was an offer I couldn't refuse. So I pivoted to the most seemingly related study area I could find: radio and television announcing. That's what they called telecommunications back then, and I picked it mostly because I thought I'd be good at it. Classes involved creating copy to read into a microphone. My dad was always telling me I needed something to fall back on, and this seemed like as good a field as any. Still, I never approached it with anything more than half-hearted interest. I think city college was as important for helping me figure out what not to do as anything else.

When I look back at that period, I see that so many pivotal moments happened on a whim. Given the era during which I came of age, it still surprises me to think that my consciousness around the Vietnam War hinged on such a juncture, but that's exactly what happened.

The story begins in the summer of 1966, just before I started college. I was on a Friday-night triple date, six of us squeezed into somebody's sedan for dinner and a show out in Hollywood somewhere. I was wearing a suit, because it was that kind of night and my date was that kind of girl. The food and the company were all fine, but as we drove through Pasadena on our way home, it struck me that I was no longer interested in any of it—the scene, the people, the whole pre-collegiate lifestyle. I was finally listening to the voice inside of me, and it was screaming, *There's gotta be something more!* Those kids were nice enough, geared toward fraternities and sororities, but I was coming to be . . . well, I wasn't sure what, but it wasn't *that*. I craved deeper meaning, and I knew I wasn't going to find it in that car.

As it happened, that thought occurred to me just as we passed a folk-dance club in Pasadena called the Tower, where I'd gone a couple of times with my pal Doug. It had a mellow, counterculture coffeehouse vibe that I liked. I asked the guy who was driving to pull over and clambered out. From the sidewalk I leaned back through the window, told my date I was done, and walked away. I never saw her again.

I went into the club with a new openness toward whatever might come at me, and I didn't have to wait long. Almost as soon as I arrived, I heard that the club's owner was about to drive some folks about six hours north to San Francisco to participate in what was shaping up to be a massive peace rally. I didn't even think about it; still wearing the suit and tie from my date, I invited myself along, jumped in the back of a cargo van alongside five or six other young people, and went along for the ride of my life.

We arrived in the wee hours, and parked on a side street to catch some sleep in the van. The scene we found upon waking up was mind-bending: thousands of people just like me, flooding the streets to protest the war. Okay, they weren't *just* like me. I was still wearing my date suit and not quite ready to burn my draft card, but I was feeling it. We chanted "Hell no, we won't go" as we marched from the Ferry Building to the Haight-Ashbury district.

That weekend was the beginning of the next part of my life. It started with my realization that the people on my date were not *my* people, and ended with a full immersion into the counterculture movement. Before that point, I hadn't put much thought into Vietnam, but as I marched it started to sink in that (a) it was actually happening, and (b) I didn't want any part of it. I realized that I needed to become more educated in the politics of the day. Being enrolled at city college had temporarily shielded me from the draft, but starting at that moment I began to consider more deeply what would happen once college ended, and how I should respond.

That would come later, though. More pressing was where I was going to stay that night. The folks I'd driven up with had scattered during the march, with a plan to meet back at the van the following afternoon. I hadn't even brought a toothbrush, let alone considered a roof over my head. Of course, Danny was living in Berkeley at that point, and I figured I could always just hitchhike across the Bay Bridge to find him.

It was hardly a solid plan; I hadn't even told him I was coming. It wasn't difficult to catch a ride, but by the time I finally reached Danny's apartment, it was late and he wasn't there. I hadn't considered the possibility that he might not even be in town. I didn't know anybody else in Berkeley, and, with no money for a hotel room, or even food, I just wandered around the neighborhood for a while. I thought about what to do if he and Sheila still weren't home when I returned. I could knock on doors, asking Danny's neighbors if they knew where he was. At the very least, some kind soul might offer to let me sleep on their couch. In those days, that wasn't such a wild thought, especially in Berkeley. If that didn't work, maybe the Jefferson Airplane was playing at the Jabberwock on Telegraph Avenue, which would at least give me something to do. Maybe I could sit in, and that would lead to some conversations, and the next thing I knew I'd be crashing at Marty Balin's place. And sleeping with Grace Slick. As long as I was dreaming, why not take it all the way, right?

Luckily, it never came to that. When I returned to the apartment a couple of hours later, Danny was back from wherever he'd gone. We ended up talking late into the night about my revelations over a joint and a bottle of red wine. Danny explained that if I really didn't want to go to Vietnam, I had options. I could go to Canada. I could go to jail. I could be a conscientious objector. "If you don't want to go, then you won't," he said. He was trying to prepare me for the consequences should I choose to resist, but all I really heard was, "You won't go."

With the clock ticking on my college exemption, there was a lot to think about. From that moment on, however, I knew I wouldn't be going to war. I didn't know how it would happen, but it was a certainty.

LA WAS A GREAT PLACE for an aspiring musician in the late 1960s. There was rock 'n' roll *everywhere*. I saw Arthur Lee & Love at the Whiskey a Go Go, but what I remember most from that night was the house band that opened up. I knew nothing about the Doors—almost nobody did—but Jim Morrison was pure charisma and his songs were otherworldly, like nothing else I'd heard. When he sang, he did this thing where he wrapped himself around the mic stand like he was making love to it, and let loose with total, mindless abandon. He was so involved, so honest. I knew immediately that he was a star. I want to do that, I thought. I want to be that guy.

I never became Jim Morrison, of course—never even tried, really—but I did attempt to emulate the honesty he expressed onstage, the way he became totally immersed in his music. I was drawn to Pete Townsend for similar reasons. I saw the Who at the Shrine Auditorium, and when they performed "My Generation" I believed every word of it. As I sat in the back of that room I understood what rock 'n' roll was meant to be: the truth.

Another seminal moment came at the Hollywood Bowl in 1968, when Doug and I saw Jimi Hendrix. Back then, the Bowl had a big reflecting pond in front of the stage, and at some point a guy in a fringed leather jacket climbed into the water and started splashing. I remember Noel Redding warning him that there was enough electricity onstage to power the entire city, but Jimi didn't seem to care. His next song, "Fire," had the lyric "You got a new fool, ha! / I like it like that," but instead he sang, "The guy in the pool, ha! / I like it like that." That was all it took; within moments, dozens of fans were in there splashing around for the rest of the show. I think they cemented over the pool shortly thereafter.

The other place I liked to frequent was the Troubadour, a funky little club filled with wooden tables that was far less polished than some of the area's other music venues. The place held a couple of hundred people, with upstairs seating that offered a great view of the stage. On the floor level you could get elbow to elbow with the performers. I saw Cat Stevens there at the beginning of his run, just him and a bass player, and he all but mingled with the audience, playing songs just a few feet away. It was intimate, like being in his living room, and allowed a tactile sense of what his music was all about. I've tried to recreate that atmosphere within my own shows over the years. It's a great feeling to get that close to the audience.

I saw James Taylor at the Troubadour when he was touring his *Sweet Baby James* album. Doug and I went on opening night, and I guess James wasn't that well known, because there were only about fifty people in the place. He came out solo with an acoustic guitar and played three or four songs—tunes everybody knows by heart now—and then introduced Carole King for a duet. Then he switched over to electric guitar and the rest of the band came out and joined him. Little did I know that I'd follow the same format in the very same venue with Loggins & Messina not long thereafter.

Another Troubadour memory involves a duo called Longbranch/ Pennywhistle, which was Glenn Frey and J. D. Souther before their Eagles days. Somehow, the Hollywood musicians I was hanging around with at the time ended up at Frey's house after one of their shows. He and I had never met—I was still just some kid from Alhambra—but those guys were all friends, and the vibe seemed mellow enough. We passed a joint around, and Glenn played us some of their new demos—and then made the mistake of asking what we thought. Maybe I shouldn't have taken the question so literally, but I did have some ideas, musician to musician. Oops. When I suggested a different ending for one of the songs, Glenn stood up, looked at me and shouted, "Who the fuck is this guy?" That was the only hint I needed. I hit the road, and I don't think our relationship got much better from there.

(As if to prove the small circles of the LA scene, Souther would also team up with Chris Hillman and Richie Furay in the Souther-Hillman-Furay Band. Furay had been in Buffalo Springfield, and would form Poco alongside a fellow named Jim Messina, with whom I would become quite familiar over the coming years. There was an awful lot of talent hanging out around there back then.)

A few months after the peace march in San Francisco, I took another road trip with my new friends from the Tower. This time the destination was Monterey, a beautiful coastal city just north of Big Sur, for a pop festival held in 1967. On the first day, I saw Janis Joplin and Big Brother and the Holding Company, the Jefferson Airplane, and Canned Heat. The group that really impressed me, though, was Moby Grape, a so-called supergroup from Northern California that never quite broke through nationally. Their music was powerful and melodic, but it was their stage presence that caught my attention. They had three or four frontline singers, and whoever wasn't on the mic would take a few steps back when one of the other guys stepped up to sing. That was how the set went: up and back, up and back, the lead singer standing his ground while the harmonizers darted out of the spotlight, all while playing guitars. The stage was constantly moving, morphing, evolving. It was the first time I'd seen a band do something more than just stand there and get wrapped up in their instruments. *That looks really cool and totally pro,* I thought. I decided the guys in my band should do that, too. Shit, yeah.

At one point, I was walking around the festival grounds and wandered into a merch tent to unexpectedly find Stephen Stills, David Crosby, and Micky Dolenz. As I walked by, I heard Dolenz introduce himself to the other two. Stills shook his hand and asked if he was in a band. Dolenz, of course, was already famous as a member of The Monkees. I think Stephen was fucking with him; rumor had it that Stills himself had auditioned for The Monkees and didn't make it. Also, he'd told Peter Tork—who did make it—about the auditions in the first place. When I heard Stills's line, I cracked up. What a great moment. I wish I'd had the nerve to introduce myself, but I was barely out of high school and wasn't yet a performer. Not really. I certainly didn't see myself as one of them.

Speaking of outdoor festivals in Northern California, a couple of years later I saw the Rolling Stones at Altamont—legendary for different reasons, unfortunately. I remember wandering through an audience that was huge and getting huger by the hour, drawn by acts like Santana, the Jefferson Airplane, and Crosby, Stills, Nash and Young. The Stones headlined, and for some ill-advised reason hired the Hells Angels to run stage security, which went about as well as one might expect. Toward the end of the day, so much agitation had built among the crowd that the Grateful Dead—who were supposed to go on just prior to the Stones—canceled their appearance, not wanting to perform amid such hostile vibes. In the middle of the Stones' set, a Hells Angel actually killed a guy up front. I wasn't anywhere close, but when it happened we could feel the wave of energy sweep across the audience like a cold shiver. At that point, there was nothing to do but leave. We took off after only a couple of songs.

Some of my most memorable Bay Area music moments came with Danny. One of them was seeing Traffic at the Fillmore in San Francisco. *Mr. Fantasy* had just come out, and even though I really liked it, I didn't know quite what to expect when they took the stage. I was surprised to see that Dave Mason, an integral part of the record (and a guy who I would become quite friendly with over the coming years), was not in the band. Then there was Steve Winwood, a skinny little fellow in this white chiffon Edwardian shirt with a flowery bow down the front. When the band started to play, Winwood opened his mouth and out came this *huge* voice, like nothing I'd ever heard. It was like a young Ray Charles was trapped inside his body. We were sitting on the floor, which was how you saw shows at the Fillmore in those days, and rows of people in front of me were practically blown over backward by the power of Winwood's voice. Just like I'd done with Jim Morrison at the Whiskey, I thought, I want to be *that*. Unlike with Morrison, this time I felt like I actually stood a chance. Winwood really influenced me as a singer, probably more than anybody. I wanted that same big voice. I wanted those high notes.

My favorite seeing-shows-with-Danny story also happened in San Francisco, at the Winterland Ballroom. By that point, Danny was working as a manager at Discount Records in Berkeley, which got him primo passes to all kinds of shows. That night we had front-row balcony seats for Crosby, Stills, Nash and Young, and Danny suggested we eat a bunch of acid to commemorate the occasion. By the time the show started, we were high as shit. I really loved those CSNY harmonies, and figured they'd be great fuel for my trip. What I didn't anticipate was the opening act, a countrified folk-jazz outfit I'd never heard of called Joy of Cooking. I'll allow that I might have approached things differently had I been sober, but in my altered state, the band's three-man rhythm section was not what my head needed to hear. It was pure cacophony, running counter to the vibe Danny and I had been building. Honestly, it was all I could do to remain in my seat. I took to gripping the handrail in front of me as tightly as I could, trying to make something cool out of the noise coming from the stage. My mind over their matter.

It didn't work. I had to escape. I told Danny I needed to use the restroom, the logic of too much acid suggesting that if I changed my environment, I'd be able to relax. I was ready to give myself the quintessential moment from *The Trip*, a movie in which a dosed and paranoid Peter Fonda flees the safety of his surroundings to wander the Sunset Strip. Luckily for me, Danny read me expertly. "No you don't," he said, smiling. "This place is a zoo. You'll never find your way back."

So I stayed. And endured. I grabbed that rail and screwed up my face, trying hard to find a way to dig anything about what I was hearing. As the set dragged on, I grew exhausted from the effort, soaking through with sweat as the heat of the ballroom combined with the drugs and the tension to wring all the moisture from my body. At least I knew I wasn't bothering anybody—there was only empty space between myself and the stage below.

When they finally wrapped up, preeminent Bay Area concert promoter Bill Graham ambled to the mic to make his standard batch of announcements regarding upcoming shows. That much I expected. What caught me by surprise was the way Graham concluded. "Would the person in the balcony who's bringing us all down please leave?" he said before heading to the wings.

What? Wait a minute. He couldn't have been talking to *me*. There's no fucking way Bill Graham himself could have seen me struggling way up in the balcony through the darkness of the room. In that moment I had a brief flash of sanity. I *must* be hallucinating, I thought. Bill Graham doesn't tell people to leave. "It's gotta be the acid," I said quietly to myself. "It's only the drugs. It's only the drugs." I began to relax.

Much to my relief, CSNY started their set a short while later. I had just begun to melt into the strains of their opener, "Suite: Judy Blue Eyes," when I was startled by a brusque voice from somewhere to my left, barking, "Excuse me, excuse me!" I turned to look and was astonished . . . and dismayed . . . to see Bill Graham himself tromping down the aisle, directly toward me. I kept trying to rationalize. There was no way the promoter's sudden appearance in the balcony could have anything to do with me.

But Graham kept advancing, right to the front row. To *me*. I'd begun to wonder whether I might be hallucinating this, too, when he pointed his finger directly at me and barked, "See me after the show!" *Poof.* The top of my head exploded and a little bit of smoke curled out.

If Graham wanted to see me after the show, that meant I had *not* hallucinated his reproach from the stage. And if I hadn't been hallucinating, then somebody from Joy of Cooking—or *everybody* from Joy of Cooking—had noticed me in the balcony acting like their music was freaking me out.

I was literally dumbstruck, unable to utter a word. It didn't matter. As quickly as he'd arrived, Graham spun around and stomped back up the stairs. I had no idea what was going on. I turned to Danny and croaked, "Did Bill Graham just tell me to see him after the show?"

Danny howled with laughter. "No," he said. "He was talking to *me*." Discount Records was an outlet for Winterland tickets, and the promoter wanted to do some accounting of that night's receipts. I didn't realize we'd been sitting in Graham's personal seats, which is how he knew where to find us.

Suffice it to say that I have a *lot* more respect for psychedelics today than I did back then.

ONE OF THE GUYS in the Second Helping had a big sister named Robin. She was pretty, freckled, and brunette, about four years older than me. She was also an ex-girlfriend of Danny's, so of course I was interested in her. When she decided that she wanted to teach me the rules of love-making, it was about the best day of my teenage life.

It began after one of our shows at the Ice House. She was hanging out with the band, which I thought was pretty cool, and seemed really inter-ested in talking to me. I think she was attracted to the music, the songs, the image I offered as a poet, such as it was. It took me years to think of myself as good looking—and to this day I'm pretty sure that I wasn't back then—but I think she enjoyed the idea of being an older woman shepherd-ing a boy into manhood. She started by turning me on to her books and her music. From her I got J. D. Salinger, Vonnegut, Vivaldi, and Richard and Mimi Fariña.

Then Robin took me to meet some of her friends, a couple she knew from college. When we arrived at their house, we walked right into their bathroom while they were in the tub. I'd never seen anything like it, never met anybody so easygoing. It wasn't like we were going to have sex with them—they just didn't care that we were present. That was very cool for me. I really felt like those were my people. Robin and I ended up spending the night together in a garage apartment, where she showed me all the ropes I could have hoped for.

For me, it was like growing up overnight. We dated for a short while after that. She took me to a love-in gathering at Griffith Park, full of hip-pies, guitars, flutes, music, pot, and diaphanous dresses.

Groovy.

THANKS TO THE group of talented musicians I met at Pasadena City College, the late 1960s were an incredibly fertile, creative time for me. We'd hang out during the day at the Pit (the part of campus where hippies congregated), then play music together at night at one house or another. I was writing songs almost as fast as I could get them onto paper, mostly in my room at my folks' place at the Villa Roma apartments in Alhambra.

One time, my guitar-playing pal, Doug Ingoldsby, challenged me to make up a song on the spot. We were in the car, and at that moment happened to pass an off-ramp to the Pasadena Freeway called Marmion Way and Avenue 64. I immediately made up two songs, "Marmion Way" and "Avenue 64," and still remember the ending line to the latter: "You only hear the motor roar / On the Avenue 64." Doug probably still has the lyrics to them someplace.

In those days, you could do pretty much whatever you wanted when it came to writing music. Nobody cared about rules. I would get high and make up songs in real time, singing them as if they already existed. I inherently knew what a good melody felt like and how to structure a chorus. Let's just say that I didn't trip over myself trying to find the perfect lyric, but that's okay because I wasn't judging my music too harshly back then, which helps explain my prolificacy. I dreamed music into being. Songs poured out of me. Many of them weren't all that great, but some of them were, and, hell, it didn't matter—nobody was going to hear them anyway. All I cared about was that they kept on coming. My only audience was a circle of friends who met on weekends to swap new tunes, and I always wanted to have something to bring to the table. (I still write with spur-of-the-moment lyrics, although these days I usually swap them out for something more considered. There's a famous story about how Paul McCartney's "Yesterday" began as "Scrambled eggs . . ." I call them my "work lyrics.")

I played constantly, with Doug, or at parties, or out in the foothills of Pasadena. Anytime I could pick up a guitar and sing, I did. It was hardly a necessity, but ready access to psychedelics lent additional layers to the experience. Doug and I spent many afternoons out along Angeles Crest Highway in Eaton Canyon, or in the desert, with nothing but guitars and mescaline that was being made by some friends with access to a Cal Tech lab. Ah, the collegiate lifestyle. Out in the San Gabriel Mountains one afternoon, a couple of guys wandered over while we were jamming. After about an hour, one of them said, "Are you Stephen Stills, man?" Well, that day I was pretty close to it: the blissed-out rock star I wouldn't become for several more years.

I actually did my first-ever solo gig at the Tower after one of those afternoon acid trips. The owner was opening up the adjacent café as a performance venue, and I was his first-ever musical act. One thing working against me was my misguided theory that I could take the thing Doug and I did out in nature and make it work inside a small, smoky room. Another was that, in order to build a crowd for the show, the club's owner shut down the folk-dance side of the venue and forced everybody to come watch me. My perspective is a bit warped, but I can remember feeling the resentment pouring from their Greek and Middle Eastern opa-lovin' souls. It was a disaster from my very first notes; I all but imploded under the bad vibes. To make matters worse, I'd invited my parents, who didn't realize how altered I was until many years later when I told them the story. I thought it was funny by that point, but they never quite saw the humor.

The good news was that I got to keep half of the money collected at the door. The bad news was that almost everyone in the audience had entered through the rear, shepherded in by the club owner himself. About the only people who dug into their wallets that night were Doug and my parents.

Doug was also part of my first recording session as a studio musician, back at Amigo Studios in the Valley—the same place where the Second Helping had gone after winning the battle of the bands. In the interim, our manager, Scotty Macquarrie, worked out a deal with Snuff Garrett to be the engineer on projects he brought me in on. Doug and I went in and laid down a few tracks, including what was probably the first-ever recording of "House at Pooh Corner." I still have the acetate demo tape someplace. On the sleeve, I wrote: "Ingoldsby and I." A couple of the other songs include "Tuesday Morning" and "Yukon Railroad," the latter of which ended up on the Nitty Gritty Dirt Band album *Uncle Charlie & His Dog Teddy*. More about that in a minute. First, I had to take a brief diversion on an East Coast tour with an actual rock band that didn't go quite the way any of us would have liked.

ONE OF THE many people I'd met during those early days was a song-writer-pianist named Jeremy Stuart, who was dialed in to the local music scene in ways I was only beginning to understand. Jeremy was always hunting down opportunities, and in one memorable instance saw fit to share one with me. The result was my first taste of rock-star life, with a psychedelic rock band called the Electric Prunes.

The Prunes were a pretty well-known outfit from the San Fernando Valley, with hits like "I Had Too Much to Dream Last Night" and "Get

Me to the World on Time." In 1968, they released the album *Mass in F Minor*, then broke up in the middle of the ensuing tour. In order to avoid refunding tickets, their manager undertook an emergency lineup revamping. The Prunes' bassist, Mark Tulin, knew Jeremy from someplace or other, and roped him in as not only the new keyboard player but also the music director tasked with finding replacements for the departed musicians. Needing a singer and a guitar player, Jeremy asked if I had any interest in hitting the road.

The terms were pretty good: I'd go on tour with a successful rock band, and we didn't even have to learn a bunch of Electric Prunes songs. Instead, Jeremy and I would work up our own tunes. What could possibly go wrong? I was in the middle of my second year at Pasadena City College, and thought hard about this opportunity.

That night, I discussed my options with my father. He was concerned about what he viewed as an impetuous decision, but I saw the situation with crystal clarity. "Dad, I'm spending ninety percent of my time studying to do something I don't want to do, and only ten percent doing what I love, which is music," I told him. "This is an opportunity for me to fix that. I want to make music for a living."

It didn't take long for my folks to come around, if not in outright support then at least in acceptance. Maybe my father had reached a similar point in his own Hollywood aspirations, and this was his way of traveling the path he never took—another shot at the dream, through me, perhaps? Besides, what parent wouldn't want a Prune for a son?

The next day, I dropped out of school and joined the band.

Before I knew it, I was on an American Airlines jet headed to Montreal and the first gig of a three-week tour. I was utterly in awe—right up until we disembarked and discovered how alone we actually were. The band's manager, Lenny, had somehow forgotten to assign us a road manager, so we had to scramble to secure transportation to the gig. Also, we had to figure out where the hell the gig was. Lodging hadn't even been booked, and we discovered that no hotels in our price range had enough rooms for all of us, so we broke ranks and checked into three different places. Mark Tulin had to sleep in a flophouse in the poor part of town, and complained about bedbugs for the rest of the run. It was an inauspicious way to start a tour, and that wasn't even the worst of it. Not even close.

The drummer Jeremy had hired dropped out at the last minute, leaving us no time to find a replacement. Rather than pull the plug, Jeremy insisted we could still make it work. After all, he explained, we still had "natural rhythm" from the bass and piano. Um . . . okay. I think his real motivation was that Lenny—the guy who'd failed to make any arrangements for us—threatened to sue if we quit. We found that part to be very motivating. So much for the rock-star life.

Our first show was at a hole in the wall called Admiral Alfie's Lighthouse Carnaval in downtown Montreal. Once we figured out where it was, we arrived to find a crowd drawn by a bunch of Electric Prunes songs we would not be playing. Not only did we not sound like the actual Prunes, but without a drummer we didn't even sound like a real rock band. Our manager didn't care. He had contracts to fulfill.

That show was where, for the first time in my career, I realized I was not bulletproof. Our show was structured so that about halfway through the set the band would leave the stage and I'd sing my surefire crowd pleasers, "Danny's Song" and "House at Pooh Corner." I was stunned when the audience responded with near silence. It's easy to see now that I was playing to teenagers who wanted only to rock 'n' roll, but I'd never bombed before, and that reception was shocking, a real blow to my confidence. It seemed like half the audience left while I was playing—and I'm surprised the rest of the band didn't take the opportunity to leave, too.

For our encore, Tulin, embracing the cutting edge in what was either a last-ditch effort to reposition the "New" Prunes as an art-rock band or a fuck-you to an indifferent crowd, had us turn up our guitar volumes and lean the instruments against the amps, creating a an ear-blasting feedback howl that blanketed the room like toxic fog. We left those things shrieking and walked offstage. Not many people remained by that point anyway, but that move managed to clear the place out. Quickly.

After that, we called Lenny and begged for a road manager, explaining that we couldn't pull off the rest of the tour the same way we'd staggered through day one. For some reason, he listened. The guy who showed up was a born-to-be-wild biker type with a big red beard named Buddha Miller, who years later would become Jackson Browne's manager. Buddha, a fun-loving guy with a grounded, take-charge personality, removed pressure from the logistical end, but he couldn't help us escape the hostile receptions to our performances. By our next stop, in Philadelphia, we were ready to try anything. I think it was Tulin who came up with the brilliant idea of wearing black armbands onstage and telling the audience that it was a memorial tour for our recently deceased drummer. Suffice it to say that didn't improve the mood of the room, save for a handful of nuns who showed up to see a performance of *Mass in F Minor* and seemed slightly sympathetic. Maybe. Truth be told, they didn't stick around long enough for us to ask.

The tour was mostly horrible, and even though I can laugh about it now, it took me years to get over bombing like we did. When Jimmy Messina and I were first preparing to take our new band on the road, I literally had nightmares about being onstage with the Prunes and watching the audience leave.

That said, I was nineteen and for the first time in my life enjoying the fringe benefits of being in a rock 'n' roll band. Like, for example, the company of groupies. There's a mystique about being onstage that appeals to a certain subset of young women, and I tried to encounter that subset wherever we went. I met a mysterious French girl after that first show in Montreal who took me back to her loft. We sat around and smoked hash with her artist friends, all of whom seemed to wear groovy sunglasses and fur vests like Sonny Bono. That night felt very romantic to me, as if I had been cast as the lead in a French art-house film. I was the traveling troubadour of my fantasies, roaming the world in my thirsty boots, lookin' for adventure in whatever came my way. Also, I got laid, which was nice.

For me, the most enduring aspect of the tour was Darla, a free-spirited young hippie I met when we played Philadelphia. Somehow, a one-night stand—at that point, going two-for-two had me naïvely imagining a career of one-night stands—turned into a multi-year relationship when she followed me back to California some months later. Darla was the quintessential hippie ("You don't have any middle-class hang-ups about sharing a toothbrush, do you?"). She was sexy but extremely high-maintenance, and needed lots of attention. Even though she had a tough, street-chick exterior, she was quite insecure, and tried to make herself indispensable. Too hard, actually. This manifested in her being sexually available all of the time; whenever I wanted it, there she was. I found that part of the relationship to be . . . invigorating. (As it turned out, she was there for a few of us, but I didn't learn those details until later.) Some women try to please in that way because they're nurturers, but not Darla. She just didn't want me to kick her out of my house.

I brought Darla home to meet my parents one Christmas, and she went straight to the refrigerator. Without pausing to question the appropriateness of what she was doing, she took out the last piece of steak, heated it up, and gave it to me. She was probably trying to prove how well she took care of me, but instead she just pissed everyone off. It was obnoxious. Darla was a bull in a china shop in that way. She tended to hype up her own importance to make people like her, but it came off as braggadocio, and people kept catching her stretching the truth. My future wife, Eva, who I met while I was still with Darla, summed her up with the phrase: "Hello, she lied."

My friends didn't like Darla. My family didn't like Darla. My bandmates didn't like Darla. Hell, I'm not sure *I* liked Darla, but I couldn't seem to get her to leave. We reached the point—several times, actually—where I literally threw her suitcase out the window. She just picked it up and came right back in. After Loggins & Messina formed, it wasn't long before everybody in the group began referring to her as "The Thing That Won't Go Away." What can I say? I was young and horny and unschooled in the ways of the world. Darla ended up living in my house for close to four years. Holy shit.

Ultimately, the guys in the Prunes couldn't quit that tour fast enough. We met with our manager, Lenny, and told him to fuck off, that we were done. He had to stifle a laugh. As it turned out, we played right into his hands. By that point, he'd fulfilled his contracts with promoters and was more than happy to show us the door. I doubt he bothered putting another Prunes lineup together after that debacle. The world grieves.

DROPPING OUT OF school to tour with the Electric Prunes had deeper implications than my ongoing education (or lack thereof). Without course credits to my name, I became eligible for the draft, and was saved from Vietnam only by . . . my buck teeth.

The late 1960s were the right time for a kid like me to be on the scene. Growing my hair out allowed me to cover up my big ears, leaving my teeth as my primary point of personal embarrassment. Getting braces took care of that. It also took care of the army.

A number of friends from high school had been drafted, and several were killed in action, including our class president. The more I learned about the war, the less sense it made to me. I didn't support an invasion of a country that was not a threat to the United States. I never saw it as anything close to the moral equivalent of World War II, which had so affected our parents. When we asked big questions about why we were fighting, we got no answers beyond "this is your country right or wrong—love it or leave it." If you didn't offer blind obedience, you were treated like an enemy by the establishment. That made no sense to me. When the National Guard started shooting kids at Kent State, it became a very real issue—of good vs. evil, the old guard vs. the younger generation.

I remember standing in a long line of young men at a pre-induction physical in downtown Los Angeles one sunny afternoon, listening as the sergeant recited a long list of questions designed to weed out the undraftable 4-F losers. "Anyone here with flat feet?" he yelled. "Hernias? Metal in the mouth?" He went on and on, but my attention never left the phrase "metal in the mouth." What the hell could it mean? The more I thought about it, the more sense it made. There was probably no such thing as an army orthodontist, and since braces were so damn expensive, I figured the military wouldn't want to be on the hook for replacing them after your service ended.

My childhood braces were long off by that point, but I hadn't worn my retainer as instructed, and my teeth had begun another slow journey forward in my mouth. It was a perfect exit strategy. I went to my parents, told them I didn't believe in the war, and they agreed with my stance. Also, they agreed to pay for new braces. I had them reinstalled.

Knowing that hundreds of young men had to show up for those induction physicals in Los Angeles, and having heard that the LA draft board didn't accept many exemptions, I began to worry they'd somehow learn that my braces were a recent addition. So with the help of a friendly college professor who let me use his address in Fresno, I changed my board to the northern part of the state. Mark Tulin, the Prunes' bass player, drove me up there in his Datsun convertible. There were only about twenty guys in my group, and sure enough—armed with a letter from my orthodontist—I was given a temporary draft exemption. Luckily for me, when the lottery system was implemented shortly thereafter, my number was so high that there was no way I would be drafted.

I left the braces on until my teeth were straight, which was perfect timing. Just a few months after that I was on the road, touring for the first time with Loggins & Messina.

That would come later, though. Back home following my Prunes experience, I tried to melt back into the scene as seamlessly as possible. I jammed at the same parties I'd jammed at before, and increasingly wondered what I would do with myself. I was still living in my parents' apartment and going stir-crazy. I felt like an arrow pulled back in a bow, ready to be released. All I needed was a target. It didn't matter that my time with the Prunes had been difficult; I was readier than ever to commit myself to a career in music.

Enter Colin and Mac. Colin Cameron and Malcolm Elsensohn—a bass-drums duo who were so ubiquitous together that in my memories they appear strictly as "Colin and Mac"—were all over the LA scene. They'd played in Southern California bands for years, backing all sorts of musicians along the way. I first met Mac at the Glendale Ice House after a Second Helping show; I guess he was impressed enough to introduce himself, and I'm really glad he did. He opened some vital early doors for me as I tried to make a name for myself. Notably, Mac was the one who introduced me to Jeremy Stuart, my conduit to the Electric Prunes. Mac was also the drummer who dropped off of the tour at the last minute, having received a late offer to record an album for Elektra Records with a singer named Diane Hildebrand. Needless to say, Colin was also on that record.

Colin and Mac were my mentors in the world of pro musicians, showing me things like how to prepare for auditions and studio sessions. Seeing my desperation to leave my parents' apartment, and knowing I had no money for my own place, they let me stay at their pad in East Hollywood for about six months. That was a seminal period. We were either playing or listening to music at all times. I felt like I was finally living the dream.

One night after we dropped some acid, a young woman knocked on the door. None of us had ever seen her before. She looked angelic to me, beautiful in a California way. Best of all, she was holding a guitar. "A friend of mine told me to come and sing my songs for you," she cooed. Hell yes. We invited her in and she began to play and sing, casting a deep spell over the room. Her songs were part folk, part jazz, and one hundred-percent magic. It was as if Joni Mitchell herself had decided to drop in on a bunch of stoned-out strangers, just to blow their minds. I'm pretty sure it *wasn't* Joni, but that's the kind of impression this girl left. After an hour or so, she departed as mysteriously as she'd arrived. Somehow, even though everyone in the room was blown away, none of us had the presence of mind to get her name or phone number. To this day, I have no idea who she was. That night might have ended up as the mythology of a collective hallucination had I not asked her to teach me some of her chords, which I used the next day to write a song called "I Ain't Gonna Stay Here." I never finished it, but it would prime my jazz-pop pump for many years to come.

One of Colin and Mac's regular gigs was backing Don Dunn and Tony McCashen, who played together under the name—wait for it—Dunn & McCashen. They were recording an album for Capitol Records, and Mac brought me in to play lead guitar on a few songs. I don't remember much about the session, except that I wasn't really a lead guitar player. I mean, I had my moments, but the environment had to be just right, and I had to be feeling it, and then things had to flow—otherwise the possibility of disaster was significant. What Mac suggested—and what I ended up doing—was listening to a demo of their songs the night before the session, and then humming lead guitar ideas into a tape recorder, which I then used to work up my solos.

Another thing that happened during the session was a studio drop-in taking note of my singing during the few minutes he spent in the recording booth. His name was Jim Messina, and he knew a few of the guys in the band. He liked what I was doing well enough to get my name, and then promptly forgot it until we put two and two together some years later while rehashing our histories for an interview.

That session must have gone pretty well, because the group asked me to play lead guitar for them at some of their shows. This might have worked in smaller rooms, but Dunn & McCashen had landed a gig at the Forum opening for Sly and the Family Stone. I was a big fan of Sly, and knew it would be a huge audience. I'd never come close to performing in front of that many people. The Pasadena Civic, where the Second Helping had appeared with the Association, held three thousand people and was half empty when we played there. The Forum held nearly eighteen thousand, and Sly Stone knew how to fill a room.

That gig was like going to the big leagues for me. I wanted to make sure we presented ourselves in a professional way, so when we were working on a new tune of Tony's, I jumped in and suggested an arrangement. I had an idea for a solo section where each instrument would take one beat to start the breakdown in the middle of the song: Colin would hit beat 1 on bass, I'd hit beat 2 on lead guitar, etc. Honestly, it was a pretty cool idea, but when it came time to perform it onstage, Tony completely blanked out. He was supposed to be the fourth guy to enter, on rhythm guitar, but he began early, which changed the arrangement in disastrous ways. We all tried to scramble to cover for him. I know now that you have to practice the shit out of an arrangement like that.

That was the final song of the set, the big closer, and it fell apart. As it turned out, that wasn't the only thing that fell—so did my belt. I really wanted to look like a rock star, so I bought a mock-silver conch belt that I wore low on my hips. Trouble was, nobody told me I should secure it to a belt loop or something, because during my final solo, with the spotlight firmly on me, that damn belt slid down over my hips and around my ankles, and stayed there until the final note of the song. I was so focused on not fucking up that I didn't even have the wherewithal to step out and kick it away. It just stayed there like rock 'n' roll manacles. Don't think about the belt, I told myself. Don't think about the belt! This mostly ensured that I did nothing during my solo but think about the damn belt. At least I didn't try to walk. When the song ended, I quietly bent over and pulled it up enough to shuffle offstage with the rest of the band.

Actually, that belt was a pretty good metaphor for my playing: If I didn't seriously study my options before showtime, my solos tended to slide downhill in embarrassing ways. I was self-taught, and such an optimist that I trusted my fingers to find their way to whatever amazing solo I was imagining—only to discover that I didn't have the slightest clue how to translate my ideas to the fretboard. I was all about feel. If I was in the zone, or if I'd had the time and self-discipline to work things out in advance, I could usually pull it off. Too often, though, any good licks I laid down were equal amounts of practice and luck. If I started to think too much about what I was doing, I would panic. It was almost as if I suddenly remembered that I didn't know how to play lead guitar. I'd get lost, and with minimal technique to find my way back, all those frets would start to look like a corn maze. Way too many of my solos ended up in ashes. I tend to be overly self-critical, but I'm pretty sure I'm not exaggerating here.

I managed to get through that slot opening for Sly, but had less luck with a subsequent show at the Ice House's other location, in Pasadena, after which Don Dunn pulled me aside and said, "Look, Kenny, you're way too good to be standing in the shadows with our backup band. You should have a band of your own." Don was a good friend, and that was a classy way to fire somebody. Also, it was damned good advice.

Still, I kept on trying. I auditioned for a Bay Area band called Sunbear, but got so high while waiting my turn to perform that I could barely speak, let alone play guitar. I auditioned my songs for a spot on the Moody Blues' label, Threshold Records, but they weren't looking for my kind of acoustic music. Years later, I met and wrote with Justin Heyward, and he told me the band never heard my audition tapes. Hmmm. Colin and Mac helped land me an audition for Linda Ronstadt's band. I loved her music—I'd seen her play at the Troubadour a half-dozen times—but for some reason I sabotaged myself by not boning up on her repertoire. That would have helped, given my inability to read more than a simple chord chart. Linda was sweet and encouraging, but I never had much of a shot at the gig. I think I was mostly hoping for a chance to show her a few of my tunes. Then again, becoming her backup guitarist might have actually been an unnecessary detour from the path I was about to take.

My theory about auditions is that if I'm not where I belong, I suck. Totally. That's always been true. I think some part of me just knows when something is right, and that's when the magic happens.

Much of the money I made in those days came through studio work—small-time demo sessions paying scale, not big record deals—that Colin and Mac helped arrange. I wasn't cut out for that either, because I couldn't read charts quickly enough. I remember sidling up to Colin in more than one session and asking questions like, "How do you play this?" and "What's that part there?" He would quietly talk me through the piece, and I'd play it by ear. What I really wanted was to be a singer on one of those dates, even just as backup, but that never happened.

For me, the real money began when Jeremy, the guy who'd hooked me up with the Electric Prunes, came through again. He knew somebody at Wingate Music, a publishing house over on Gower Street in Hollywood. They shopped songs around for artists to record, and wanted to bolster their stockpile of material. I happened to be a songwriter, and Jeremy knew I was desperate for dough. When he told me that Wingate had just given a friend of his a writer's contract, I wanted to know more.

A few days later, I was sitting across the desk from Bob Todd at the Wingate offices. Bob was in his late thirties, with the obligatory record-exec goatee and shaggy, longish hair. I was surprised by his spartan office—no gold records on the wall, or any adornments at all, really. Then again, he was on the publishing side of things, which is a different beast. I unpacked my old Kay acoustic and played Bob my best stuff: "House at Pooh Corner," "Danny's Song," "Yukon Railroad," and "Vahevala." I didn't know it at the time, but musicians rarely performed their songs live in the office for this type of meeting, opting instead to send in recorded demos. I was innocently optimistic and really wanted that gig. And I didn't suck. My voice was strong and relaxed. I was in the zone. Oddly, Mr. Todd kept shaking his head *no* while I sang, yet kept smiling approvingly. I was totally confused until it dawned on me. "Mr. Todd," I said between songs, "I know that you're keeping time with your head, but could you try to do it up and down instead of from side to side? I keep thinking that you're shaking *no*, and it's kind of demoralizing."

"I'm so sorry," he stammered. "No one's ever said that to me before."

Years later, Bob told me that from that day on, whenever a songwriter played something for him, he nodded *yes* instead of shaking *no*. I don't know if any of his other musicians appreciated it, but I sure did. Also, I got the gig.

Bob and I enjoyed a great working relationship from that day on. I got $100 per week on a three-year contract, and there wasn't even a monthly quota—I just gave Wingate songs as they came to me. That's hardly any dough for even one song like "House at Pooh Corner," let alone everything I ended up writing for Loggins & Messina under that publishing deal, but it was exactly what I needed at that stage in my life. Becoming a professional musician was validating, even if it was behind the scenes. Believe it or not, I'm still grateful. The rights to those songs eventually reverted to me, so it all ended well.

The one song I held back from Wingate was "Danny's Song." I used to joke that I kept it because it always got me laid, but the reality is that I knew it would become an important tune for me, and I simply wasn't willing to give it away.

As a bonus, I got free demo time in Wingate's pro-grade, 24-track studio, which was one of their hooks to lure young talent. It worked. They cut actual hit records there during working hours, so I'd come in at night with Colin and Mac and other musicians—even Jimmy Messina now and then, once that relationship started—to work on my demos. In exchange, Wingate used those demos to try to sell my songs to established acts. It never really worked. Bob eventually told me that my songs were too rangy for most pop acts, and the only person who should sing them was me.

I did encounter one problem upon signing with Wingate. Our deputy-sheriff manager with the Second Helping, Scott Macquarrie, had locked us into a contract of his own, in hopes we'd break big and give him a train to ride for a long while. We were high school students at the time, and he'd positioned the deal as essential to our relationship. This provided a stumbling block for Wingate over who actually held the rights to my music. At that point, Jeremy came through yet again, sending me to an up-and-coming young music business lawyer named Lee Phillips, who proposed a simple resolution: I'd been under eighteen when I signed that deal, so it wasn't valid. It took only one paragraph on Lee's letterhead to void the contract with Scotty. I had no money for legal fees, and didn't pay Lee a penny until a few months later, after my $100-per-week salary started rolling in. I couldn't pay the entire bill at once, so I sent him an initial payment of twenty bucks. Lee called me immediately upon receiving it.

"Why did you pay this bill?" he chuckled. "I'd already written it off!"

I sent Lee a bunch of checks for $5 and $10 over the coming weeks, to the point that it became a running joke between us. No one had ever done that before, he said—people either ran out on a bill or they paid it in full, but he'd never known anybody to split the difference. The moral of the story is that Lee has been my attorney ever since, representing me through my entire career. I even gave him one of my Grammy Awards. He refused to accept it as a gift, but said he would watch over it for me. It's been in his home, on a shelf, for more than twenty years. Lee continues to refuse ownership.

MY FIRST BIG SALES for Wingate didn't come from the company shopping my demos, but through my own connections and a bit of luck. At one of the parties where I regularly swapped songs with area musicians, I happened to trade tunes with a couple of guitar players, Jeff Hanna and Jimmy Ibbotson, from a group called the Nitty Gritty Dirt Band. They had released five albums at that point, a career's worth, but what excited me was that they were talking about their sixth, and how they needed songs for it. I played them some of my tunes, and they liked them so much that they invited me to meet their manager, Bill McKeuen, at his home in Laurel Canyon. Bill's brother John was the group's banjo player, and he was there, too. I played a bunch more songs for them, and before I knew it, they said they wanted four of them for their new album, *Uncle Charlie & His Dog Teddy*: "House at Pooh Corner," "Santa Rosa," "Prodigal's Return," and "Yukon Railroad." I didn't know it at the time, but the sound of that album was inspired by a new country-rock group named Pogo, which would soon change its name to Poco, and which featured a guitar player named Messina. The guy kept coming into my life before he ever actually came into my life. We were satellites circling in increasingly closer orbits.

Before the album could be released, though, a problem emerged: Walt Disney Productions denied the band permission to use "House at Pooh Corner," claiming copyright infringement. Their attorneys decreed that outside artists—especially artists with a name like the Nitty Gritty Dirt Band, I thought to myself—would not record songs about one of their cornerstone characters.

"House at Pooh Corner" was the best song I'd given to Wingate. If Disney wouldn't let it be recorded, where did that leave me? I even considered changing the first line—"Christopher Robin and I walked along"—to "Christopher Loggins and I walked along," to try and skirt the copyright issues, but that destroyed the magic. The song had to be what it actually was for it to work.

Enter my pal Doug Ingoldsby. Doug was old friends with a girl named Marnie Walker, whose father, Cardon, happened to be COO of Walt Disney Productions. (Within a couple of years, Card Walker would become the company's president and CEO.) Doug made a call, and before I knew it we were grabbing our guitars and heading out to the Walkers' house in Glendale.

Marnie took us to her father's den, where he was reading the newspaper on a couch. She sat on the floor with Doug and me as we played some songs. When we got to "House at Pooh Corner," Card put down his paper and listened attentively. "That's a really good song, boys," he said.

Doug took it from there. "Well, Cardon, it's really interesting," he said. "Kenny wrote that song, and it *is* a great song, but evidently there's something going on with the legal department at Disney. They won't let him record it."

Card looked puzzled, then chuckled. "Call my office on Wednesday," he said. I'm pretty sure he figured nobody would ever hear the thing. No way could a kid from Alhambra be a threat to the Disney machine.

I did as instructed, and the next thing I knew, "House at Pooh Corner" had been cleared to become a centerpiece on *Uncle Charlie & His Dog Teddy*—and, even more importantly, on the first Loggins & Messina album two years after that.

COLIN AND MAC'S PLACE, where I'd been crashing for six months, was next door to Don Dunn and only a block from Jeremy Stuart, so it was pretty much the center of my musical universe for a while. I had some amazing times there, but after too many days spent stepping over the guy who slept on the living room floor and didn't pay rent (that would be me), they suggested very gently that it might be best if I got a place of my own.

They also helped me find it. One of their friends, Dann Lottermoser, lived in a little hillside duplex in East Los Angeles, and the unit next to his was vacant. The place overlooked the train yards and was in a crappy neighborhood, but rent was all of $65 per month, which I could afford . . . even if I had barely any money left over for groceries. I would occasionally hear gunshots at night, and more than once I walked in on somebody trying to rob the place. Finally, my mom insisted that I get a guard dog. Her friend's pup had just had a litter of spaniel-mutt puppies, and I picked out the biggest, most rambunctious of the bunch—the first to the food bowl, which I figured showed a strong survival instinct. He'd need that if he was going to be *my* dog. Given his relative size, I named him Moose. He was far too sweet to guard anything, and he'd be my best friend for the next fourteen years.

When Moose was still tiny, I piled him into my shiny red Land Cruiser, and drove down to Don Dunn's house to pick up Colin and Mac for a beach day. Well, as we packed my car with their stuff, I plumb forgot that I had a dog and left Moose behind. We were halfway to the beach when I screamed, "Shit!" and spun the car around. We'd been gone from the house for maybe twenty minutes, but when we pulled up there was Moose, sitting inside the open garage, waiting patiently. He was just a puppy. From that day on, he always kept one eye on me, staying aware of where I was at all times. I tried to return the sentiment. That skill came in handy when I eventually had kids.

Moose was smart and loyal, and I took him with me everywhere, including recording sessions. (He once got kicked out of Sunset Sound because he chased a fly into the control room window while tape was running.) That dog was psychic or something. When we'd go to friends' homes or big outdoor concerts, even though he'd be off-leash all day, I always found him by my car, curled up asleep, somehow knowing when it was time to go.

After I'd had him for a year or so, I wrote a song called "Moose Is a Good Dog." Jimmy Messina always wanted me to record it for L&M, but I didn't think it was up to our standards. Years later, I added some lyrics and a bridge, changed the title to "Moose 'n Me," and recorded it for my children's album *All Join In*.

I blame myself for Moose's hearing loss in his later years, because his resting place of choice in the studio was behind my amp, which was always a bit too loud. Then again, lots of dogs lose their hearing as they get older, so who knows? Moose lived for fourteen years, enough time for him to be by my side as lots of important things started to happen.

DANN LOTTERMOSER WAS a good guy to live next door to. He'd been in a San Diego surf band called Deep Six with Mac, Don Dunn, and Tony McCashen, which released an album on Liberty Records in 1966. I mention it here because a song on that record, "Rising Sun," featured a seventeen-year-old Jim Messina, who even as a teenager was such a production savant that he handled every instrument on the track except for drums. As huge as the Southern California music scene was in the late 1960s, sometimes it seemed very, very small.

Dann and I were neighbors for only a few months, but that was a creatively fertile time for me. I loved having musician friends over to jam, and Dann lived just across the deck. The group of us would light some candles, smoke a joint or two, pass around a bottle of cheap cabernet, and play together on whatever ideas emerged. They flowed like wine, stream of consciousness, continuously moving from notion to notion. When a chord progression caught my attention, I'd sing over it, making up the melody as I went. The trick was that I recorded everything on my trusty cassette machine, knowing that in our drunken, stoned reverie, we'd never remember a thing. The next day, I'd go through the tapes, pick out the best moments, and turn them into songs, crediting whoever was jamming with me as co-writers. I was very free with those credits; if you played something that I built a tune out of, your name got attached. I was such a hippie that I'd even give you a writer's credit if you did nothing more than stand in the background and bang on a tambourine. I figured that everyone in the room added to the energy, and so, to my cosmic reasoning, they must have had some influence on whatever emerged. I remember Dann coming home from a gig one night, sticking his head in an open window, saying with a smile, "Hey, buddy, what did I write today?"

Looking back on it, those days seem like a dream: creative, fun, and wildly absurd. I can't overstate my naïveté. I wanted to feel like we were a kind of artistic family, a gathering of talented musicians sharing ideas in an unfiltered, noncompetitive way. And in many ways we were, even if I was doing most of the heavy lifting. I never accounted for the work it took searching through a four-hour jam session to find thirty seconds' worth of inspiration, nor did I value the talent necessary to craft a bridge, a chorus, and words. That would take me years to put together. It wasn't until money started to come in from those songs that I recognized how much I was diluting my paycheck. I was giving away my work, my talent, and, eventually, my income.

Actually, I didn't come to think of my work as valuable until Columbia Records boss Clive Davis referred to me as an artist. Only then did I begin to see myself as somebody who didn't make up songs but *wrote* them. At that point, I stopped giving credit to folks who happened to be walking through the room while we jammed. A few of the tunes we worked on that summer, including "Vahevala" and "Sailin' the Wind," ended up as Loggins & Messina staples.

After Dann moved out, a rotating cast of characters cycled through his apartment. First was a singer-songwriter from Baton Rouge named Duke Bardwell, who went on to play bass in Elvis Presley's band. After Duke was an old high school buddy of mine, Jimmy Recor, who had just returned from a stint in the air force. On his move-in day he tried to get an upright piano into the place and, symbolic of the disrepair of our duplex, it fell right through the rotted planks of the porch onto the hillside below. Welcome to the neighborhood, Jimmy. The landlord's solution was to remove Jimmy's bathroom door and lay it across the chasm. Problem solved.

The other issue Jimmy faced was that the hillside was slowly sliding down onto his side of the apartment. His bedroom was in the rear, and when he opened the curtains one day, he found dirt piled halfway up the window like an ant farm. It was disconcerting, to say the least. When Jimmy moved out, the landlord decided to leave the apartment empty rather than risk the hillside busting through the wall while somebody was sleeping there. That decision was fine by me, because the unit's living room was unaffected, and now I had unlimited access to it. It became my party house. I made a huge dining table out of plywood and bricks, and would have a dozen people at a time over for dinner and late-night jam sessions.

One night, Colin, Mac, and I were jamming, loud, like rock stars. It was an extremely hot LA evening, and we had the doors and windows open. I don't think we realized how effectively loud music can filter down a hill. The guys left after midnight, and only moments later there was a knock on the door. Through the open window I saw two police officers on the porch. "One second," I called out, as I gathered up the pipes and headed to the bathroom to flush what little remained of my pot.

The racket was clearly over—hell, I was alone in the place—but it didn't take much for the cops to notice the lingering scent of marijuana through the open window. The strangest thing was that, even as we shouted to each other through the closed door, we were looking at each other right through that window. Eventually, they simply reached through, twisted the door lock from inside, and let themselves in. All that was left at that point were a few boxes of seeds Doug and I planned to toss around San Marino after the next rainy day, but that was enough for them to call in a team to search the house. Over the next hour or so, the arresting officers and I got to know each other. I think they might even have grown to like me. They arrested me anyway, of course, and took me downtown in handcuffs, where I spent the night in a holding tank with about fifty other guys, trying to make myself as invisible as possible.

It was the first (and last) time I was arrested. I'm not sure why, but I never wrote a song about the experience, maybe because the charges were dropped shortly thereafter. I remember one of the cops asking if I'd learned my lesson. "Oh yeah, I'm done with getting caught," I said. They laughed.

It was only a couple of months later that I set out for a weekend in Palm Springs—complete with a big bag of weed, of course—and was pulled over for a broken taillight just a few blocks from my house. I'd been smart enough to stash the pot in my suitcase, but dumb enough to leave my wallet in there next to it. Jeez. To get my ID I'd have to expose my stash. Even worse, when I got out of the car, I saw that it was the same cops who'd arrested me before.

"How you doin'?" one of them said.

"Uhhh . . . great," I stammered. "Headed to Palm Springs. Driving. Obviously."

While I talked, I was desperately trying to figure out a way to open my suitcase while shielding its contents as I snatched up my wallet. Luckily, it never came to that. One of the cops said, "Don't bother with your ID. We know who you are. Just fix your taillight. See you around."

Boy, did I learn a lesson that day. I never kept my wallet near my stash again.

MY FIRST TASTE of real recording—not just demos but an actual album, and not just one track but the whole thing—came courtesy of my boss and benefactor at Wingate, Bob Todd. Bob had his fingers in many pots in the local music scene. Country-rock was burgeoning thanks to the likes of Poco, Buffalo Springfield, Linda Ronstadt, and Emmylou Harris, all of whom were recording in Los Angeles at the time, and Bob wanted in on that action. He hooked up with Dee Barton, a well-known LA big-band leader, and gathered up a bunch of session musicians to cut a country-rock record. Because they needed songs . . . and a singer

. . . he inducted me. Even though we were all from Southern California, Dee tried to swampify us as best he could, going so far as to call the group Gator Creek. I guess it worked, because Mercury Records agreed to release our album.

Almost as soon as I'd joined the group, they hustled us out for a photo shoot in what, on the record cover, looked like southern marshland. In reality it was Malibu Lake, the gated community where Dee lived. At one point, somebody propped a floppy farmer's hat on my head. When they asked me to walk into the water for a picture, I cut my foot so badly on a submerged shard of glass that I had to go to the hospital for a tetanus shot. That was the end of the photo shoot for me.

Gator Creek existed for only a short time, first in the recording studio, and then at an industry showcase we did for the press. I appeared on a couple of songs, both of which I wrote: "Long Tail Cat" and "Danny's Song." It was not the passion project of my dreams, but it gave me exposure as a performer, and was my first experience in a pro studio with top-level musicians. Most importantly, it was my introduction to a keyboard player named Michael O'Martin, who, apart from me, was the least-known player in the group. Boy, was he great on those tracks. After changing his name to Omartian, Michael ended up joining Loggins & Messina for our first three records.

The other lasting thing to emerge from Gator Creek was the first real recording of "Danny's Song." It's not great. I came late to the project, and I suspect they were running low on budget, so instead of taking the time to rehearse the tune with me (I offered; they refused) the musicians just decided to read it off the charts in the studio. I assumed they knew what they were doing. I counted it down, sang the first verse, and they were off and running. It would have undoubtedly turned out better had we taken the time to map out a more nuanced approach.

Mercury barely promoted the album, not that the Gator Creek musicians cared all that much. They were all living off of studio gigs and didn't need this record to hit in order to make a living. I didn't care that much either. It wasn't my band, and I just wasn't into it the same way I would be with groups to come.

CHAPTER 3

MESSINA AND ME

I WAS BANGING AROUND Los Angeles, picking up studio work on pop sessions for artists no one remembers, writing tunes that were never picked up by anyone, and trying like hell to figure out how to make a go of this music thing. Like they say, it's good to be good, but it's better to be lucky.

I knew that I could write quality songs—the Nitty Gritty Dirt Band proved as much, and the fact that people continually wanted to hear "Danny's Song" and "House at Pooh Corner" reinforced the notion—but I was floundering with my career. My Wingate songs weren't selling, and I had a strong feeling that the missing piece was my voice. If I wanted anyone to listen to my stuff, I needed to be the one singing it, just like Bob Todd had said. I just didn't know how to make that happen.

Enter Danny.

My brother didn't introduce me to Jim Messina, per se. I'd known Messina's work since I first saw Poco at the Troubadour in 1969. That was a really good band—Richie Furay, Rusty Young, and Jimmy could all play. Hell, Messina and Furay had been in Buffalo Springfield together. They were bona fide. I was a fan.

When Poco announced a show at Pasadena City College a few months after that Troubadour gig, I wasn't gonna miss it . . . and I turned out to be one of the only people to feel that way. Only about fifteen people showed up, spurring Furay to ask the crowd, "Did anybody work on the publicity for this show?" An empty room was fine by me; I got to zero in on Messina through the entire concert. He wasn't what you'd call a showman—he didn't own the spotlight or anything like that—but his country-style electric-guitar picking was uniquely his own.

The Buffalo Springfield connection was what really drew me to Jimmy. As a teenager he'd worked as an engineer at Sunset Sound, where the Springfield cut their records, and was so competent that he somehow ended up as the band's producer *and* bass player. Between that and Poco, I really felt that Jimmy would relate to the music I was making. I even wrote him a letter in which I talked about wanting to show him my stuff—but I sent it to the management address on a Poco LP jacket, and I'm sure he never saw it.

This is where Danny comes in. My brother's gig as a manager at Discount Records in Berkeley paid off in multiple ways. CBS owned both Discount Records (the record-store chain) and Columbia Records (the label). Danny, along with a co-worker named Don Ellis, transitioned to the Columbia A&R department, where they became trainees under the legendary Clive Davis. Later, Danny would head the company's London division for a few years, during which time he signed Mott the Hoople and Rod Argent of the Zombies. Ellis would eventually lead Columbia's entire A&R team.

At about the time that my brother transitioned to Columbia, Jimmy quit Poco. He was tired of the life of a touring musician and wanted to become a staff producer for the label, which would allow him to stay home and develop artists.

So Danny talked me up to Don, and Don talked me up to Jimmy, who agreed to meet with a youngster to discuss his rock 'n' roll aspirations. (Was it odd that the aspiring youngster was Jimmy's junior by all of one month? Yeah, but he was experienced and I was not.)

It was December 1970. A dinner meeting was arranged at Jimmy's North Hollywood apartment. I wore baggy jeans and a velour shirt, and I think my beard might have taken him aback. Jimmy told me later that his first impression was, Gee, they must want a rock star. I guess I looked the part.

Jimmy's wife, Jenny, made tacos, after which we were supposed to review my music. Jimmy thought I was going to bring some demo tapes, but I figured that I'd play my stuff live. I brought my old Kay, but was so embarrassed by it that I left it in the car, hoping that Jimmy would offer me one of his. (Jimmy didn't share his first thought—What kind of amateur shows up to play music for somebody without a guitar?—with me until a couple of years later.) So he handed me a gorgeous Gibson acoustic and fired up his reel-to-reel recorder. I played him "Danny's Song." I played "House at Pooh Corner" and "Vahevala." I played a few songs that we never ended up recording, including "Santa Rosa" (which was covered by the Dirt Band) and "My Love's Gonna Tumble On You" (which I eventually performed with jazz/pop vocalists Clark and Marilyn Burroughs on *The Smothers Brothers Comedy Hour*). I thought things were going well; Jimmy and I seemed to hit it off, and my voice was strong. But something wasn't quite connecting.

I learned later that Jimmy was not impressed. I mean, he liked me well enough, and he liked my music, but I'd brought him a bunch of folk songs, and he wasn't looking for folk songs. Also, I was completely raw, with no manager, no agent, and no experience leading a band. Hell, I didn't even own a decent guitar (or *any* guitar, as far as Jimmy knew)—all of which meant a lot of extra work on his end that he wasn't certain he wanted to take on.

So he auditioned other people. Olivia Newton-John ended up at his house, as did Andy Williams, but neither was a great fit. At that point, Jimmy was under contract to handle six records a year for Columbia, and he hadn't even found his first artist. The guy he came closest to producing was Dan Fogelberg, who went on to chart four top-10 hits over a multi-decade career. When Jimmy asked what he wanted out of a potential relationship, however, Dan said he wanted to make music that sounded like Poco, which was exactly what Jimmy *didn't* want to hear. Messina had spent years making records that were too country for the rock charts and too rock for the country charts, and wanted to avoid another go-round with that particular headache.

Which is when he began to reconsider the hippie kid from Alhambra. Jimmy liked that my voice was versatile enough to sing folk, country, and soul. He gave me one of his songs, "Peace of Mind," to try on for size. He clearly liked the results, because the next thing I knew, he offered to produce my record.

This was the break I'd been looking for. Jimmy was very encouraging, and kept me comfortable while showing me the ropes. He'd been through the rock 'n' roll ringer, and knew things like how to put a band together and build a tour itinerary. He knew the music business: What are the percentages for managers and agents? How do you rehearse, and for how long? How do you pay for rehearsal time? When he told me he'd been touring for six years, I couldn't imagine being on the road that long. (Now that I've been touring for more than fifty years, it's a whole lot easier to picture.)

I had a lot to learn, and Jimmy was about to become my mentor in many ways. We started meeting at his place almost daily. Early each morning I'd drive my girlfriend to work in my old VW camper, then park on the street outside Jimmy's apartment and go to sleep in the back of the van. When I woke up, I'd stumble bleary-eyed up the stairs to Jimmy's door. It was time to play.

Jimmy was focused and intense. He claimed that he didn't listen to rock 'n' roll on the radio because he didn't want to be influenced. He'd never even heard Led Zeppelin, which blew my mind. This professional seclusion became comically clear a couple of years later when Loggins & Messina went on the TV show *The Midnight Special*. Wolfman Jack had Jimmy introduce the Guess Who, and Jim read the cue card like it was a question—"Coming up next: guess who?" Oh yeah, I thought, he's probably never heard of them. During my first visit to Jimmy's apartment, I found that the most recent LP in his collection was *Sgt. Pepper's*, which by that point was three or four years old.

When it came time to audition musicians, we made our headquarters at Barry Sullivan's home at the top of Mulholland Drive. Barry was Jimmy's father-in-law, and had been a successful Hollywood actor since the 1930s. His place had a pool house just big enough for a rock band to set up. (Only a couple of years earlier, I had seen a feature in *Los Angeles* magazine about Sullivan's daughters, Jenny and Patsy, and thought about how pretty they were, and wondered why I couldn't meet the kind of attractive neo-supermodel who got featured in magazines. Almost before I knew it, Jenny was making me tacos.)

Finding the right mix of players for our band was important to us. This would be our group for the record and on the road, and the fit had to be right, both musically and temperamentally. The audition process took months.

We found our first member before we even got started. Al Garth was a gifted saxophone player who lived below Jimmy, literally, in the downstairs section of a two-unit house. The stairs to Jimmy's apartment ascended directly outside Al's front door, and Al couldn't help but notice when I kept showing up at Jimmy's place and making music with the neighbor he had yet to meet. One January afternoon, Al was standing by his open front door as I arrived, and called me over. I'd seen him through his window on occasion, sitting at a Fender Rhodes piano, so I knew he played a little. We got to talking. He was eager to meet the guy at the center of those upstairs sessions that kept bleeding through his ceiling.

I invited him up to meet Jimmy, and Al was smart enough to bring his saxophone. Neither Jimmy nor I had even considered a sax as part of our sound, but when Jimmy started playing a song called "Nobody But You," Al jumped right in, ad-libbing horn parts. Jimmy and I both loved it. When Al mentioned that he also played viola, the deal was sealed. Never mind that he hadn't touched the instrument in fifteen years; suddenly we had a sax player *and* a fiddle player in one package. If the guy wasn't a musical genius, he was awfully close—a description that's even more appropriate for our other multi-instrumentalist, Jon Clarke.

Jon had played sax with Don Ellis (the jazz trumpeter who'd accompanied the likes of Charles Mingus and Eric Dolphy, not the Columbia

Records exec who worked with my brother). He was a musician's musician, an oboe prodigy who played in orchestras until we convinced him that he needed to learn rock 'n' roll. (We probably destroyed his classical credibility when we got him to join our band.) Jon wasn't even eighteen when we met him, and needed his parents' approval to join us, but boy did we want him on board. He had amazing jazz chops, and in addition to oboe he played English horn and bassoon, and all the flutes from baritone on up. The guy could play two recorders at the same time. Early on, Jon pulled me aside and confided that he just didn't understand rock music. Well, he made up for lost time.

The duo of Garth and Clarke was a difference maker for our sound. They could both write charts, and between them they handled pretty much every non-rhythm instrument besides guitar. They'd jump from brass to woodwind to fiddle between songs, sometimes even during songs, lending unbelievable depth to our sound. We were one of the first country-rock bands, if not the first, to use those sorts of reed instruments, and got a lot of attention for it.

Jimmy knew a drummer named Merel Bregante from a local band called the Sunshine Company, which had regularly opened up for Poco. Merel left town after the band broke up, but Jimmy liked him so much that he flew him down from Sacramento to audition, even putting him up in his apartment. I guess this gave Merel a leg up on the competition, which was fine with me, because I *loved* the way he drummed. His style was pure groove. It was perfect.

Another benefit to Merel was that he came pre-loaded with his own bassist, Larry Sims, also from the Sunshine Company. Those guys knew each other's styles inside and out. Larry was also a fantastic vocalist, giving us a third part for harmonies, not to mention the occasional lead (which was itself impressive in a band named for two vocalists). That's Larry singing the biblical quote at the end of "Golden Ribbons" on our second record: "What does it avail a man to gain a fortune and lose his soul?" A lot of people think it's Stephen Stills, thanks to Jimmy's Buffalo Springfield roots, but man, Larry was just as good. Jimmy liked his voice so much that he gave him the lead on "Keep Me in Mind," from our *Mother Lode* album.

As it happened, Jimmy wasn't the only person in the band with ties to the Sunshine Company. I'd actually opened for them with Second

Helping, when we both appeared at something called the Teenage Fair in Hollywood, in the booth sponsored by Standel amplifiers. (The Second Helping secured our spot by winning that KFWB battle of the bands competition.) I have an indelible memory of Larry's performance that day.

That was the year Standel introduced DDL (digital delay line) to their amps, and Larry accidentally plugged his bass into the delay port, making everything he played a half second late. Larry was so high on acid that he figured it was his brain and not the technology. The impressive part is that he compensated by playing everything—the whole show—a half second ahead of everybody else, while still singing perfectly in time. He just assumed that the drugs created a bizarre wrinkle in time, and he was such an extraordinary player that he was able to adjust accordingly. Now that's what I call a fluid mind.

That talent came in handy because Jimmy was a damn good bassist himself, and had already come up with most of our bass parts. The approach he'd used in Buffalo Springfield involved the deft touch and muted rhythm that he'd picked up from Stephen Stills, and Larry had to learn that style from scratch. The result was ideal for our sound.

I brought in Michael Omartian from Gator Creek. He was an abundantly talented keyboardist, who like Jimmy wanted to produce records more than he wanted to star on them. I could see it from the very first time we recorded together; I never knew what he looked like because the piano faced the wall, and he never once turned around. During our vocal sessions, Michael actually had to tell me who he was. Soon enough, though, I introduced him to the joys of tequila and we became fast friends. I talked him into joining Loggins & Messina, but he agreed only to play in the studio, never on tour. That schedule gave him lots of time for side projects, which he gobbled up until L&M became a side project as his production career took off. He played on our first three albums before moving on to produce records for the likes of Whitney Houston, Donna Summer, and Rod Stewart. Michael won three Grammys for his work on Christopher Cross's "Sailing."

I've gotten to play with a number of world-class musicians over the fifty-plus years of my career, which has given me perspective to look back on the L&M guys and realize how lucky I was to start off with such a talented group.

WE WERE VERY much in alignment for those first few years, Jimmy and I. Our creative interplay made the band work, and I appreciated where he was coming from musically.

When it came to the direction of the band—the difference between the Kenny Loggins Band with Jim Messina, as we were sometimes billed early on, and the now familiar Loggins & Messina—the tipping point was the song "Peace of Mind." Before we worked that song up together, Jimmy and I treated the project as a solo album; afterward, we saw it as a duo. It's Jimmy's song, but I got the lead vocal because at that point he was still only the producer. It turned out so well that Jimmy introduced more of his songs, and we realized the record would be better with them than without them. And if we were going to use Jimmy's songs, well, Jimmy ought to sing them. "Peace of Mind" was the last time Kenny Loggins sang a Jim Messina song. From then on, he sang his tunes and I sang mine.

The first songs Jimmy brought to the project were ones that never got recorded by Poco. He'd written "Golden Ribbons," for example, for Richie Furay to sing, but Richie never embraced it. It showed up on our second album.

With our relationship running significantly deeper than the typical artist-producer arrangement, Jimmy and I reconsidered our approach. Instead of this being the solo project we'd first considered, Jimmy and I came up with a format that had been widely used on jazz records in the 1950s, in which one musician sat in on the session of another. We decided to call the record *Kenny Loggins with Jim Messina Sittin' In*. This would allow me to maintain my status as a solo artist while clearly acknowledging Jim's significant contribution to the record. It would also allow Jim to nurture my growth in an extremely hands-on way before moving on to his next producing project. And if adding his name to the record drew the attention of Buffalo Springfield and Poco fans, well, that'd be just fine. Once I became established, the plan was for Jimmy to cede the stage to me, most likely producing my second album as a solo effort.

In addition to lending his expertise, Jimmy also lent me his guitars. I still didn't have a decent one of my own, so he let me bang around on his Martin in the studio. Jimmy really set me up by arranging a visit, early in our first tour, to the Ovation headquarters in Hartford, Connecticut, where Jim Hennessey graciously gave us the acoustic guitars we would use onstage for years to come. Ovations have unique, rounded plastic backs that sound great, but when you sit down to play them they have a tendency to slip off of your lap. I never stopped wrestling with that thing during concerts, up until I added a corduroy patch to the back that held the guitar in place atop my jeans.

I also bought myself a Gibson 330 hollow-body electric with open F holes. I'd been raised on acoustics and didn't know what sound I was after, let alone what kind of sonic role my electric guitar should play in L&M. Jimmy probably could have helped more in that arena because he was the guitar guy, and I still don't know why he didn't—although to be fair I never thought to ask for his advice. I think I was just too embarrassed by my ignorance to admit to it. Whatever I picked, we both knew that its sound should not compete with Jimmy's bright, punchy Telecaster. Jimmy encouraged that 330 because of its warm jazzy tone, but its hollow body ended up feeding back when we turned up the stage volume, emitting a howl that was impossible to control. Before too long, Jimmy sold me a Gretsch Country Gentleman that he'd purchased from Stephen Stills. I think Stephen got it from Neil Young. That sucker had *pedigree*. It was stolen, along with several other guitars, from a storage facility in Hollywood in the mid-1980s. I still grieve the loss.

It took me years to understand guitars and amps enough to figure out the kinds of features I could sink my teeth into. Ultimately, I settled on classic Fender Stratocasters, especially ones made in Mexico. (Among Fender aficionados, Mexican-made Strats are accepted as sounding better than the American versions.) That became my go-to guitar for studio recording, most notably on my opening riff for "Footloose." When I got older and developed some shoulder problems, heavier guitars caused me to lean forward when I played, making it harder to breathe and affecting my singing. My solution was to hire a second guitarist to cover most of my parts, and to commission a few lightweight guitars from Bill Wise, a luthier out of Nashville who does amazing work with his company, Charis Acoustic. Where a classic Martin might weigh eight pounds, Bill's Charis clocked in at three pounds—the lightest guitar in its class, and a joy to wear onstage.

TO SAY THAT Jim Messina was detail oriented is an understatement of epic proportions. The guy meticulously prepared for everything, especially when it came to recording. A Jim Messina session was not some free-flowing, let's-mess-around-and-see-what-happens kind of affair. Rehearsal time was free and studio time was not, so we drilled for our first album like military cadets. We didn't come close to the studio until we'd arranged and memorized every note of every song, practicing five days a week in Barry's pool house, sometimes all day long, for the better part of a year. It was exhausting. I can still hear Jimmy saying, "Downbeat's at one p.m. We will rehearse until six p.m. Be there early." (Yeah, we usually went past six.) I began to worry that we were rehearsing the spontaneity out of the songs, which became the first real bone of contention between Jimmy and me.

Jimmy's rehearsal ethos was never more clear than on our third album, *Full Sail*, which we rehearsed so relentlessly and for so long that the band eventually rebelled. One day the guys went to Jimmy as a group and said, "We've rehearsed enough, man. We know these songs backward and forward, so let's go record because this is becoming a pain in the ass." Jimmy thought about it for a minute and said, "You're right, we've rehearsed this long enough. . . . We'll only rehearse for another month."

The quantity of rehearsals may have been overkill, but the need for solid preparation, especially in those early days, was beyond question. With a group of musicians as disparate as ours, trying to play in a style that we more or less invented as we went along, we needed a lot of time to figure things out. Jimmy or I would present a song, we'd work out arrangements for guitars, bass, drums, and the occasional keyboard, and the boys would write their charts. I loved to make up horn parts with Al and Jon, so we'd sneak off to kick around ideas while Merel and Larry worked on grooves with Jimmy. We also had vocal rehearsals, not only for Jimmy and me, but for Larry and Al, too. We even worked out arrangements for live solos—sometimes the exact notes but more frequently the cue lines the player would use to let the rest of the band know he was wrapping things up.

It was always exciting to see what this group of prodigies could do with my songs. I'd written "Back to Georgia" for Wingate in hopes it would be recorded by Aretha Franklin (who I don't think ever heard it), but whatever vibe I'd given it back then was replaced by something way cooler: a kind of country boogie spearheaded by Jimmy's Texas-style guitar roots and highlighted by Michael Omartian's piano virtuosity. I approached the horn parts with Al and Jon as if they were vocal parts for a band like Sly and the Family Stone. That's why one of Jon's lines was like a bass voice, played on baritone sax, followed by a line on Al's alto. While Al was playing, Jon switched over to soprano sax for the final line, which he played way up in the stratosphere. That sure was flashy when we did it onstage.

Jimmy's touch was substantial. He turned "House at Pooh Corner" into the ballad we know today, a tune dissimilar from my original up-tempo version the Nitty Gritty Dirt Band had put out a year earlier. Our recording of the song was delicate and layered, with a tick-tock, time-is-passing feel that really suited it. We worked on that sucker for months, orchestrating our guitars to intertwine rather than duplicate each other, rehearsing with a metronome as if it was a classical guitar duet. Jimmy told me later that he looked at the song in part as an exercise to gauge whether I could keep up with what he was doing. I passed the test. That level of detail was eye-opening for me. Orchestrating two acoustic guitars to play different things—even just to capo one and play in a different inversion—was far more complicated than I'd imagined. So *this* is what professional musicians do.

Jimmy's arrangement for "Vahevala" went the other way, rocking it up with a perfect bass line that propelled the chorus and worked as a hook all its own. His suggestion of the steel-drum section in the middle was the kind of originality and innovation I'd dreamed of working into my material. "Vahevala" itself is just a word I made up, the name of an imaginary island where the hero of the song, a sailor named Billy, liked to jump overboard now and then to swim ashore and party with the locals.

I practiced the shit out of the guitar part Jimmy wrote for "Angry Eyes" every night for a month before I had it down. It's in a drop D with both of the E strings tuned down, and it calls for a precise picking pattern that was doubled on clavinet. The double was exact, and had to be played perfectly; if one of us messed up, the entire thing would go off the rails. That was how Jimmy worked: with precision.

Once I started going to school on Messina, I wrote "Till the Ends Meet," with a guitar line of my own. Soon that kind of thing became part of my writing process. I learned that from Jimmy.

Messina also taught me the art of arranging, hearing how instruments play off of one another. I paid close attention to new voicings, which was a total turn-on. Before long, I was hearing not only the main chord structure of songs I conceived, but also the various counterparts as well. I learned to think in layers from Jimmy, too.

This was all great for my musical education, but it wasn't easy on the band. For the better part of a year, participation was a volunteer effort, based largely on Jimmy's confidence in our eventual success. He spoke in terms of *when*, not *if*, but until that happened—until Columbia bought what we were selling—there was simply no money to go around. So the guys showed up for free, five days per week, for nearly ten months. For somebody like Al Garth, it was not so difficult. He had a day job as a computer programmer for the city of Los Angeles, and never had trouble making his rent. Jon still lived at home with his parents and wasn't worried about money. For guys like Merel, though, things were more tenuous. That's one reason he moved into the duplex next door to mine for a short while when it went vacant; it was one of the few places within twenty miles that either of us could afford.

I had my own money coming in thanks to my $100-per-week deal with Wingate, and while that didn't turn out so great for me in the end—they kept the early royalties for a bunch of songs L&M ended up recording—it did manage to keep Loggins & Messina afloat until our Columbia advance came through. That's because my Wingate deal included making demo recordings for them to shop around, and I brought in the L&M guys to cut the tracks. Even Jimmy played on one. They earned "demo scale" for that—something like $60 for three hours—which at least put some change into their pockets.

Speaking of demos, in addition to endless rehearsals, Jimmy had us cut *Sittin' In* as a demo—twice—to pin down the details before we recorded it for real. We recorded live in a borrowed studio, after which he edited and re-edited until he was satisfied with how it sounded. Through Jimmy's years as an engineer, he had seen innumerable bands enter innumerable studios without a clear picture of what they wanted to do, then fritter away costly hours while they tinkered. He would not make a similar mistake.

Finally—finally!—we took the guys down to the Columbia recording studios off of Sunset Boulevard in Hollywood. Jimmy brought his engineer's sensibility to the sessions, including a recording technique he'd honed with Buffalo Springfield. He had these old RCA BA6A compressors that would resonate in wild ways, especially on acoustic guitars, getting progressively louder the longer chords were held. He would chain two or three of those compressors together, and the sound just exploded. I think Jimmy invented that. I spent years trying to replicate that sound, and none of the engineers I worked with ever figured it out. We chained our own compressors, linking them up one after the other, but it never worked the way it had with Jimmy. The secret, I eventually learned, was that digital compressors can't do it; there's something about the recovery time of analog tubes. You can really hear it on Jimmy's guitar solo on "Same Old Wine," which was also helped by the microphonic pickup on his early-'50s Telecaster. When he turned that thing up, it would bleed out of the studio speakers and loop right back through the pickup, feeding back every note. It was a really cool sound, like the guitar was breathing.

To add some groove and good vibes, Jim brought in renowned percussionist Milt Holland, who'd been an LA institution since the 1940s. Milt showed up with two trucks full of percussion gear—two fucking trucks—and he left them out back for us to dig through. It was like a treasure hunt, finding crazy, interesting things to bang on. My favorite was an instrument made from an old swimming pool thermometer, with the temperature gauge replaced by a spring. Milt would scrape it with a thin metal rod, making it "talk" by opening and closing his hand around the device. That was one of about a zillion handmade gems he presented to us. Milt spent a lot of his time teaching tabla in India, and the rest of his time in LA working on movie scores. We were lucky to have him.

Because we'd rehearsed the album so thoroughly, the entire thing took only about two months to record. The band then mixed the tracks for another few weeks in all-hands-on-deck sessions. There were no computerized mixers back then, so we'd each take a batch of faders on the huge board—two or three for each guy—and adjust them as needed. Jimmy told everyone what the moves were, of course, but the guys and I would cheat a bit to get more of the sound that we each wanted. We almost always mixed the entire thing in one pass, top to bottom, because Jim and I wanted to treat songs like living creatures. I learned early on that you can't ever let a musician—especially a sax player—mix his own track, or that'll end up being the loudest thing on the song.

By the time we finished, I was mentally exhausted. Luckily, there was some time before Columbia put the record out. My girlfriend, Darla, was about to visit her parents in the Poconos and invited me along. It was a loaded proposition, given that I still wasn't sure how I felt about her, but it was an excuse to leave my surroundings and take in some mountain air. We hopped on an airplane the day after L&M wrapped in the studio.

About five days after we arrived on the East Coast, I had my first anxiety attack. My hands started to shake and I couldn't sleep. Before long I wasn't holding food down, and found myself entirely unable to interact with people. I got some respites with hikes we took and when we rode her family's three-wheel ATVs through the woods, but other than that my condition was constant. It dominated my days. I had no idea what was happening. Anxiety turned into panic. I felt like I was having a full emotional meltdown.

When I considered what it might be about, what I came up with was this: after a year of intensive rehearsing and recording, all of a sudden there was nothing on my schedule. Going from hyperactivity to no activity at all can fry a nervous system. My lifelong dream of recording an album had finally happened. My band had signed with Columbia, which by itself exceeded most musicians' expectations. Whatever awaited in the future was nebulous, and there was no dream remaining to fill the void of the old one. I felt like I'd fallen into a hole with no air in it, and couldn't figure out how to escape. Where do I go now? What am I supposed to do? *Who am I now?*

Twenty-one seems awfully young for an existential crisis, but I'm pretty sure that's what I was having. After a week, I went to a local emergency room where they gave me a stomach relaxant. That helped.

Trying to piece me back together, Darla and I decided to get out of the mountains before the stillness drove me even crazier. Our destination: New York City. I'd never been there, but I was far too anxious to be very excited about it. We ended up doing mostly touristy stuff, including taking in a Broadway play about Lenny Bruce. It was the first real stage production I'd ever seen, and I was in such a raw, emotional place that I ended up weeping in my seat. I've loved the theater ever since.

The next day Darla and I walked past Carnegie Hall, and I commented about how amazing it would be to play there someday. If I'd known in that moment that I'd be there in less than six months, it might have helped ease my worries. Looking back at it now, that synchronicity seems like a mirage. You see it, you say it, it happens, like optimistic foreshadowing in an old musical: "Gosh guys, wouldn't it be swell if . . ."

After staying in Manhattan for a couple of days, we decided it would be best if Darla stayed back east with her family while I returned home. I needed space to figure myself out. Space helped, but not as much as meditation.

My friend Doug—the guy who I took acid with while we played guitars up in the San Gabriel Mountains—was deep into the transcendental meditation movement by then. He got me started with a mantra, the sound you use to calm and center yourself when your brain is too active. You move in and out of it and finally sink beneath it, losing track of thinking, of time, and, ultimately, of yourself. The goal is to be entirely absent of thought. Back then, the TM folks recommended two fifteen-minute sessions each day, but I ended up meditating three or four hours per day, or more. My nerves were so thoroughly fried that it was the only peaceful place I could go. I still wasn't sleeping well, but meditating off and on through the night could make me feel as if I had.

On my bed I propped up an old down sleeping bag I'd had since I was a kid to envelop me when I sat down. It became my cocoon—a safe place to be when things seemed overwhelming. I meditated in it, and made sure to wrap myself in it on the rare occasions that I allowed a friend to visit. Those were my Brian Wilson moments, calm and safe in my little sandbox. At the same time, I began reading books like *Siddhartha*, which led me to more of Herman Hesse's books, and *Autobiography of a Yogi* by Paramahansa Yogananda. That was the beginning of my connection to Eastern spiritual philosophy.

At that point, the song spigot turned on for me. I'd been writing three tunes a month, maybe four, but all of a sudden I found myself writing three songs a week for weeks on end. I didn't tell anybody in the band about my anxiety attacks, because I didn't want them to worry about my ability to fulfill our coming commitments. They'd volunteered nearly a year of their lives in service of *Sittin' In*, and now their financial livelihoods were dependent on my emotional well-being. To be honest, I had no idea what was happening to me, so I was in no position to explain it to anybody.

Just before L&M went into rehearsals for our first-ever tour, we all took a road trip up to Murphys, a Gold Rush–era mining town in the Sierra Nevada foothills of Northern California. Jimmy's actress wife, Jenny, was filming a movie there called *The Other*—a 1930s period piece—and Jimmy got the idea to shoot the album cover on location. The movie's wardrobe department decked us out, and we set up a photo session at Murphys Historic Hotel. To kill some time during a lighting change, one of the guys broke out a deck of cards and we started an impromptu poker game. Before we knew it, we were all pretending to be card sharks like in a scene from *Maverick*, and the photographer couldn't get enough. That ended up being our cover image. I don't recall the big winner that day, but I'll say it was Jimmy and me, if you know what I mean.

CHAPTER 4

KENNY'S SONG

SITTIN' IN MET immediate success upon its release. Even though we never turned "Danny's Song" into a single—or "House at Pooh Corner" or "Peace of Mind," for that matter—FM radio played the shit out of the whole album. The format was only four or five years old at that point, and geared toward commercial-free rock 'n' roll that allowed DJs to play whatever they wanted. The FM jocks particularly took to our longer tracks, during which they had plenty of time to step outside for a smoke. I sure heard about that in all sorts of grateful terms when we made in-studio appearances. On March 11, 1972, *Billboard*'s Nat Freeland called *Sittin' In* "the new breed of country rock, rural songs played by urban long-hairs without any element of condescension or embarrassment." We were hoping to sell fifty thousand copies, and moved five times that many within the year. We were delighted, of course, but we didn't have time to soak it in. We had a tour to prepare for.

L&M's first real gig came sooner than expected. We were in the process of booking an East Coast swing when a slot unexpectedly opened up at our local club, the Troubadour. Curtis Mayfield had already sold the place out, but his opening act, R&B singer Donny Hathaway, dropped out at the last minute. This is where recording for a label like Columbia paid dividends. The Troubadour was owned by a guy named Doug Weston, who'd helped launch the careers of Elton John, the Eagles, and Joni Mitchell, among many, many acts. He was close with label boss Clive Davis, and when Clive asked whether there might be a spot for us on the calendar, Doug happily complied.

When Jimmy got the call telling him that we'd be playing the Troubadour in just a few days, it was like a bolt of lightning hit the band. We went into overdrive to get ready, spending long hours at the pool house, practicing our set again and again. That's where Jimmy hit upon the notion of having me go onstage first, alone, to warm up the audience. I never fully understood it because we'd worked out all these killer two-part harmonies that we couldn't use when I was up there solo, but this was a Kenny Loggins show, and Jimmy felt the tactic would help me establish a rapport with the crowd. It was a good idea. People ate it up, and it let me dive into my quieter material before the band came out and blew everybody away. Then again, knowing we'd be in front of a Curtis Mayfield crowd, Jimmy might just have wanted to throw me out there to see how it went. (Joking, Jimmy. Sort of.)

Going out by myself wasn't easy for me to get my head around at first. I was nervous about performing, partly because of my recent meltdown and partly because of my experience with the Electric Prunes, when people literally got up and left while I played those same songs. Add to that the fact that this was Curtis Mayfield's audience, and we were not exactly an R&B act. Yet there I was, onstage alone. As I played, though, the audience seemed to like it. I was in the middle of "Danny's Song" when I noticed two attractive women up front, right at my feet, kind of moaning and shaking their heads back and forth, swaying to the music while they chanted, "Get down, get down."

Well, what do you know, I thought, they're digging me! Things were going better than expected. Encouraged by the positivity, I turned up the charisma, singing with as much mojo as I could muster, and the audience response got better and better. By the time I introduced Jimmy and the band, I was exuberant.

It wasn't until later when Jimmy pulled me aside and said, "I don't know how you made it through that," that I began to recognize what had actually happened.

"What do you mean?" I asked.

"Those girls in the front," he said, pointing from the wings.

"They loved it," I told him. "They were chanting, 'Get down, get down' the whole time."

"Yeah," he said. "They hated you. They were telling you to get down off of the stage."

Oh.

Still, that show was magical. Even a crowd primed for a funkier sound than ours came around to our rhythm and horn sections. When Al started in on his first sax solo, they went absolutely nuts. We won them over to such a degree that Weston immediately booked us for a four-night run as headliners just two weeks out. We sold out every show. Richie Furay came in from Denver for one of them, even though his artistic disagreements with Jimmy had hastened the demise of Poco. Still, they played together like old friends, breaking out some Buffalo Springfield numbers like "Child's Claim to Fame" and "Kind Woman." The crowd ate it up.

One day at about that time, I was listening to the radio in my duplex on the hill when the DJ said, "Well, we know who Jimmy Messina is, but who's this Kenny Loggins fella?" So I called the station. "Yeah, so, that's me." We didn't have a deep conversation or anything, but they got a kick out of the fact that I was listening. It was that kind of industry back then.

FOR OUR FIRST TOUR, the Kenny Loggins Band (we wouldn't be called Loggins & Messina until our next album) was the opening act for Delaney & Bonnie and Billy Preston. We spent a couple of weeks rehearsing for the gig at my old school, San Gabriel Mission High, which was kind of surreal for me. One of our roadies (and future road manager),

Jimmy Recor, was also an alum, and had briefly been a teacher there. He called in a favor and got us nighttime access to the auditorium.

Those sessions gave us a chance to tighten up our set to an appropriate length for an opener. One of those rehearsals also served as an audition for Schiffman & Larson, a prominent management company Jimmy had worked with during his Poco years. Those guys didn't want anything to do with an unknown like me, but somebody made a call on behalf of Columbia—I think it was Clive Davis, looking out for me yet again—saying they were about to release my record, and Schiffman & Larson might want to rethink their position. We chucked the idea of working out new ideas that night, opting instead to blow the goddamn doors off of the place. Which we did.

Todd (Schiffman) and Larry (Larson)—who made an impression by pulling up in a gold Rolls-Royce—took us on as clients.

That wasn't the only way that Columbia intervened on our behalf. For the first time ever, at least in Schiffman & Larson's experience, L&M's first tour was bankrolled by the record label. We were making only $500 per gig as an opener, an unsustainable fee for a group like ours. We never could have undertaken that tour if the label hadn't chipped in for things like plane tickets and rental cars and feeding the band and *paying* the band. We saved money by staying at an awful lot of Holiday Inns bordered by highways, dumps, and storage lots. One was across from an automobile factory, with a giant neon sign that blinked on and off through our blinds all night long. Livin' the dream.

To make sure that Columbia got a return on its investment, Steve Popovich, the label's brand new, thirty-year-old VP of promotions, had Columbia's regional promoters hammer the record in cities like Dallas, San Francisco, St. Louis, Chicago, Cleveland, New York, Miami, and Houston. Things progressed so quickly that within a few months we were regularly pulling in $7,500 per show, and sometimes as much as $10,000. We did that in part by betting on ourselves, taking a low flat fee plus as much as 70 percent of the gate after expenses. That kind of deal kept promoters confident they wouldn't take a bath on us, and it kept our agents—who quickly learned we could fill houses across the country—on their game.

Opening on that tour was a sweet gig. Delaney & Bonnie had just jumped to Columbia Records, and were notable for the fact that Eric

Clapton occasionally sat in with them, both in the studio and in concert. (One of their records is even called *On Tour with Eric Clapton*.) For that matter, my old pal Leon Russell (who we last saw adding fuzz-tone guitar to our Second Helping release) sat in with them, too, as did Duane Allman, Dave Mason, and Tina Turner. (Bonnie had gotten her start as a teenage "Ikette," touring with Ike and Tina back in the day.)

None of those cats were on tour with us, though. Delaney and Bonnie and their huge band traveled by bus. Not even a tour bus, but a Greyhound-style commuter with no beds or tables. With that kind of transportation, overnight travel was not really an option—which was good, because Bonnie and Delaney, who were husband and wife, fought *all* of the time. It was pretty fucking dreary. The album they were promoting would be their last together. They split up later that year.

Bonnie Bramlett was a tough cookie. The lady liked to drink so much that she kept a case of bourbon under her seat in the back of the bus. I never saw it affect her performance, though. The first thing Delaney would do when he got on board was shout, "Johnny, I want a cheeseburger!" at which point his road manager, Johnny, would have the driver find a White Castle on the way out of town. That's when I discovered the late-night joys of a square five-cent burger.

Billy Preston must have had his own way of getting around, because I don't remember him on that bus with us. I do remember the huge Sly Stone wig he put on for shows. You wouldn't recognize him without it, which might have been the point.

We went from Montreal to Maryland to New York City, where we visited Clive Davis at the Columbia offices. This was before they moved to their Black Rock headquarters in Manhattan. I was appreciative of all that Clive had done for us, but the stories people were writing about *Sittin' In* all seemed to include him taking credit for discovering us. Well, that wasn't the case. My brother and Don Ellis had hooked me up with Jimmy and brought me to the label. Apparently, I mentioned this to some reporter along the way, and Clive got wind of it. When we met in his office, he cut right to the chase. "Why are you telling the press that I didn't discover you?" he asked. I explained about Danny and Don, and Clive quickly dismissed my reasoning. "Those guys worked for me, so therefore I discovered you," he said matter-of-factly. "They played your demo for me. I listened to it. I signed you to the label, not them. If you'd come from another label, maybe that wouldn't be the case, but Columbia Records broke you, and I run Columbia Records."

It was the right of royalty. I accepted the premise, and Clive accepted us.

Our visit to New York City overlapped with the Grammy Awards taking place at the Felt Forum at Madison Square Garden. Clive thought it would be good publicity for me and Jimmy to make an appearance, so he got us tickets, rented us tuxedos, and sent us off to mingle. Being in a room with so many musical luminaries was intoxicating, and made me feel like we were in rarified air. Things were happening amazingly fast. (The feeling returned even stronger the following year, when we were nominated for Best New Artist and played "Your Mama Don't Dance" in front of a packed house.)

Actually, that first tour was full of indications that we'd arrived. Two days after the Grammys, L&M played Carnegie Hall. Sure, we were only the opening act, but it felt like an arrival considering that only a few months earlier I'd been standing on the sidewalk outside, telling Darla what a fantasy it was to play there someday. Now here we were. After the show, Clive threw a midnight party for us and 450 close friends at Tavern on the Green in Central Park, where we played a set for WCBS radio. While people mingled beforehand, I was talking to some industry folks when Bonnie Bramlett brushed past in a low-backed dress. I liked Bonnie, and felt a camaraderie with her. I'd also had a bit to drink and was, shall we say, overly excitable. I took a quick step to catch up and . . . licked her back. I don't know why I did it. I wasn't trying to come on to her. It was more like a bratty little-brother thing to do, and as with many of my faux pas, it seemed like a good idea at the time. Let me tell you, it was *not* a good idea. Bonnie spun around and snarled, "Who the fuck did that?" The only reason she didn't deck me was that I'd immediately walked away as if nothing had happened, then pretended to be as confused about the situation as she was. At that point, I wasn't about to confess. I should have pointed at Jimmy.

During that same stop, we also played for the Intercollegiate Broadcasting System's convention at Columbia's 52nd Street studios in New York City, which the label recorded and sent as a two-disc set to college radio stations across the country. We were smokin' that night, and the distribution plan worked like a charm. The recording was never released commercially, but we saturated the collegiate market with it, and before we knew what had happened we'd exploded nationwide. It seemed like everybody was playing cuts off of that LP. It didn't hurt that we made personal appearances at just about every FM and college radio station in the cities we played. After some gigs we'd jump into a car and drive forty-five minutes outside of town just to shake the hand of the late-night jock at some little station, play a few records with him, and then drive all the way back to our hotel. We were working fools and wanted to make sure we had as many people on our side as we could get.

In the middle of everything, CBS decided to pull us out of upstate New York and sent us to Miami for an unexpected appearance at the CBS convention. Leaving blizzard country for a few days on the beach? That was fine with us. They barely gave us enough notice to make it to the airport, however, and there was so much snow on the ground that the road was all but invisible as we sped through high winds toward the airport. "We're gonna make it, we're gonna make it," our tour manager, John "Johnny P" Palazzotto, kept muttering as he struggled to keep the car on the highway. The label put us up at the Playboy Club in Miami, all expenses paid for four straight days, all so we could play a single showcase set. By the time Johnny P signed the tab at the end of the run, we'd racked up $27,000 worth of food and drink. Talk about living like rock stars. Columbia then flew us right back to New York to rejoin Delaney & Bonnie.

It was difficult not to be affected by all of this. *Sittin' In* was getting a ton of airplay and fame came quickly. It's a funny balance when you're twenty-one years old, because for some reason I expected it. You make a record and then you become a star, right? That's how it's *supposed* to work. Still, I couldn't stop thinking about how to keep the ball rolling. Where should I go now and how will I get there? Who should I write with? How do I achieve the next thing? What *is* the next thing? When I was eighteen years old I wrote a song called "Where Do They Go When Their Hits Are Gone?" Even then, a part of me realized that fame does not last forever. That idea has kept me moving forward over the years.

L&M spent about a month with Delaney & Bonnie before setting out on our own, sometimes opening for various acts, sometimes headlining our own gigs. Stops on that tour included an appearance on *American*

Bandstand with Dick Clark, where we lip-synched "Nobody But You" and "Vahevala." We played the Spectrum in Philadelphia with the Kinks, and made a stop at the Philharmonic Hall at Lincoln Center, for which on November 11, 1972, *Cash Box* magazine's Robert Adels gave me one of my favorite early write-ups:

> This stately concert hall tries very hard to book the most respectable rock attractions—those for whom fans sit patiently and quietly, with all decorum. Well, they didn't get that from the Loggins & Messina crowd. Aside from the mellow moments of Loggins' acoustic opening, everyone was on their feet for the Columbia duo. The reaction is the kind that makes superstars.

We also made a triumphant return to Southern California, playing the Hollywood Bowl where I'd seen so many shows as a teenager, and the Santa Monica Civic Auditorium. We also did a gig at the Arcadia High School gymnasium where I'd played basketball games as a teenager. That show is noteworthy mainly because my second wife, then in high school herself, was in the audience—a detail I wouldn't learn until many years later.

I remember playing a gig in Santa Barbara early on, and taking my friend Doug Ingoldsby backstage. Just before the show started, I brought him right up to the edge of the curtain, then walked onstage by myself, guitar in hand, without an intro or anything. The crowd went bonkers. I turned toward Dougie with a grin and shrugged my shoulders as if to say: Can you believe this?

A notable test came about a month into the Delaney & Bonnie tour, at the National Guard Armory in Waterville, Maine. Just getting there was an adventure. Jimmy, Johnny P, and I had stayed behind in Boston for some promotional appearances, while the rest of the band made the three-hour drive up the coast; we then caught a late flight to Waterville to meet them. The weather was terrible, and the plane rattled so violently en route that I was certain we were going down. I soon learned that when somebody flies as frequently as I would, that kind of situation is pretty common. That was the first time it happened, though, and it made a hell of an impression. We finally caught up with the band at the venue, where we all hunkered down in the gym locker room waiting to go on. For some reason, Delaney & Bonnie never showed up. I heard it had something to do with wanting their money up front and the promoter's refusal to pay. The venue was packed with boisterous college kids, and we were already an hour behind schedule waiting for the headliners, watching it snow through the skylights. We could hear the crowd grow more and more agitated. Eventually, somebody grew tired of waiting, went outside, and threw a rock through one of our windows. At that point, we freaked out, and Jimmy decided our best move was to start playing before things got any more dangerous. And by "our best move," Jimmy meant "*my* best move," given that I opened our set alone. When I reached the stage, I said, "I don't know about anybody else, but I came here to play." The audience ate it up.

As it turned out, Delaney & Bonnie were on to something. The promoter didn't pay us either, at least until the lawsuit was settled later. In court he insisted that my statement about coming to play was an admission that he had no obligation to fork over any cash. Luckily, the judge didn't agree. After that, I was more careful about what I said in front of crowds.

Another questionable encounter, albeit in a very different context, cropped up not long thereafter, when the band was in Detroit. I met this pretty flower child—not even at a show, just out on the street—who invited all of us for dinner at her place outside of town. It was a crash pad, six or seven people living together in a sort of farmhouse with a real hippie vibe, with imported Indian pillows and throw rugs all over the place.

The evening was memorable mostly because of the heavily loaded fly strip that hung perilously above the dining room table. The band ended up sitting around for what seemed like hours waiting for food to be served, which gave us plenty of opportunity to consider the insect magnet above us. By the time our hostess emerged with a pan of lasagna, it was well past nine o'clock and we were all starving. Just as she slid the dish onto the table, that thing fell off its hook—and directly onto the top layer of cheese. Yuck! Fuck! Talk about conflicted! All six of us L&M guys sat there wide-eyed, staring back and forth from each other to the fly strip, from the fly strip to each other. We can't eat that! Can we eat that? Well, hunger won out. We resignedly pulled the strip away and carefully ate around the sickening situation—even Jimmy, who has a notable aversion to flies in his food. He didn't freak out, but he did turn a bit green. Come to think of it, we all did. I suspect that was the last time any of us accepted a dinner invitation from a stranger. Even a cute one.

Among more pleasant memories, my first notable on-the-road-with-L&M moment came while we were still in upstate New York. After our opening set, Merel, Al, and I went into the crowd to watch the other bands, and fell in with a group of kids in the back of the auditorium. I started dancing with this girl, and we hit it off pretty quickly. I must have gotten extra friendly at one point, because she stopped dancing, looked at me, and said, "What do you think you are, a rock star or something?" It was too perfect. "Well," I replied with a grin, "yeah, I am." She giggled, then she melted. That moment has stayed with me through the years because it was so natural and innocent, completely uncontrived. It was as if I was declaring the version of myself I'd always known but never owned, and here it was in Technicolor. Because I shared a hotel room with Messina, I ended up taking the girl back to Jimmy Recor's room. Thankfully, Recor, old college pal that he was, dutifully pretended to be asleep for the next few hours. I guess I wasn't yet the rock star I imagined myself to be. Still, I was so inspired by the experience that the next morning I wrote a song about it, which I never recorded and won't name here because its title is the girl's full name. But you can bet I still remember it. She made quite the impression.

In those early days of L&M, I didn't know anything about using an alias, so I was always on the rooming list as Kenny Loggins. That led to occasional late-night knocks on my door. Actually, it happened more than you'd expect—or exactly as much as you'd expect, given my line of work. I didn't know what to do at first. I mean, the sex part was clear, but after twelve years at an all-boys Catholic school, I still didn't really know how to interact with girls. It was all very new to me. Were we supposed to get to know each other? Should I buy them dinner? Eventually, one of the crew guys set me straight. "Kenny," he said, "if she's knocking on your door past midnight, she's probably not there for dinner."

As I became more famous, this occurrence went from golden opportunity to annoyance. After enough girls have knocked on your door in the middle of enough nights, sleep becomes preferable to whatever the next stranger might have to offer. Within a tour or two I started checking in at hotels using any name but my own.

THAT JUNE WE were scheduled to drop into Kansas City in between the East Coast and Las Vegas. Our gig was an opening slot for our label-mates New Riders of the Purple Sage—a Bay Area band that had emerged alongside, and frequently played with, the Grateful Dead. When I heard we'd be on a bill with them, my mind kept going back to a Grateful Dead song I liked to break out at parties called "Friend of the Devil." The Dead played it as a toe-tapping bluegrass number, but my version was much slower, more like a CSNY kind of thing. I'd debuted it publicly when we played the Winterland Ballroom in San Francisco a couple of months earlier. That was the first time I'd been to the venue since I sat in the balcony with my brother, stoned on acid, and I figured the Dead fans in the crowd would appreciate my cover. I sang it to the seat I'd occupied years earlier, envisioning a younger version of myself, high as a kite and gripping the rail with everything he had, waiting to hear something he could get off on. It worked. The audience went nuts.

Loggins & Messina didn't do too many covers, so I put the tune back into my quiver for a while, until I broke it out for our slot with the New Riders. It would have been entirely uneventful and certainly not worth revisiting had it not been for one person in the building that night: Betty Cantor. Betty was the recording engineer for the New Riders, a job she'd landed in part because of the body of work she'd put together taping Grateful Dead shows over the years. Not only did Betty capture my performance that night on tape, but she brought the recording back to the Bay Area and played it for Jerry Garcia. As the story goes, he loved it. Since releasing the song, the Dead had transitioned to a heavier electric sound, at which point they'd dropped "Friend of the Devil" from their regular rotation. Thanks to Betty's tape, however, Jerry reimagined the song so that it closely resembled mine, and reinserted it into the band's live act. Look no further than 1981's *Dead Set*, recorded at San Francisco's Warfield theater (by one Betty Cantor) for an example of a slower, more deliberate version than the original.

I didn't know any of this at the time. It wasn't until many years later, when Garcia publicly credited me for the inspiration, that I got a clue—and it wasn't until thinking about it for this book that I managed to put all of the pieces together.

That Winterland gig where I first played "Friend of the Devil" was memorable for one other reason. We were coming off of a two-week break, during which our drummer, Merel Bregante, nearly ended his career. He lived in Tujunga Canyon, about twenty-five miles outside of LA, and was cutting some trees on his property. Merel has always been outdoorsy like that. Unfortunately, one of those trees landed on his foot and nearly took his big toe clean off. Alone and desperate for help, Merel drove down the hill until he stumbled upon a Chinese family-practice doctor. The guy had been a trauma surgeon back in Beijing, and he managed to put Merel's foot back together right there in his office. It was Merel's kick-drum foot, and Winterland was his first show back. Though he had to be pushed around in a wheelchair, he got through our set by propping his foot on a pillow, which ended up soaked with blood by the end of the show. He didn't miss a gig.

Loggins & Messina spent about two hundred days on the road that year, and it became sort of a lifestyle for me. It was cool. It was fun. It was what I'd dreamed of doing since high school, and now I was living it. The guys in the band felt similarly, though a few of them took the whole rock 'n' roll thing to another level. One morning, we found Jon Clarke passed out on the floor in front of his hotel room door, his key broken off in the lock. Probably seemed as good a place as any to call it a night. Another time, Johnny P got a 3 a.m. phone call from Al Garth telling him to hurry and collect Jon from the hotel swimming pool, where he was cavorting with two half-naked co-eds. "If the police show up and catch him with those underage girls, we're all going to jail," Al yelped. (It probably wouldn't have made a difference that Jon was underage himself at the time, or pretty close to it.)

At the Hyatt in Albany, New York, Merel ordered a room-service seafood dish they called "the President." He got so sick that we had to stay in town an extra couple of days waiting for him to stop throwing up. Luckily, we didn't have another show booked until the middle of the following week.

Through it all, Jim Messina and I turned out to be pretty good road companions—most of the time. We were twenty-one years old and working as a duo while searching for our individual identities. For the first couple of years we happened to have very similar aesthetics. We'd walk into a clothing store in some town and find ourselves competing over who got to buy what. "I like this color shirt." "Yeah, well so do I." This was actually a boon for our music because I liked a lot of his ideas and he liked a lot of mine, though we ended up battling over damn near everything else. We even occasionally hit on the same girl after a show, which led to its own unique brand of tension.

With me and Jimmy battling over differences *and* similarities, the friction that built between us emerged in unfortunate ways. One time we got into a fight—an actual, physical fight—over the arrangement of a song . . . or maybe it was where to have lunch. Who even remembers anymore? It happened in the back seat of a station wagon during a too-long ride through the Midwest. Jimmy and I started arguing, and before I knew it he was pulling on my beard and I was biting his hand. That's what Jimmy Recor—our road manger by then—saw when he turned around from the front seat. In his infinite wisdom, he treated us like a couple of five-year-olds, pulling the car over and separating us by putting me in the band car. Yeah, I was pissed off by that move, but my anger was nothing compared to the rest of the group, one of whom had to take my spot in the lead car. Nobody wanted to ride with Jimmy, whose anti-drug stance tended to put a damper on whatever fun they were having in their own vehicle. We kept up that arrangement for a while, with the band rotating shifts in the lead car. Ultimately, the role fell to Merel, maybe because he was the easiest-going among them.

When you live that closely and work that hard, intra-band fights happen. Luckily, Messina and I didn't end up in too many other head-banging (or hand-biting) brawls.

Later in the tour, L&M went to England for a showcase, which presented us with a new set of issues. Loggins & Messina never really hit in Europe, largely because we didn't take the time to break the territory. The country-rock thing struggled to gain traction in the United Kingdom, and instead of trying to influence things, Columbia Records just gave up. Without any sales or radio support in Europe, starting over as an unknown touring band would have been extremely challenging. We'd have had to play smaller venues for a lot less money than we needed to break even, instead of the damn good living we were making in the States. Nobody, us or our managers, wanted to threaten that payday.

Our gig at the Crystal Palace Bowl, outside of London, was different. It was a one-off affair as part of an annual rock festival known as the Garden Party, held at a park with a sizeable lake between the stage and the audience. We shared the bill with the likes of Roxy Music and Edgar Winter, though the most intriguing band to me was a group called Stone the Crows. Just a few months earlier, their guitar player had been electrocuted to death by faulty wiring onstage at a show they'd been playing in Wales, and they were only just returning to performances. It's a terrible story, and people were still in disbelief about it when we arrived. It was a beautiful day, though (which I'd later learn was a bit of a rarity in London at that time of year), and people came out in droves to see us.

With a few days to knock around town, a bunch of us went to Carnaby Street and bought suits. On the way home, I cagily tried to walk my purchases past US customs without declaring them, as if a long-haired twenty-one-year-old always traveled with four English suits in his luggage. The agents thought that was hilarious. They busted me, of course, calling me out in front of everybody and slapping down a healthy fine. I could easily afford it by that point, but it was enough to prevent me from trying to sneak anything through customs again.

Ultimately, I never considered the possibility that Loggins & Messina wouldn't succeed. I tuned out the idea that the industry was a hard one to break into, and that it wasn't nearly as rewarding for most people as it had been for me. My first business manager, Patty Dennis, told me the usual lifespan of a pop act is three years—and I never once considered that as words of warning. She couldn't be talking about *me*. Like so many kids my age, I was ten feet tall and bulletproof. Even through my debacle with the Electric Prunes and my existential crisis in the Poconos, I never once felt like I wasn't going to make it. After I left college, I never even entertained a backup plan.

Thank God I never needed one.

CHAPTER 5

I AM THE RIVER AND
YOU ARE THE SHORE

OUR FIRST TOUR made me feel like such a rock star that I ditched my VW van and bought myself a BMW, transforming overnight from a hippie to a yuppie. (Joking. Yuppies wouldn't exist until the 1980s, and whatever I was at that point was definitely *not* yuppie.) When it came to cars, I'd had so many clunkers, so many radiators burned up, I swore to myself that if I could ever afford it, I'd get a real car—something with style. Well, thanks to L&M I finally could. After a show in 1972, I found myself shooting the shit with a professional race car driver, a friend of a friend who was hanging out backstage. I seized the opportunity.

"If you could have any street car, what would it be?" I asked.

"That's easy," he said. "A BMW three-liter coupe. Sweetest ride out there." Loggins & Messina had become the darlings of FM radio, and I was feeling the flush of rock stardom. It was well after midnight, but I didn't hesitate, calling my business manager and leaving a message to find me one, ASAP. The decision was spontaneous, emotional, and tequila fueled.

The next day she called me back, exuberant. "I tried all over," she said, "and found *one*. It's silver blue with blue leather interior. It's in Scottsdale. And they don't deliver."

"No problem," I said. I didn't even know what the car looked like, and it didn't matter. I was living in half of a crummy duplex in East LA for sixty-five bucks a month and carried no real expenses. Thanks to our sudden music success, I'd become flush with cash almost overnight. Buying that car was the first real rock 'n' roll thing I ever did. It wouldn't be the last. When I told L&M's road manager, Jimmy Recor, about it, he chuckled knowingly, then went above and beyond by traveling to Arizona to pick it up for me himself.

That car was beautiful, and I mean *beautiful*. Low, sleek, two doors, big motor, with a pretend back seat that was better for a small dog than a large human. Or any human. I'd never even sat in anything so exotic. I was almost afraid to drive it. I won't say that it was out of my league, but the driveway where I parked it wasn't even paved. To this day, it's my favorite car I've ever owned. Like the Gretch from Stephen and Neil, it's long gone but I sure wish it wasn't.

Believe it or not, that was pretty much it for my early celebrity indulgences. Sure, I bought my folks a car, and a year or two later I bought them a modest home in Alhambra. But as Patty Dennis warned me when I met her: "Be careful, Kenny—it's easy when you move up, and much harder to slide back down." Luckily, I'd learned a lot from my dad about achieving balance, and fame never went to my head the way I've seen happen with so many young artists. Too many people forget the law of gravity in this business. Columbia Records president Clive Davis used to call it the emotional bends: people rising so quickly that they go emotionally haywire. That wouldn't be me. For example, a couple of years later we were on the road and I needed a suitcase. Recor suggested I buy two. "What do

I look like, a millionaire?" I said to the guy who was literally in charge of counting receipts each night. He knew better than me what I could afford.

Another thing keeping me grounded was the uncertainty of our label support. *Sittin' In* had been an undeniable success, spending months on the *Billboard* charts and earning tons of radio play, but when Jim Messina informed Clive that our next record would be another Kenny Loggins solo effort, he met a brick wall. Jimmy's participation on the first album—writing songs, doing arrangements, producing the entire damn thing—was great for me, but worrying for Clive. Loggins & Messina was a proverbial bird in the hand, and he didn't want it to fly away. He realized that even if it had always been Jimmy's plan to stay in the background, our success made it imperative to consider equal billing. As a producer, Jimmy was bound to move on to other projects, and without him onboard, I was back to being a longshot for the label.

"I'm not going to invest money in a band that's going to break up," Clive told us. He advised us that a partnership like ours might come once in a lifetime, and demanded a six-year commitment. If Columbia was going to back us, he said, they needed certainty. The days of sittin' in were over. From that point forward, Jimmy and I were to be a band—and with that, Loggins & Messina was officially born. (I'm pretty sure the existence of *Sittin' In* is the only reason I got top billing when we named the duo. Jimmy had seniority and name recognition; it would have made all the sense in the world to call the group Messina & Loggins.)

I had no clue what working with Jimmy for six years would be like, but the relationship was functioning well artistically and emotionally, so I agreed. What would come back to haunt us was that even though we were now a duo, Jimmy and I had individual contracts, each negotiated by our own attorneys, and they were miles apart in terms of value. Jimmy told me that it would be better for us to keep our deals separate. Bands get into legal battles over shared contracts, he explained, and he assured me that distinct contracts would protect our autonomy. Made sense to me.

Jimmy was already under contract to Columbia as a producer, and his new role with Loggins & Messina gave him an opening to negotiate as an artist. We were positioned to break huge, and he milked whatever he could out of the situation. Which is as it should be. What wasn't right in my book is how it was done.

As best I can tell, the only way Columbia would meet Jimmy's new demands (whatever they were) was by preventing him from telling me what he was getting, for fear I'd make them match it. His contract literally barred him from sharing financial details. From Jimmy's perspective, it was a hedge against Columbia taking money away from his end to make our deals equitable. From my perspective, it was a shortsighted way to structure a partnership if Columbia Records wanted us to endure.

Jimmy was up front with me about his renegotiations, but I didn't understand the ramifications of all that secrecy. I was brand new to the business and trying to make sense of pretty much everything. Looking back, I wish my attorney had laid down some demands, like no new records until our deals were equitable. Messina has said similar things to me over the years, telling me that my slice of the pie, whatever it was, had nothing to do with how much he made. I get it. Jimmy was a free agent whose career vision never included being half of a new duo, and he went for the best package he could get. He drew a hard line and felt it was up to me and my legal team to draw a hard line of our own. Still, I can't help but think that Jimmy should have refused when Columbia contractually short-circuited an equal partnership. The label had a responsibility to make things even between us, which they completely ignored—if they were aware of it at all. I was already under contract with Columbia Records, and he, renegotiating his producer's deal, was not. His clout with the label could have been *our* clout, had we negotiated together. I didn't have that kind of power. He did.

To understand Jimmy's side better, he'd been through a messy separation with Poco and didn't want to be contractually tied to anybody at that point. He argued that his solo deal was his autonomy. Of course, at that point he could have convinced me of anything. He even asked me to tell Columbia that I was okay with not knowing how much his contract was worth. I went along with it, but the whole thing felt very manipulative. It inserted doubt into our partnership and made our future differences of opinion over things like song arrangements and who got more tracks on an album more contentious than they had to be. It was difficult not to be suspicious of ulterior motives. You can't have a good partnership without trust, and those financial decisions didn't have a lick of trust in them.

In my opinion, that first contract effectively set up the demise of Loggins & Messina. By giving Jimmy a deal they couldn't—or wouldn't—duplicate for me, Columbia Records sowed seeds of discontent that wouldn't fully flower for several years. There are a lot of fluid dynamics in any relationship between twenty-two-year-olds, but those negotiations cut deep. Jimmy and I worked closely together for a long time to come, and whatever acrimony we eventually developed began with those deals.

Clive Davis saw that, too. It just took him a while to acknowledge it. He must have known such an arrangement was a time bomb, and once it went off it would mean the end of the band. Clive never did tell me what Jimmy was getting, but about two years later he called my attorney, Lee Phillips, and said he was willing to renegotiate. Clive could smell what was cooking and wanted to keep me happy. It worked. I still had difficulty accepting how Jimmy's team had negotiated around me, but I let it go. Our partnership was fruitful. We were making hit records and selling out shows. Why make trouble?

OUR RESPECTIVE CONTRACTS were only one sign of the imbalance of power in my relationship with Jimmy, which was growing more pronounced by the day. Messina's role as producer gave him extra sway, and while he tried to be fair, he was also concerned about his image, his career, and the effect Loggins & Messina had on it all. Jimmy is controlling by nature—look no further than his excessive rehearsal demands—and before long I started to see it as repressive. After our first shows at the Troubadour, he cornered me backstage and told me not to talk to the audience during gigs because they didn't get my humor. (I think it was Jimmy who didn't get my humor.) He even went so far as to have me rehearse *interviews* with him because he didn't want me going off-message when talking to reporters. I wasn't to talk about religion or politics or sex or drugs or pretty much anything that did not have directly to do with whatever we were promoting at that moment. His grip grew tighter and tighter. Soon Jimmy was telling me specifically what to say, and if I strayed I was sure to get a lecture. Imagine going along with all of that. Tom Nola put it well in *Rolling Stone* on February 27, 1975:

These two who so markedly complement one another onstage have a decidedly different rapport in this informal situation. When they perform, Kenny is the center of attention, leaping in the air, bouncing and bobbing to the beat, gushing over with infectious enthusiasm; Jim, the master musician and engineer, strikes an intense, single-minded, silent counterpoint. Out of the spotlight, the emphasis is reversed: Messina dominates the conversation, while Ken seems happy to defer to him, as if this is Messina's due. He listens intently to Jim, nods, laughs, amplifies his remarks; when Ken is talking, Messina watches him unresponsively. It feels like a marriage where much is hidden, buried beneath an accommodating facade; not a rancorous union, but one in which partners have quickly learned or been taught their place—an old-fashioned, closed marriage, where one person gently but firmly leads and the other is "happy" to follow.

This really wasn't a big deal in the early days, when I was soaking up whatever Messina had to say, but as I found my feet as a musician and began to grow my own ideas and opinions, his dominance began to wear on me.

Our interpersonal hierarchy and the resulting finances were one thing, but how it affected the band proved to be another concern. L&M's musicians were absolutely vital to our sound, but we were not a band in the truest sense of the word. Loggins & Messina was *not* a democracy. Jimmy had experienced that dynamic with both Buffalo Springfield and Poco, and, wanting to avoid those kinds of arguments, we did not share decisions and profit equally among members. Instead, the band effectively worked as salaried employees of Jimmy and me. At twenty-two years old, of course, I thought about the relationship in terms of creativity, not business. We all wanted to make great music, I figured, and the money would work itself out. I never stopped to consider that Jimmy and I could hire whoever we wanted to back us up. Our guys were our guys, and I liked it that way.

As it happened, our guys *didn't* like it that way. They wanted more say in the band's musical direction, and probably a bigger slice of the pie. I hadn't yet considered the idea of royalty participation, and when a couple of the players approached me one day with a question—"Well, we're a band, right?"—the answer seemed obvious. Musically and aesthetically, we *were* a band. Jimmy and I weren't going to record with anybody else. I probably should have gone to Messina for some clarity, but instead I answered emotionally, not practically, with what came immediately to mind: "Of course we're a band." It was hardly a commitment to splitting proceeds six ways, but that might be how they took it. It never ended up in anything as drastic as a court case, but it got pretty tense, especially for Jimmy, who was much more involved with financial issues than me, and I didn't know enough to even take ownership of my gaffe. So Jimmy came in and eased the tension by offering them points on our subsequent albums. I was fine with that.

The guys must have been fine with it, too, since they all stuck around until the end, or close to it. There was an occasional quote in the press about feeling like sidemen, and how me and Jimmy would sometimes override their opinions. Still, we always considered their musical ideas. I can point to many creative additions the band brought to our records, all of which Jimmy and I appreciated. Ultimately, of course, we *were* called Loggins & Messina. Having a band and a duo at the same time required some fancy ego juggling, but it was the balancing act between two separate leaders and the creativity of an ensemble that made L&M different and special. Despite any differences between us, I am forever grateful to Jimmy and the guys for their creative generosity and musicality that served as the cornerstone of my musical education in the '70s.

ONE THING MY DEAL had in common with Jimmy's was that we were both obligated to Columbia to deliver one record per year—an absurd demand that too often forced creative compromises to satisfy deadlines. The months after *Sittin' In* came out were devoted to touring, and because neither Jimmy nor I wrote much on the road, we had to scramble once we got home. We'd had a trunkload of material for the first album, but now we had to come up with stuff on the fly. I think this is why so many bands suffer from the sophomore jinx. They empty the trunk for their debut and then have trouble refilling it.

I did have a few songs lying around for the next album, which we'd title *Loggins & Messina* in acknowledgment of our new contract, a way of publicly proclaiming Jimmy and I were officially a duo. "Long Tail Cat," which I'd written for Wingate, was already part of my solo acoustic opening set for L&M shows. It was easy to play and I sang it with a bluesy twang. Best of all, the song's ending was a great place for the band to come onstage and join in. Like much of our early stuff, I now think the original version is way too fast, pumped up by early-twenties hormones (something I like to call "teenage urgency").

The most noteworthy track on that second album is "Your Mama Don't Dance," which Jimmy and I had written while making *Sittin' In*, but decided not to record for that album. We came up with it while killing some time before rehearsal. Jimmy already had the title and opening verse, and I helped fill in everything else. We finished it in a day. Originally it had a swing to it like a cross between Wilbert Harrison's old rockabilly classic "Kansas City" and Elvis's "Don't Be Cruel." Both of us saw the song as a fun ditty, and didn't include it on *Sittin' In* because we felt it was inconsequential.

Well, it took all of one live performance to learn otherwise. We decided to play the song toward the end of our first-ever Troubadour gig, and people immediately stood up and began to dance. Hmmm. Maybe the song was better than we thought. Because it brought so much energy to the room, we soon slotted it as our first encore.

It's said that hit songs feel immediately familiar, and "Your Mama Don't Dance" fits that bill perfectly. I've held that experience as a yardstick ever since. Whenever I have a new up-tempo song, I'll throw it in as an encore, and if people dance I know there's something there. (We performed "Mama" on Wolfman Jack's TV show, *The Midnight Special*, and suffered from a severe case of teenage urgency, blowing through a three-and-a-half-minute song in under two minutes. Talk about hyped up.)

We were as surprised as anyone when "Your Mama Don't Dance" shot to No. 4 on the *Billboard* pop chart. The song is short and snappy, while we were a group that liked to explore lyrical ideas and complex arrangements. Just like that, though, our first hit single came to define Loggins & Messina as something we were not, a perception we never really shook.

The song set a precedent we should have ignored, but didn't, especially when our label tried to elicit similar magic for our next single by urging us to revisit a formula we didn't much like in the first place. They repeatedly pounded on that peg, never stopping to think about the shape of the hole. If an artist isn't emotionally invested in a song, it probably ain't gonna fly. We saw "Your Mama Don't Dance" as a kind of novelty song—a conduit to a bigger audience and greater success—but I was less fine with the sound-alike track that Jimmy and I came up with under pressure to write something similar.

The song in question was a jaunty piece of crap called "My Music," which we wrote at Jim Guercio's ranch in Colorado. We started with the same old-fashioned rock groove as in "Mama," which was our first mistake. The lyrics were sophomoric, which was our second mistake. I never did much like the song, but Jimmy did, so it's on our third album, *Full Sail.* I'm pretty sure Al Garth agreed with me. We never discussed it, but his hokey, 1940s-style sax duet with Jon in the middle of the tune—which I think he initially intended as a joke, and somehow made it into the final cut—sounds to me like a giant fuck-you to Jimmy, and probably to me, too. Al knew a turkey when he heard one. Interestingly, a number of radio stations took it upon themselves to edit the sax section out of the single, which probably helped—a little. That song actually charted at No. 16— our second-biggest hit ever—but I felt our credibility draining away with every spin of the turntable.

That wasn't even the worst of it. Columbia so badly wanted a follow-up to "My Music" that Jimmy had us rerecord one of his songs, "Thinking of You," as a single. I liked the original version from our second album, but the suits wanted something more radio friendly, with a faster tempo and a big hook. Jimmy gave them what they wanted, and I was disappointed with the result. Suddenly, there were castanets in there that bugged the shit out of me. The original had a kind of soul to it that was stripped away in the new version. What was originally a moody, romantic song became just another chipper pop ditty. It did okay but not great, reaching No. 18, even while I wondered whether the album version would have done just as well, if not better. I didn't feel good about that compromise—changing a song we liked to make it a hit, especially when it didn't really become a hit—and we never did it again. In fact, that experience inspired Jimmy and me to tighten our standards about that kind of thing. We stopped playing "Your Mama Don't Dance" on TV, save for the notable exception of the Grammy Awards. We wouldn't play any song on TV without the band. And we never again shape-shifted a tune to try and fit into an AM radio–friendly box.

One thing "Your Mama Don't Dance" did do was give me the financial ability to finally move out of my crumbling duplex in crime-ridden East LA to a beach cottage in Santa Barbara. Talk about a lifestyle reboot. My new place was a tiny turn-of-the-century two-bedroom Victorian that I rented by the month. It was hardly lavish but it was right on the sand. Some of my happiest times were in that house. I was literally footloose, with the world stretched out before me like the ocean horizon I could now see through my living room window.

WHILE WE WERE RECORDING *Loggins & Messina*, our road manager, Johnny Palazzotto, told me that management was seriously considering an offer for us to play the famed Whiskey a Go Go nightclub on the Sunset Strip in Los Angeles. I didn't frequent the place—it drew more of a hard-rock crowd, and I was more in tune with the Troubadour vibe— but I'd seen Love and the Doors there a few years earlier, and knew what the place was like. And I was worried. So Jimmy and I went with Johnny P to check it out. Sure enough, the headliner that night—some intense metal band I've long since forgotten—was shaking the room with volume. The frenetic energy of the crowd was in stark contrast to the mellow atmosphere at the clubs we normally played, where country-rock bands like ours could perform acoustically without fear of audience revolt. Sitting at a back table and sipping my Cuervo, I began to see the future—and it looked like our heads mounted on stakes in front of the stage as a warning to other folkie fools who dared test the patience of the Hollywood rock gods. Just then, Johnny leaned in and yelled into my ear: "Better not try to sing anything mellow here." It was a throwaway line, but the next day I turned it into a song. "Whiskey" ended up as the second track on our sophomore album and included the lines: "Don't do anything mellow at the Whiskey / Johnny says you'd best take my advice / Cause the stony little crowd will get to talkin' even louder / And they'll smother you in hissin' / And if they do, your musical insurance better be paid up." I guess I was flashing back to my Electric Prunes experience. I know what it's like to be eaten alive.

We never did end up playing there.

Fortunately, the audiences we played for appreciated what we delivered. And we got to deliver with some pretty great company. During those first couple of years, the Doobie Brothers (pre–Michael McDonald) opened for us, and then we opened for them (also pre–Michael McDonald). Steely Dan was on some of those bills, which is noteworthy because their guitarist, Skunk Baxter, jumped to the Doobies at about the same time as Michael. (I've wondered ever since if Skunk met those guys during that tour.) We played with Carly Simon, Dave Mason, Taj Mahal, and the Beach Boys. We opened up for the Allman Brothers. Looking back, I really wish I'd gone into the audience to watch more of those shows.

A very young Billy Joel opened for us at the Berkeley Community Theater in 1973. I remembered him from a promoters' convention in Dallas we'd done the previous year, a private showcase where bookers decided who they wanted to play their venues. Billy wasn't even on a proper stage; somebody stuck him in the hotel lobby, with people walking right past as he played. Not a soul was paying attention. I didn't know anything about the guy, but boy did his music floor me. I thought he was the second coming of Paul McCartney. I promptly ignored whatever else I had going on and sat down to listen. When Billy finally took a break, I went over to talk. "What the fuck are you doing here in the lobby?" I asked, just like he would later write in "Piano Man." He muttered something about "my goddamn managers," and "this goddamn thing." Grumble, grumble. He was hating it, and I didn't blame him. What a shitty way to showcase an act. (In 1977, when I was working on *Celebrate Me Home*, my producer, Phil Ramone, asked me if I was familiar with Billy Joel. By that point, "Piano Man" had been out for a couple of years, but Billy hadn't yet achieved superstar status. Phil told me that Billy wanted him to produce his next record. Based on our early encounters I gave a full endorsement. I don't know how much influence I had, but Phil ended up producing Billy's next six records, including his breakout, *The Stranger*.)

L&M also played a show with Leon Russell at the Ontario Motor Speedway that I remember mostly for what Leon did in the middle of his set. We had already wrapped up, and I was watching from the VIP area in front of the stage. A fight broke out someplace behind me, and within a moment Leon silenced his band. "I've had enough of that shit at the clubs in Tulsa," he said. "I don't need it here." I thought that was about the coolest thing I'd ever seen. Of course, fights at rock 'n' roll shows weren't uncommon. The first time Loggins & Messina played Madison Square Garden, a fight broke out among literally hundreds of people. That place is so huge that we could barely hear any of it from the stage. We had no idea until later that there had been a near-riot during our set.

EARLY IN OUR 1973 TOUR, the Grammys called.

Unlike the previous year, they wanted Jimmy and me to be more than spectators. L&M had been nominated for Best New Artist, and we were asked to play "Your Mama Don't Dance" on the telecast. Sort of.

The producers wanted us to sing it live, but over a prerecorded instrumental track instead of with the band. I guess that cut down on the chance of technical mishaps, and also insured against musical freelancing. It was a guaranteed way to keep things on time. It was fine by us; if nothing else, it would keep us from taking the song to the races, which we tended to do when playing live back then. The problem was, we didn't have an instrumental track to play over. Thankfully, we had some off days at just the right time, and a generous offer from Jim Guercio (the producer of Chicago) to use the studio at his Colorado ranch. (This is where we wrote the aforementioned "My Music.") It was wintertime in the mountains, and there was no way a bunch of harebrained musicians from Southern California were going to sit still in the snow. Guercio had snowmobiles, which we raced all over the place—until our bassist, Larry Sims, drove one straight into a tree. He was okay, but he busted up his face pretty badly. When we took the Grammys stage a couple of weeks later, he was still bandaged up. I swear I saw blood dripping down his cheek while we performed.

But that's only part of the story.

We'd been planning to record several shows for a live album at just that time. On March 1 and 2, we taped at Carnegie Hall in New York City, a venue we chose because of its pedigree and amazing acoustics. Unfortunately, we didn't realize the contract required local union workers to set the stage, and Jimmy had already lined up roadies for the job. We ended up hiring union guys to watch *our* guys set up. It ended up costing us twice as much to record there as anyplace else in the country.

We canceled our next stop, at the Spectrum in Philadelphia, so we could get to Nashville for the Grammys. Our compressed schedule had us arriving in Tennessee at 10 a.m., just in time for rehearsal. Well, our flight was on time but the Grammys weren't; we arrived to find a five-hour schedule delay. Even our consolation naps were ruined when the organizers called almost as soon as we'd checked into our hotel, telling us they were just about ready for us. By the time we returned to the venue, they'd decided they were no longer ready for us, and we waited around for another four hours. Grrrr.

Almost as soon as Jimmy and I sat down for hair and makeup, the power went out. With a live broadcast looming, we found ourselves tended to in a dark room by makeup artists with brushes in one hand and lighters in the other. The blackout, which didn't seem to affect the front of the house, wreaked absolute havoc backstage, with stagehands crashing into each other as they raced around blindly. Nobody seemed to be listening to anyone else's directions.

The show started on time, and we got to play—or at least sing over that instrumental track. We didn't win any awards (America took Best New Artist), and the next morning caught a three-hour flight back to Boston, where we had a gig that night at the Orpheum. Energized by the Grammys, we ended up playing one of the best sets of the tour. Wanna hear it? It's on *On Stage*.

THE *LOGGINS & MESSINA* ALBUM went platinum. So did *Full Sail*, the record after that. I was steadily developing as a songwriter and musician, which included forming my own ideas about what a rock band should look like. Sometimes these ideas were compatible with Jimmy's, and sometimes they weren't. This is not to say that I was right and he was wrong, but rather that our creativity was beginning to lead us in different directions.

For example, "A Love Song." It was inspired by a girl I met at a party, a waitress at the Troubadour who I wanted to ask out. That's why I wrote the song. I was going to play it for her the next time I saw her, but by then she'd already found herself a boyfriend. Still, it was a good song, and I proposed it for *Loggins & Messina*.

Well, Jimmy wasn't crazy about it and refused to put it on the record, a decision that cut to one of our core issues as a duo. While we were ostensibly equal partners, whenever we disagreed on something, the tie-breaking vote went to our producer—who was Jimmy. It had been that way from the beginning, and I couldn't much complain about it. I'd *agreed* to it. The system worked fine early on, but when I developed opinions of my own, the imbalance in our partnership became a liability. In the little picture, it's why "A Love Song" didn't make it onto the *Loggins & Messina* record. In the big picture, it's why Jimmy and I eventually had to split up. My own creativity was taking me further and further away from the style Jimmy had so carefully crafted, and as the guy in charge he didn't want me to stray too far.

I eventually played "A Love Song" for Anne Murray backstage at one of our shows. Anne had clocked a massive hit with a fine cover of "Danny's Song," and since I'd written "A Love Song" in a similar finger-picking style, I figured she might like it. She did. And just like she'd done with "Danny's Song," she recorded her own gorgeous version. And just like she'd done with "Danny's Song," she turned it into a hit—No. 1, in fact, on the adult contemporary charts—and won a Grammy for it. At that point, I went back to Jimmy. "*Now* does it get to be on the record?" I said. Anne made my point. "Love Song" is the fourth track on *Full Sail*.

Of course, Jimmy occasionally had songs I didn't like, either. The difference was that those songs always made it onto albums. Take "Lahaina," also on *Full Sail*, which he'd written about a sleepy little dream of a town we'd discovered on Maui in 1971. I thought the song was too sophomoric for L&M—more of a children's tune than a credible album cut for us, and certainly not up to the standards we'd set for ourselves. When he was composing it he said to me, "I'm writing a song that acknowledges how beautiful Lahaina is, but I'm throwing in a part about a centipede crawling on your feet so that people won't want to go there." He chuckled as he explained that he wanted to keep tourism down. When Jimmy insisted on recording it, I suggested a CSNY-style harmony refrain so the song would at least have a memorable, singalong-style chorus. To Jimmy's credit, they loved it in Hawaii.

Also on *Full Sail*, and also inspired by the tropics, is the song "Comin' to You," on which Jimmy brought in a string section and fashioned his version of a reggae song. This was confusing to those of us in the band who hadn't yet heard much reggae. Messina encouraged us to pick up some Jimmy Cliff and Bob Marley records to understand the genre better. I became a big Bob Marley fan because of that, for which I'm grateful, but there's no mistaking that Loggins & Messina was *not* a reggae band. The steel drums we'd used so effectively on "Vahevala" became corny this time around. Whatever its merits, "Comin' to You" was unique in our repertoire, with mixed results at best. With Jimmy, though, debates about our musical direction were off the table, so into reggae we dove. I can't say we nailed it, but we sure gave it a hell of a try.

Speaking of the tropics, "Lahaina" (and much of the *Full Sail* album, including the cover) was inspired by our visit there during our first tour. The cover photo was taken on a classic wooden-hulled sailboat called the *Flying Cloud*, an antique schooner owned by George Walker of the Merry Pranksters. It seemed to fit, somehow, and Jimmy's idea to craft the record around that theme sure resonated with our audience.

One thing that emerged many years later from *Full Sail* was the yacht-rock phenomenon. I'll get into that more later, because inadvertently becoming a face for a movement that I had no idea I was helping to create had more to do with the music I made later in my career, but in 1974 we helped get the ball rolling. The idea started with the California-based, adult-contemporary sounds of the 1970s, which somebody later morphed with the image of wealthy guys cranking tunes on their luxury cruisers, making nautical themes prominent within the genre. At that point, the term "yacht rock" was still forty years away from being coined, but calling our record *Full Sail* and featuring a cover photo of us on a sailboat, plus songs like "Lahaina" and "Vahevala" put us in a place of prominence when people began to backfill the category.

My song "Sailin' the Wind," also off of *Full Sail*, added to the mystique despite it being about flying kites, not sailing boats. Then again, while we were in the studio recording it, Jimmy found that if he turned up his amp and rubbed his leather guitar strap against his wooden Telecaster, it sounded like creaking ropes on a sailboat. Then we turned over a steel drum, filled it with water, and our percussionist, Milt Holland, dipped a big bell into it, making a haunting Doppler sound, like a ship's bell floating past on a foggy night. Those effects lent a clear impression of sailing, and were so cool that I was happy to let the sailing theme eclipse the kite one.

ONE THING I'VE never understood about my partnership with Jimmy is why we didn't write more songs together. He doesn't understand it, either. I'd helped him a little bit with the three-song medley "Trilogy" off of *Sittin' In*, but our first real collaborations came on the *Loggins & Messina* album. One was "Your Mama Don't Dance." Another was its polar opposite, "Angry Eyes," which I think is one of L&M's best songs. That guitar intro is an unbeatable hook.

Jimmy wrote that riff before we'd met, for the soundtrack of a western comedy called *Evil Roy Slade*, and was slowly turning it into a song about somebody he'd once worked with (though he never told me who). When I heard him noodling on it one day before a show in Santa Barbara, I jumped in to help write the second verse and the bridge. Jimmy had been sitting on that song for a long while, and I think my enthusiasm helped create the impetus he needed to finish it. Luckily for me.

One of the L&M collaborations I'm most proud of is "Watching the River Run," which we wrote in the back seat of a station wagon on the road someplace between our hotel and whatever venue we were playing that night. I'd recently had a dream in which I was wandering around an island somewhere, observing a kind of songwriting convention. In this dream, people played a game that involved writing down four bars of a melody and passing the sheet music on to somebody else, who would write the next four bars and pass it on again. After going through enough hands, the composition would be complete. Something similar happened with the lyrics. The songs were then performed by an orchestra and choir. (It was a long dream.) I told Jimmy about it and we decided to try it out. I already had a melody and we took turns writing lyrics. The trick was that we were not allowed to discuss what the song might actually be about—it had to write itself. Jimmy started with the lyric: "If you've been thinking you're all that you've got." I wrote the next line: "Then don't feel alone anymore." Jimmy came right back with: "'Cause when we're together, then you've got a lot." I followed with: "'Cause I am the river and you are the shore." Wow, I thought, this is a good game. I'd recently read

Herman Hesse's *Siddhartha*, whose main character lived beside a river as his path to enlightenment, and I was drawn to that spiritual imagery. We finished the lyrics in less than an hour. I frequently feel that my songs have minds of their own as I write them, that they come *through* me more than *from* me. This was that—a song that clearly knew what it wanted to be about.

Strangely, even though Jimmy and I both loved the process, we never worked that way again. For reasons I still don't understand, "Watching the River Run" would be the last song Jimmy and I truly wrote together. Maybe we each got too wrapped up in our own stuff to continue giving a shit about what the other guy was doing. We'd always seen ourselves as separate artists thrown together by happenstance and Clive Davis, so we were bound to drift apart artistically. Let him do his thing, and I'll do mine. We also grew increasingly territorial over our songs, effectively guarding our borders rather than letting each other in. I wouldn't call that a perfect partnership, but it's what we ended up doing.

As a side note, I performed "Watching the River Run" years later for the launch of Maharishi Mahesh Yogi's television station in Los Angeles. Afterward, Maharishi asked me to sit with him for a final camera shot. "That is a most beautiful song," he said. "Perhaps someday you can write a song about meditation." I looked at him quizzically for a moment.

"I thought that I did," I said.

LOGGINS & MESSINA did a *lot* of promotion on tour, visiting radio stations and doing more meet-and-greets than I could ever remember. We also did some noteworthy television gigs on shows like *The Midnight Special* and *Don Kirshner's Rock Concert*. The best of them let us stretch out a bit and demonstrate what our live show was all about. The worst of them . . . well, there was only one worst of them.

In the early 1970s, Sandy Duncan was a huge star, the squeaky clean girl next door. That's probably what led to the variety show TV special *Sandy in Disneyland*, which was precisely as wholesome as its title sounds. Because it aired on CBS, and because CBS owned Columbia Records, Jimmy and I were booked as musical guests. Lip-synching "Watching the River Run" in front of an artificial Disneyland lake while sitting on barrels and wearing suspenders was a small price to pay for some pretty massive exposure.

The truly steep emotional cost came later in the program, with a comedy routine that was one of the more embarrassing moments of my life. Jimmy and I played competing Prince Charmings, dressed in full pastel Shakespearean regalia, tights and all. In the skit we argued over who got to wake Sleeping Beauty (played by Ruth Buzzi, a terrific comedienne not necessarily known for her exquisite looks, buried under a layer of blankets) with a kiss. As I approached, Ruth began to loudly snore. Scared off, I deferred to Jimmy, and the same thing happened to him. Thoroughly rattled and kiss undelivered, we began discussing how a handshake might be better—at which point Ruth popped up with a snarl from under her covers and shouted for us to argue someplace else because she was trying to get some sleep. Hilarious. It was a great way to lose rock credibility in an instant.

For whatever it's worth, the Jackson 5, Michael included, also appeared on *Sandy in Disneyland* dressed in their own ridiculous outfits. At least we were in good company.

SHORTLY AFTER RECORDING *Full Sail*, Jimmy and I both went in for surgery—me to correct a deviated septum, him to have his tonsils out. We took care to book our procedures for the same time to minimize the impact on our upcoming tour.

I'd broken my septum in a car crash when I was seventeen. I was driving an old Ford Fairlane that belonged to a friend's parents, which, unbeknownst to them, he loaned me to go on a date. I never made it, thanks to a head-on collision on the way to pick her up. It was a rainy night, I was new to driving, and the car that hit me had veered into my lane with its left headlight out, so I initially thought it was a motorcycle. Both cars ended up totaled, and so did my nose, which crunched into the steering wheel on impact. At first the cops thought I'd stolen the car, and they held me until everything got straightened out. I sat on the curb for what felt like hours with an ice pack on my face because I was bleeding like crazy. Needless to say, my date wasn't pleased about getting stood up, and my friend's parents liked me even less than my date did.

That accident literally crushed my hopes to sound like Steve Winwood. My singing voice became much more nasal, and I had to live on Afrin to maintain whatever I had left. You can hear it clearly on the song "Peace of Mind." It wasn't until the surgery in 1973 that I was able to open up a little bit, and my voice became more chest based and mature. By the time I recorded "Celebrate Me Home," which is stylistically similar to "Peace of Mind," my voice had really evolved. I think the difference is stark.

HOWEVER GOOD OUR records may have been, L&M really shined as a live act. We intentionally left sections in our songs that created opportunities to stretch out, especially for Jon Clarke and Al Garth. Those moments onstage made all those hours of rehearsals worthwhile. Jon, Al, and Jimmy brought an alchemy to our performances that consistently captivated the audience.

Songs like "You Need a Man" and "Angry Eyes" were golden opportunities for the guys to create some unique interplay for extended stretches. There were moments when we would disintegrate out of time to the point that we were just making bird calls and creaking sounds with our guitars, waiting for somebody to play something musical that could bring us back home. Concerts were unpredictable, spontaneous trips for all of us. It was all extremely rehearsed, of course—not the jams themselves, but the intros and end points that told us when a soloist was ready to rejoin the pack.

With that in mind, it made sense for L&M to release a live album early in our run. What made even more sense was that it counted as a record delivered against our contract. By then, Jimmy and I had scraped the cupboard bare of original songs and needed time to come up with new material. *On Stage* bought us that time.

The album was culled from the shows we'd recorded around our Grammys appearance, plus a set from the Winterland Ballroom in San Francisco. Our goal was to offer listeners a sense of our concerts, which our studio stuff had a hard time capturing. We presented the songs in much the same order as our set list, including my two opening solo acoustic numbers, "Danny's Song" and "House at Pooh Corner." "Your Mama Don't Dance" appears second to last, in its standard first-encore position.

In between, we hit all the favorites. Had we waited to record it until after *Full Sail, On Stage* could have effectively been a greatest-hits album.

Of course, sticking to the classics didn't prevent us from getting carried away. *On Stage* was a double album, and we used that space extravagantly. The entirety of side three was a twenty-one-minute version of "Vahevala." Also included were a twelve-minute "Trilogy" and a ten-minute "Angry Eyes." Man, we sure got away with some crazy shit back then. By that point, Loggins & Messina had achieved enough success that the suits were willing to let out our reins and give us some freedom to experiment.

Playing "Vahevala," with its multi-layered structure, was probably the closest we ever came to being a jam band. Messina really liked to stretch out on that one, even though he wasn't a natural improviser. Jimmy's solos tended to be similar from night to night, pulling from a grab bag of ten or twelve well-rehearsed ideas that he would juxtapose on top of each other. Unlike Jon Clarke or Al Garth, Jimmy didn't trust his chops enough to play whatever he was feeling. There must have been a lot of pressure in being the lead guitarist for a band as musical as ours. A representative moment occurred at rehearsal a few years later, when Jimmy was getting frustrated by the chorus of voices offering opinions about an arrangement. At one point, Larry Sims said, "I've got a question," and Jimmy snapped, "I'll ask the questions because I know the answers!" To me, that was quintessential Messina. What he was really trying to say was, would everybody please give me a minute so I can figure this out? But that's not how it came off. Larry's benign question happened to be the one that broke the dam. Jimmy's answer made sense, and it also illustrated the level of control he tried to maintain. To this day, we still chuckle about that snafu.

During one of our reunion tours in 2009, Jimmy would occasionally lose track of the beat during his solos, so instead of coming in on the downbeat on one, he came in on the second beat as if it was one, which would automatically turn the beat around and force the whole band to adjust. All of a sudden the cue line preparing us for the next transition was inside out, and we'd have to figure out a way to follow it. As you can imagine, that can be nerve wracking. The band was going nuts, and asked me to talk to Messina about it. So the next time we had a quiet moment I said, "Jimmy, if you get lost, just stop playing and we'll let you know where we are." But he couldn't do it. Even though the cue line was completely its own thing—you could stop and take a two-bar rest, then come in at the right spot without anybody knowing any better—he would just jump onto whatever was there and say, "Follow me. This is where it is." I could see the confusion on his face, but it wasn't in his personality to cede control.

I bring that up because of the conversation I had with the band over dinner one night, while Jimmy was someplace else. One of the guys pulled out a newspaper and read a review of the show we'd just played. "This is the best part," he said. "It says, 'Jim Messina is obviously the leader because the band watches his every move during his guitar solos.'" Everybody howled at that. We *had* to pay attention. Jimmy was the front car of the train, and wherever he went you'd better follow. I don't recall him doing that back in the 1970s, so maybe it's a product of aging—his *or* mine, given that I don't remember things the way I used to. There's no way I'm calling Jim a bad guitar player here—he's really good at what he does—but it did become an adventure waiting for that three-bar beat to jump out at us like a mad jack-in-the-box. My hat's off to Stevie "D" DiStanislao, the drummer on that tour, for figuring out how to quickly turn the groove right side up during those hairpin moments.

AS IF JIMMY'S CONTROL of our production, arrangements, song selection, and concert set lists wasn't enough, he also decided to take charge of the recording process—the *entire* recording process. He bought a ranch in the Ojai hills, about an hour northwest of Los Angeles, and transformed it into L&M's de facto studio. This made some sense given Jimmy's history as an engineer, producer, and noted stickler for detail, in that it gave him control over factors as granular as where band members slept while we were recording. Jimmy converted the stables into a bunkhouse, transforming horse stalls into mini bedrooms, complete with antique beds and furniture. Facilities were down the hall.

The "studio" was in the den of the main house, with an ad hoc isolation booth set up in an adjoining hallway, and another on the lanai. A baby grand piano was placed in the wood-paneled living room. Jimmy would call the Haji remote recording truck up from Los Angeles when it came time to cut the tracks. While tape was rolling, you had to remember where you could or couldn't walk and which toilets were okay to flush.

The idea behind the place, which he named Mother Lode Ranch after the first record we made there, was the dream of one big happy rock 'n' roll family. In Jimmy's mind we were a band of brothers, spending time together away from the outside world, our only responsibilities being to make the best music we could. The acreage was beautiful and the sky was clear.

The reality, though, was a bit different. We were a bunch of twenty-something guys sharing too much personal space. We worked on the *Mother Lode* album for about four months, during which time our access to friends, family, and the familiarity of our own homes was mostly limited to weekends. Whatever sort of camaraderie Jimmy may have envisioned came off in limited quantities. Guys resented being put up in horse stalls, no matter how well those stalls were appointed. But we did get a lot of work done.

Jimmy and I had it easier than the band members in one regard: he had an entire house to live in, and I didn't stay on the property. Because there were only so many beds to go around, I booked myself a bungalow in a nearby motor court out on Mallory Way. It was only a few minutes away from the ranch, and it afforded me some privacy. The main downside was that the only form of air conditioning in the place was a freestanding swamp cooler. Summer days in Ojai frequently exceeded a hundred degrees, and I would wake up soaking wet from all the moisture that box emitted during the night. I found out one morning that the place also had woodpeckers in the tree just outside my door. At 7 A.M. I'd hear *knock, knock, knock*. I'd get up, open the door, there'd be nobody there. Close the door. *Knock, knock, knock*. Fucking woodpeckers.

Still, there was a lot to love about the setting. We were surrounded by trees and country air that was so crisp it surprised me every time I stepped outside. There was also a hot tub on Jimmy's property, and the Matilija Hot Springs just thirty minutes up the road. Soaking proved to be an excellent relief for whatever tension might have built up.

The other thing I loved about being in Ojai was Jimmy's new assistant and bookkeeper, who I'd met during our early rehearsals in Barry Sullivan's pool house. Eva Ein was almost six feet tall, blond, freckle-faced, and an absolute knockout. She was best friends with Jimmy's wife, Jenny, and always seemed to be at Barry's house when the band showed up. When

Jimmy hired her to do some project management at the ranch for the new record, I saw it as a stroke of good fortune.

Eva was born in Sweden but her ancestry was Estonian, which is where her parents lived until World War II. That girl was full of mystique, which was surpassed only by her wicked sense of humor. It took me a while to ask her out—this was still back when we were preparing for *Sittin' In*—and I could hardly believe it when she said yes. I wrote "Till the Ends Meet" for her, which made it onto our second album, although I don't think I ever told her it was about us. I was still very shy back then.

My relationship with Eva was complicated by the fact that I was still with Darla, even though in my mind that connection was only ever temporary. She was still living in my house, but we barely even slept together anymore. I knew that I didn't want to be with her long term, but I also couldn't seem to get her to leave. One time she came with me to Berkeley to visit Danny, and for some reason played Steppenwolf's "Born to Be Wild" on his turntable over and over. I mean, *over and over.* It drove everybody nuts, and he finally snapped and kicked her out of the house. I was so annoyed that I didn't even argue. We dropped her and a girlfriend at a freeway on-ramp and told her to find her own way home. It sounds pretty damn cruel to think about it now, but we'd hitchhiked up there, and it was how we were going to get home. Also, it was the most definitive way I could think of to break up with her. It didn't work. She ended up back in Southern California—at my place. I guess that kind of thing could happen when you were nineteen years old and it's 1968.

How cavalier young men are with time. I was young, inexperienced, and way too horny for my own good. Darla was eager and easy to be with, but ours was a partnership of convenience, not love. Everybody expected me to leave her once I started dating Eva, but for some reason I didn't. Maybe it's because Eva was pretty and popular, and I was way too insecure to imagine us in a relationship. I could be with Darla because that relationship didn't matter to me. I couldn't be with Eva because I knew a relationship with her *would* matter, and I wasn't ready for it. We hooked up briefly . . . and then I stayed with Darla for four more years. Holy shit.

It wasn't until the *Mother Lode* sessions at Jimmy's ranch that things grew serious between me and Eva. L&M had released four albums by that point, and I'd been on the road for years. It was time. She was living in a guest room in the main house, and our collective seclusion kept us in close proximity. Before long, my attraction to her was undeniable, and I almost didn't believe it when she seemed to feel it, too. At first, Eva was reluctant to rekindle what we'd started all those years earlier, especially since my situation with Darla had hardly changed. But her resistance soon melted, and before I knew it I was falling in love for the very first time. The ranch became our little Eden. We would wander away to quiet parts of the property whenever we could, going for walks or to the hot springs. We grew our friendship as much as we grew our attraction to each other, and I realized this was the person I wanted to be with.

I was so wrapped up with Eva, in fact, that I completely forgot Darla was still living in my cottage back in Santa Barbara. I hadn't so much as spoken to her on the phone since before I'd left for Ojai to record, and when I finally went home and saw her in my kitchen, I was actually surprised.

"This is ridiculous," I said. It was the first thing out of my mouth. I couldn't believe she was there. I could barely believe she had been there at all.

I sat down on the couch and asked her to join me. "Why are we still pretending to be together?" I said. "It's time for you to find a new place to live." She nodded as if she understood.

"I really mean it," I said. "You need to leave, for good." I tried to be soft in saying it, but there's really no empathetic way to deliver that kind of message.

I gave Darla one more night in the house—in a room other than mine—and told her to pack her stuff come the morning. She seemed okay. As I headed off to bed, she told me she was going for a walk on the beach.

I had trouble falling asleep because a voice kept telling me that I had to go find her. She's going to hurt herself, the voice in my head kept saying. I actually responded out loud at one point, shouting, "It's not my problem!" I pulled the covers up over my head, but the voice was persistent. She's going to kill herself, it said, telling me over and over again to get up. Fuck you, I thought. She can do whatever she wants. *Get up*, the voice said. *Get up NOW.*

So now I'm getting up and getting dressed, even as I'm still saying, "Fuck you! Leave me alone." It must have been one in the morning. I pulled on a jacket and went down to the beach, where, on a moonless night, I could barely see a thing. I had no good reason to walk in the direction I did, but within a minute I found her. Darla was passed out in the sand, having taken (I'd learn later) an overdose of sleeping pills. She'd written "I'm sorry, Damien" in the sand beside her.

Who the fuck was Damien?

I didn't have time to ponder the question. Desperate for help, I tried to lift her, then ended up dragging her by her feet to a nearby house. As I stumbled through the sand, I started to talk to her as if she could hear me: "Goddamn it, Darla—I'm *done* with you!" Now I was yelling. "I'm done! I'm fucking done!" What began as anger turned into tears, and then an overwhelming awareness. I could not keep it contained. "Holy shit," I said out loud, beginning to laugh. "I *am* done with you. We've been together all these years just for this moment to happen!" I suddenly understood that our connection had existed so I might save her life someday. With that, a wave of forgiveness flowed through me—forgiveness for her pushy, annoying tenacity, and forgiveness to myself for not being strong enough to have forced her out of my life long ago. It was a karmic thing, some sort of payback that Darla had unwittingly forced upon me. I knew then that this chapter of my life had finally ended, and I felt a deep sense of relief as all emotional connection to her slid from my body. It was as if I was taking off a heavy, wet overcoat of responsibility I no longer needed to wear.

By that point, I'd reached my neighbor's house. She called 911, and the paramedics raced Darla to the hospital. They pumped her stomach and put her in the suicide ward.

It wasn't until I returned home that I found the note she'd left—not to me, but to her boyfriend, Damien, who'd been living in my house with her while I was away. There were a lot of drugs. I also found out that Damien was hardly the only one she'd messed around with. In a particularly egregious example, the first time the band went to Ojai, when I was working at the ranch, she repeatedly fucked some guy back at the motor court.

The day after Darla's suicide attempt, Damien actually showed up at the house and asked for a ride to the hospital. I had to go to there anyway to sign some papers, so I agreed.

It was a mostly silent trip. Finally, he turned to me and said the one thing he felt was essential: "I love her, you know."

"You can have her, you know," I replied.

And that was the end of that.

CHAPTER 6

THIS IS THE END

CLARITY ABOUT MY RELATIONSHIP with Darla was one thing. I was also gaining clarity about my relationship with Jimmy. I'd pretty much given up on writing songs with him, especially since we never even pulled out our guitars together unless we were recording or onstage. That was fine—he's the Messina, I'm the Loggins, you be you and I'll be me. Still, after writing seven tunes together across our first three records, that was it for us until we finally helped each other polish off a couple of songs for our last album, the live *Finale*, because Jimmy thought new material would help it sell.

Our drifting apart was due mainly to our increasingly divergent musical tastes. I was becoming more independent by the day, and less reliant on his leadership. I was no longer willing to rehearse the life out of every piece of music I wrote. I didn't want to Bambify our music with castanets and pseudo-reggae arrangements. I was moving away from the country-rock thing and toward a more R&B-influenced sound, while Messina didn't even seem to like R&B. When Stevie Wonder broke through with *Music of My Mind*, Jimmy was openly critical of it. I thought the album was revolutionary, and every guy in the band was going nuts over it. When I insisted this was the new music, Jimmy seemed to see it as threatening. "Your Mama Don't Dance" was *not* Stevie Wonder, and if Stevie Wonder was changing the face of pop radio, we'd be on the outside looking in. It can happen fast.

This is when I really began to conceive of my post-L&M life, where my music had a place of its own. I was already thinking about the kinds of songs I wanted to write once Jimmy and I split up, even though we hadn't even discussed the idea of going our own ways. Meanwhile, we were still actively recording and touring. The material spinning around in my head was dramatically different than anything I'd ever written. When L&M hit the road, I found myself ducking away before shows, jamming alone with my guitar in the shower room of whatever arena we happened to be playing, improvising melodies into a cassette recorder, one after the other. The huge echoes in those tiled spaces sent me into a hypnotic space where all kinds of music poured out.

Back home I sifted through each tape, searching for even the tiniest fragment of song potential, and cataloged it in a spiral notebook. I gave each idea a grade, described whether it was a ballad or rocker, a verse or a chorus, whether it should be written on keyboard or guitar, and who might make a good collaboration partner.

The first guy I worked with in this regard was Ronnie Wilkins, who reached out to me through my management team. Ronnie had co-written the great Dusty Springfield song "Son of a Preacher Man," which had the kind of southern R&B vibe I wanted to explore in my own music. We only spent a couple of hours together at his house in LA, but it was successful enough to whet my appetite for more of the same. The song Ronnie and I wrote together, "Growin'," became the lead track on *Mother Lode*.

Ronnie wasn't my only outside collaborator on that album, though the other one came about more through happenstance than anything. Its aftermath continues to awe me.

The guy I'm referring to is Maury Muehleisen, a guitar player who accompanied Jim Croce. L&M toured with Croce quite a bit, and I ran across Maury one day in the laundry room of the Holiday Inn where we were all staying. I had to wait out a wash cycle and so did he, so I grabbed my guitar and showed him a melody I'd been working on. I'd had a vivid dream the night before in which I watched hundreds of soldiers parachuting from planes under a moonlit sky, like an ominous scene from some black-and-white World War II movie. The thing was, everybody in this dream, including me, knew they were going to die. I *had* to write a song about that. It was dark and moody, and needed a melody to match. Over the course of a couple hours in that laundry room, Maury helped me capture the emotion. What we came up with reflected some serious heaviness: "Thunder is born in our eyes / And we see them, / four horsemen, last judgement / Lord Apocalypse is nigh." Impending death from the sky, set to music.

That song, "Fever Dream," was easily the darkest thing I'd ever written. Maybe that's what made it so shocking when only weeks later Croce's plane crashed in Natchitoches, Louisiana, killing everybody aboard, including Maury. I was at home when I got the news, and a shiver ran through me, as if the song had somehow picked him to help me write it. I didn't consider myself prophetic then, and I certainly don't now. I still have no way to make sense of that series of events. I put the song on our record in Maury's honor, but that was pretty much it—I never played it again.

Losing Maury and Croce deeply affected everybody in the band, especially because they'd died doing something we all did all the time: flying across the country from one gig to another. Actually, that part didn't bother me. About a year earlier, I'd met a psychic in Santa Barbara who after reading my palm said flatly: "You will not die in a plane crash. That is not your fate." I've always had limited faith in psychics, but I believed her. I suppose I just wanted it to be true. Still do.

After that, I began gravitating toward collaborations with different keyboard players, usually R&B-influenced writers whose voicings and chordal progressions were distinct from whatever I knew how to get out of my guitar. I would sing my cassette melodies to these guys, which they then translated into piano chords. Through trial and error we parsed out a new kind of music. My music. From that point forward, that was how the vast majority of my songwriting partnerships worked.

During L&M's later years, two keyboard players in my immediate circle were Ed Sanford and John Townsend of the Sanford-Townsend Band, best known for their 1977 hit "Smoke from a Distant Fire." Ed was friends with our drummer, Merel Bregante, and had a terrific, southern-blues style. He and John were writing their first album together, and actively seeking songwriting partners. I was a willing target.

Sanford and Townsend were still unknown at the time, and in an effort to gain some fame they took it upon themselves to enter a song we wrote together called "Oriental Gate" into the American Song Festival competition in upstate New York. I wouldn't have done something like that on my own—I had gold records on my wall, man—but I thought it was worth pursuing. It wasn't just a contest but a TV special, an entire concert at the Saratoga Performing Arts Center in upstate New York, coincidentally scheduled just a couple of days after Loggins & Messina played that very venue. It was September 1974, and since we didn't have anything else on the calendar, I stuck around. It was a big production, with old-school luminaries like Sarah Vaughn, Etta James, and the Limeliters performing the songs being judged. The venue had about five thousand seats, plus lawn space for tens of thousands more, and I was amazed at how many people they packed in. I never took the stage, though I did smile for the cameras during the early portions of the program.

That's how it started. How it ended was that a decision to perform every song multiple times for the TV cameras bogged things down so much on a cold and rainy night that by eleven o'clock much of the crowd had cleared out. That left the producers with a bunch of empty seats—not great for televised visuals—and a schedule so bloated that the winner wasn't announced until six o'clock the next morning. Whew. Glad I cut out early. So for that matter did one of the musical acts, whose name I forget; he took off before the song he was supposed to showcase came up, and it never got played. Our song can be heard on the resulting LP, performed by Sanford & Townsend themselves. A few years later they re-cut it on their *Smoke from a Distant Fire* album, including harmony vocals by yours truly.

AL GARTH REALLY didn't like the song "Changes," a coming-of-age thing Jimmy wrote about the hardships facing young men in modern society. He was really fixated on the line about Uncle Sam putting his hand down somebody's pants. It could be taken a number of ways, I guess (I always assumed it was about the taxman), but Al wanted nothing to do with it. "My son will hear this," he said. "My mom will hear it." Al and Jimmy had been at each other's throats for a while by that point; these complaints were just the latest chapter in an increasingly large book of issues.

Al was unique in his willingness to mix it up with Messina. He openly disagreed with a number of Jimmy's musical choices, and increasingly questioned his leadership. Once, he even took out his frustrations onstage by sabotaging a musical duet in which Jimmy played a lick on his guitar, which Al would duplicate on his fiddle before playing his own lick for Jimmy to copy. It was a regular part of our act, and, needless to say, exquisitely rehearsed. Well, this time Al played something he knew was too complicated for Jim. You'd have to have been paying extremely close attention, let alone be familiar with our set to even have noticed, but Jimmy left that stage embarrassed, and they ended up screaming at each other backstage.

That kind of stuff seemed to happen more frequently when Al was drinking—and Al drank a lot. As far as I know he never showed up wasted to sessions or shows, but off-hours on the road gave him plenty of time to booze it up, which was when I tried diligently to avoid him. His given name was Lester, and band members began referring to his dual personalities, sober and drunk, as "Good Al" and "Evil Lester." Even with Good Al among us, Merel would occasionally sidle over with a shit-stirring grin and goad his bandmate into a confrontation of some sort, usually with Jimmy. Theirs was a strange kinship.

We were scheduled to record "Changes" as part of the *Mother Lode* sessions, and I told Al to just skip it, that we'd record the song without him. Jimmy had recently taken me to the nearby Matilija Hot Springs to broach the subject of firing Al, which was my first inkling the situation had grown so serious. I worried that a fight over "Changes" would be the final straw, and wanted desperately to avoid that.

I didn't like the idea of letting Al go. Jimmy felt that his musicianship was not worth the headaches he caused. I disagreed. Then again, I also understood that Al's drinking was getting worse, and that any future disruptions would carry more weight, not less. By the end of our soak, Jimmy seemed more determined than ever, and I decided to acquiesce. I mean, the band was called Loggins & fucking Messina, not Loggins & Garth. If somebody had to go, it sure as hell wasn't gonna be Jimmy.

When Al was a no-show for the "Changes" recording session, it was all the justification Jimmy needed to let him go. I wasn't there for that conversation, but it was clear to me that it would have happened anyway; even if Al hadn't been AWOL, the minute he questioned those lyrics again, the hammer would have fallen.

Musically, Al was always the right guy for the band. He was bluesy and jazzy on the saxophone, very much in the David Sanborn ilk, and we panicked a bit when it came to replacing him. I guess it speaks to how essential he was that it took three guys to fill his shoes: Vince Denham on sax, clarinet, and flute; Richard Greene on fiddle, cello, and mandolin; and Steve Forman on percussion taking over the parts Al would play when he wasn't on wind or string instruments. (During that same period we also added woodwind player Don Roberts and keyboardist Michel Rubini, making our roster increasingly gigantic.) If I'd known then what I know now, I would've sat Jimmy down to discuss the decision a bit more deeply. I wouldn't try to diminish his anger or frustration, which were totally justified, but I might have pointed out how profoundly Al's replacement costs would affect the bottom line. That might actually have had an effect.

The whole band was upset by how things went down. This group started Loggins & Messina together, and the guys rightly had a sense of ownership. The whole purpose of creating a band—of sharing record royalties instead of just hiring studio musicians—was to foster a sense of kinship and pride in the work. A personnel shakeup like that disrupted morale, not to mention the distinct sound of our music. It might have been different had Al quit, but abruptly firing one guy from the group had a devastating effect. Our family vibe was lost, and I don't think we ever got it back.

Before long, Al made the most ironic of moves, joining Jimmy's old band Poco. As I heard it, it didn't take long for that group to make its first-ever unanimous management decision: fire him and start over. I'm guessing that Al eventually cleaned up his act, because he later spent decades playing with Glenn Frey and the Eagles. Things have probably evened out for him. I hope so, anyway.

ISSUES WITH AL ASIDE, we'd been doing well with our record releases, putting out four albums' worth of mostly high-quality material, all of which garnered positive reviews and sold well. It was a pride-worthy catalog.

Then we released *So Fine*.

This was 1975. Our latest trip to Jimmy's ranch had resulted in two albums' worth of songs: one of originals, and one of cover songs from our childhoods. The latter became *So Fine*. I never thought it was much of a plan, but I didn't push back like I should have, especially now that I understand how badly something like that can hurt a career.

When the president of Columbia Records, Bruce Lundvall, heard what we were up to, he came all the way from New York to talk us out of it, threatening that the label wouldn't promote a covers record. Messina was immovable. I'm not sure why, but he really wanted this to happen. Before Bruce arrived, Jimmy pulled me aside and insisted we present a unified front. For the sake of our partnership, I went along with him.

Looking back, I wish I hadn't. It shouldn't have been difficult to recognize that when the label president shows up in person to give you a vote of no confidence, it might be a good idea to rethink things. Jimmy will forever insist that his motivation came from a sincere desire to recognize his early musical influences, which I'm sure is true, but I suspect the real reason for *So Fine* is that it knocked another album off of our contract with relative ease. No new writing needed.

It was not a totally crazy concept (if Jimmy had wanted to record a klezmer album, that would have been crazy), and it contained some great songs, but my heart was not in it at all. Ultimately, *So Fine* ended up hurting our artistic credibility and turned off fans and critics alike. Jimmy and I never really agreed on our approach, even after I'd signed off on the idea.

Jimmy insisted on maintaining the arrangements of the originals, while I felt that if we were going to record other people's songs, we should at least make them sound like L&M. I kept thinking about James Taylor, who always brought unique magic to his covers, while ours seemed uninspired, more like something performed by a tribute band. As was usually the case, Jimmy's opinion prevailed.

Betrayal is too heavy a word to use in this context, but it's close to the feeling many of our fans expressed after *So Fine* came out. It simply didn't deliver the kind of quality they'd come to expect from us. A lot of people bought it without knowing what it was, and ended up returning it. I know this because they told me over and over again. At one stop during our ensuing tour, a radio DJ pulled me aside and pointed his finger into my chest. "You shouldn't have messed with the songs of my youth," he snarled. "Those are the songs I got laid to in the back seat. They're sacred, man!" What could I say? You can't argue with that.

These days, when people tell me they like that record (which does happen on occasion), I have a hard time believing it. Some people did like *So Fine*. My problem is that *I* never liked it. Ultimately, Lundvall followed through on his threat to not support the record: *So Fine* was a bust, topping out at No. 21, by far the worst showing of our career.

More than that, Loggins & Messina never really recovered. In fact, the decisions behind *So Fine* led to the end of our band as much as any direct conflicts Jimmy and I might have had. The record opened the floodgates for bad reviews in a way we hadn't experienced before, with the prominent critic Jerry Gilbert (in *Sounds*, spring 1975) beginning his assessment, "I hate this record with a rare savagery" and ending it with, "So artlessly reverent without inspiration, so vapid, so awful . . . It doesn't deserve the vinyl it's pressed on." Ouch. Even worse, only three years earlier, on October 18, 1972, John Ingham had written in the same magazine: "The Kenny Loggins/Jim Messina band is the best thing to emerge from LA in years." I felt that deeply. We all did. And the splintering began.

MESSINA SPILLED THE BEANS about *So Fine* to the *Los Angeles Times* in Dennis Hunt's February 8, 1976, article saying, "Some people told us concept albums just don't sell. They said this kind of album is a big risk and our fans wouldn't go for it and it was unwise at this point in our career. They warned us no matter how good it was, people would still say our versions of the oldies weren't as good as the originals. But we wouldn't listen to any of that talk."

The catch was, when Jimmy said that he was promoting *Native Sons*, the other record we'd recorded at the same time, which came out about six months later. (We originally wanted to call it *Native Sons of the Golden West*, but that name was under copyright.) By that point, whatever bad will we'd built with *So Fine* was being thrown right back at us. To be honest, it's not our best work as a collective or my best work as an individual. I was busy conceiving of R&B-flavored music that would ultimately feed my solo career; my attention was no longer singularly devoted to the country-rock genre.

On January 29, 1976, the *Spokane Daily Chronicle* said some of the lyrics "might appeal to a third grader." A few days later, on February 1, the *Austin American-Statesman* wrote: "Somewhere between the surface of the record and the listener's ears, the excitement disappears." On February 7, the newspaper in Binghamton, New York, said we "should have been put out to pasture" for releasing *So Fine*, and *Native Sons* was "hardly enough to lift us from those doldrums." And on February 15, Steve Pond, in our hometown *LA Times*, called *Native Sons* "overblown and needlessly elaborate." I remember our percussionist Steve Forman referring to one of the tracks as "doggy bunny music," which I'm pretty sure he didn't mean as a compliment.

It was our first album of originals featuring our new ten-person lineup, and preceded a tour for which we'd have to find even more musicians to replace some who had only signed on for studio work. Jimmy wanted me to come back to Ojai for auditions, but the process felt insincere to me. I was spending my off-hours envisioning a post-L&M landscape, so rejiggering the current roster—a move that had a limited shelf life—did not hold much appeal. Anyway, if I ended up liking different guys than Jimmy, I knew which one of us would get his way.

So I left the entire process up to him and headed off to Switzerland with Eva. It was a great opportunity to clear my head. Her Swedish aunt Lya had a vacation cottage in Switzerland, about an hour outside of Liechtenstein, which she offered to let us use. It was wintertime in the Alps, which I thought would be romantic.

Well, we arrived to find the cottage completely cleaned out by bur-
glars. Even the furniture was gone. Really, the place looked move-in
ready. Eva called her aunt and I notified the police, and we altered our
plans and continued up the road to St. Moritz, where we booked a room
at the Palace Hotel. This was actually working out for me. The place was
gorgeous, perfect for a romantic, uninterrupted week in Europe with my
new love—until, almost as soon as we got there, Eva came down with the
flu. She didn't get out of bed for the next three days, and I was left with
little to do but take long walks through town.

What I saw confused me. St. Moritz is a world-famous resort, but I
found it deserted—nobody on the streets, nobody in the shops. I ended up
spending most of my time back at the hotel with Eva, and suggested that
when she was well enough to travel, a beach in the South of France would
be more restorative than sitting around a ghost town in the Alps. So as
soon as Eva was up for it, we packed our stuff and headed to the train
station. Arriving with a couple of hours to spare, we decided to check our
bags with a porter and hop the mountain tram to a place up top called
Corviglia.

Turns out that's where the magic was happening.

When the doors opened, it was like the scene in *The Wizard of Oz*
where everything goes from black and white to color. The very first thing
we saw was a horse-drawn sleigh, with two people bundled up in furs
like in a Currier and Ives lithograph. All at once, I realized the town was
empty because everybody was up on the mountain. Eva and I looked at
each other, and in an instant decided to stick around and learn how to
ski. We checked back into our hotel, and the next day met our five-foot-
tall, fifty-something sweet little ski instructor named Ursi. She spoke only
Romansh, no English, so we just followed her down the bunny slope and
imitated whatever she did. I still don't know how I managed to pick up
anything, but that lady's lessons stuck; I ended up skiing for the next forty
years. Back home, I even took advantage of a celebrity ski event in which
they paid airfare and hotel costs in exchange for my participation. Professional skiers were on hand to teach us whatever we could absorb in a
one-day class, which is how I somehow went directly from my beginner's
snowplow to Olympic-style downhill turns. For years, that was the only

way I knew how to ski: pointing downhill and cutting fast. Stopping was never a forte, but I made do.

WHEN WE FINISHED mixing *Native Sons* in late 1975, Loggins & Messina was effectively over. We'd fulfilled our contract to Columbia with our sixth album in six years, and all that was left was to support it with a tour. Jimmy and I were growing more and more distant, but even then it was difficult to dismiss the idea of continuing a good thing, selling boatloads more records and concert seats. Boatloads were appealing. Jimmy was very much in favor of this option. "Why are we breaking up?" he asked. "Can't we find a way to ride this train a little longer?"

Well, no. I couldn't. For me, it wasn't even about getting along. I couldn't hold my new creativity hostage within the constraints of the L&M framework. I was stockpiling ideas for a solo career that was just around the corner, but it's not like I was holding back material from Loggins & Messina; these were songs Jimmy would never want on an album, which was precisely the reason we needed to split.

I think Jimmy knew it too. I keep going back to a sound check we did before a show in what must have been 1975, which we were recording for what would become our final live album. I got into an argument with Jimmy about a song I'd recently written called "Oklahoma, Home of Mine," one of two new tunes we were working up for our set. (The other was Jimmy's "Motel Cowboy.") I was looking for a Leon Russell–esque southern boogie vibe. Hell, "Oklahoma" was in the song's title specifically because that's where Leon was from. By the time Jimmy finished rearranging things into a country-rock shuffle, I barely recognized it.

I don't remember the details of the spat, probably because they aren't important. It's not like we hadn't argued about similar things many times before. This time, though, I lost it. Maybe it was because I could see the future so close and I'd run out of patience with the present. Maybe I was having a bad day. Whatever drove it, I had a harmonica in my hand, and in a fit of anger I threw it as far into the seats as I could.

Messina, to his eternal credit, took my tantrum calmly and with incredible insight. Instead of pushing back, he paused for a beat and then said quietly, "We should break up now, while we're still friends." Jimmy had been in a similar place with both Buffalo Springfield and Poco, and recognized the signs. It was selfless of him, a moment of clarity, and I knew he was right. I'd been anticipating a break from L&M for some time, but it was still just a nebulous plan. It wasn't until Jimmy said those words that I truly understood how over we were.

I took what he said to heart. We decided to split, but not without a glorious send-off. We planned a whole tour around the event, and called it *Finale*. Our publicists billed it as the last chance for fans to see me and Jimmy together, and it totally worked. Every newspaper preview of our show drove that narrative. The thing was, it was true—and it wasn't just the fans who were feeling it. Jimmy and I both put a lot of emotional weight behind that tour, and so did our band, sometimes even more so than us.

In fact, our drummer, Merel, was so invested in our success, so utterly passionate about L&M, that he couldn't stomach the thought of simply playing out the string. We were breaking up, and he didn't want to be around to see it. Merel left before that last tour got underway, more sad than angry. I hated to see him go, but I appreciated where he was coming from.

Merel had joined the band with bass player Larry Sims—they'd played together in the Sunshine Company before Loggins & Messina—and that's the way he left, when Larry decided he didn't want to play with any- one but Merel. With that, our rhythm section was gone.

Along with the recent dismissal of Al Garth and the addition of the three guys who replaced him, our band was about to look very different. Jimmy and I ended up bringing in an LA-based drummer named Wil- lie Ornellas for that last tour. We'd found Willie by happenstance while we were auditioning keyboard players, simply because he'd given his pal a ride. Well, his keyboardist buddy didn't get the job, but Willie ended up sticking around. Then again, Willie's rejected friend—the soon-to-be legendary David Foster—became one of my most important collaborators for decades, so things worked out for everybody in the end.

This left us with an entirely new look for our stage act. Only me, Jimmy, and Jon Clarke remained from the original lineup, plus one of Al's replacements, Vince Denham on sax and flute. In were Willie Ornellas and George Hawkins, a bass player from a bar band in Ojai who I'd met during one of my trips into town from Jimmy's ranch. He'd never played on the big stage, but he had serious chops (and would become one of my best friends for many years to come). The guys got along pretty well, and musically we were tight. It looked like it was going to be a good tour, until I threw a wrench into the plans.

I'd recently taken up wood carving, and was getting pretty good at it. It was a creative outlet that required total concentration, which I found to be quite meditative. I carved a miniature replica of my living room—complete with fireplace, bookshelves, and a crystal ball on a stand—into a bellows. I carved a block of cherrywood into a smoking pipe for my dad, with two doves wrapping around the bowl, meeting in front at their beaks. (My son Luke uses it to this day.)

Sitting with Eva on the beach one day, I was working on a large wooden spool, carving out vines with leaves that folded back on themselves in relief. At some point, the knife took a wrong turn and skipped across the wood, straight into my left hand. I watched, transfixed, as blood began to trickle, then pour, from the wound as if somebody had turned on a spigot. I pressed on my hand as hard as I could with a towel while Eva drove me to the hospital. Given how bloody the cut was, I was amazed at how easily they sewed it up in the emergency room.

If only things were as simple as they seemed.

What the doctors didn't realize was that my knife was so sharp, and the cut so completely clean, that I had severed a nerve sheath that subsequently collapsed, obscuring the extent of the damage. Over the next few days my hand started to clench, closing in on itself like a flower. Suffice it to say, that freaked me out. My manager, Larry Larson, called a contact at UCLA, and the next morning I found myself in surgery at Cedars-Sinai to reconnect my nerve endings. When I came to, they gave me the devastating news that the damage was permanent.

If there's a bright side to this story it's that I eventually regained about 80 percent of what I'd had, more than enough to accompany myself on guitar. Unfortunately, the steady progress I'd made as a soloist was shattered. Those unsteady leads I'd taken way back with Dunn & McCashen had been replaced by competent advances in technique. I was finally getting to the point where I could play the things in my head, which opened up a world of possibilities. After the accident, much of that was gone. I no longer had the dexterity in my fingers to pull it off. I'd already decided to focus on writing mostly with keyboard players, so I resigned myself to rhythm guitar and felt lucky to have that. It's not like I was a shredding lead player anyway, so accepting my new fate did not involve much heartache.

From that moment forward I shifted emphasis from my guitar to my voice. So much for my dreams of becoming Pete Townsend. In the meantime, L&M had a tour to do and three useable hands between our two guitarists. When I showed up at rehearsal wearing a cast, our fiddle player, Woody Chrisman, volunteered to grab a guitar and play my parts. Thankfully, he was really good. My participation on that tour was limited to vocals and some hand percussion.

The lesson of the day: guitarists shouldn't play with knives.

BEFORE L&M, JIMMY WANTED to become a producer specifically to avoid touring. As we gained popularity, though, we ended up traveling a *lot*. It seemed like we spent at least half of every year on the road, a relentless schedule that began to wear on Messina. We could see it. Actually, the hassles of commercial air travel—getting the entire band, plus our equipment, checked in on time, then dealing with standard airport hassles day after day—was grating on all of us. Finally our road manager, Jim Recor, convinced Messina about the benefits of private air travel, and how it might improve an itinerary that was becoming less tolerable by the day.

Jimmy had always been a master of thrift, having designed all kinds of money-saving measures for the band—rehearsing at Barry Sullivan's pool house and at Mission High School (both of which were free); doubling up on hotel rooms; renting station wagons driven by band members or road crew. That's pretty grassroots stuff. It's also why leasing jets was such a departure. It was somewhere around the *Full Sail* tour that Jimmy finally acknowledged being a rock star. Once he did, it didn't take much to get me on board. Kicking back in a private plane sounded good to me.

The first plane we used was a Cessna Citation. Because it had only four seats, Recor also booked a Handley Page Jetstream for the band. This caused some perception problems, because the Handley Page was a twin turbo-prop and put another level of distinction between the haves (me and Jimmy) and the have-nots (everybody else). That was only the beginning.

Jimmy was such a nervous flyer that before our first flight he decided to buy parachutes—literal parachutes—in case catastrophe struck. It might have been the strangest rock-star request our road manager ever filled. This presented multiple problems. The pilot informed us about one of them after he stopped laughing. "Jim," he deadpanned, "if you jump out the door of this plane you'll get sucked right through the engine—but only after the wing has already killed you." That was reassuring.

The other problem was more serious because it was real. At Messina's direction, we only packed four chutes: for him, for me, and for our two road managers. Not that anybody but him wanted one, but if you're ever looking for a way to show your band members how expendable you think they are, stiffing them on parachutes is a good place to start.

Also before that first flight, Jimmy pulled the pilot aside and asked about the plane's glide ratio—how far we might sail if the engines cut out. The response was equally memorable: "About the same as my car keys." I thought that was hilarious. Jimmy . . . not so much.

By that point in the 1970s, jet travel for rock stars was pretty standard. The thing was, the bands you think of with their own planes—Led Zeppelin, Elton John, and the like—tended to sell out coliseums. Loggins & Messina played mostly in arenas and performing-arts theaters. When I questioned the decision, I was told that a couple extra shows could be designated to cover those costs. Okay, then. Truth be told, I really wanted to believe it. On one tour we actually rented *two* Lear jets, which ended up costing almost every penny we made. Booking them for a tour like ours was a ridiculous financial decision, but nobody on the business end informed me (or Jimmy, as far as I know) as to exactly how much we were blowing until after the money was already spent. Management might actually have been happy about it, because they got their percentage either way, and lower profits increased the likelihood we'd tour that much more the following year. The industry is rife with tales of points-earning business managers keeping their bands hungry to prevent them from leaving the road.

For our farewell tour in 1976, we went all out and booked the *Starship*—the legendary, custom-fitted Boeing 720 that for a time was *the* means of travel for notable rock acts. It was available late in the year, so we got a deal; our premium flight package ended up costing about the same as what we'd been spending anyway on two smaller jets. Sure enough, there was the Loggins & Messina logo up there on the fuselage, just like the bands before us. It was a magnetic stick-on, not a paint job, but I must admit that was a rush.

The *Starship* was the height of luxury, and made that tour 1,000 percent easier than when we'd been flying commercial. Then again, traveling in such an overt airborne rock 'n' roll symbol did have the occasional downside, like the time we returned to the United States from Canada and watched as customs officials tore the entire aircraft apart searching for contraband. It probably shouldn't have been too surprising considering that the guy who ran the charter company made a habit of offering people in-flight "peanuts" that, unbeknownst to Jimmy or me, were really coke-filled capsules.

Luckily for us, we were tipped off to the possibility before we left the ground in Edmonton. Our manager walked around the cabin with an empty bag into which he demanded that everybody on board dump whatever they didn't plan on ingesting before we touched down in the States. This included a bunch of pot and a lot of cocaine and a heroin baggie belonging to a member of our entourage, who literally cried at having to ditch it. Before we took off, the pilot tossed the entire mess through his little cockpit window at the far end of the runway. Boy, was Messina pissed when he saw how much we'd collected.

Jimmy set an unmistakable tone for the rest of the band when it came to drugs, especially considering how much pot the rest of the guys managed to smoke behind our backs. I never knew this at the time because Jimmy and I were somewhat removed from the group, but our band smoked a *lot*. I found out years later that they'd gather in the wings during my acoustic opening numbers before a show, and as soon as Jimmy walked onstage to join me they'd inhale the fattest joints they could, as quickly as possible. When we traveled it was often me, Jimmy, and the road managers in one car, and the band in another, and it doesn't take much insight to guess which vehicle became a hotbox as soon as we hit the road.

When it came to drugs, Jimmy was like a stern parent who our musicians wanted to avoid. (I think I was more like a substitute teacher, mostly oblivious to their mischief.) I'd stopped smoking pot in earnest by the time L&M began, but I wasn't about to dictate drug policy for anyone else. Still, on the occasions that I rode in the band's car, I never found anything amiss. They must have been worried about my presence, too, because they were always on their best behavior when I was around.

When we were recording our second album at CBS Studio A in Los Angeles, our percussionist for hire, Milt Holland, ended up smoking hash with the band. Messina came over, miffed at the idea of getting stoned while recording. "What are you guys doing over here?" he said accusatorily. Milt didn't miss a beat. "What the fuck does it look like we're doing? We're smoking hashish." I don't think anyone in the group, myself included, could have gotten away with that, but Milt could. "Oh," said Jimmy. Then he went back into the control room.

Much, much later, Merel told me there's not a single track on any of our records where the band played straight. That's how they performed best, I guess, and to judge by their output it worked out fine. Merel in particular was adept at playing altered, something he proved back on our first tour when he took a big bite of a hash ball before a gig in Central Park. He was hungry, and somebody facetiously offered him what he mistook for a pastry. He ended up playing well enough, but by the end of the set he couldn't manage to get off of his drum stool. One of our road managers, David Cieslak, had to literally drag him off the stage and then drag him back for an encore. The audience, thinking it was part of the act, roared with approval.

There was also cocaine. My own coke days came later in the 1970s, after L&M split up, but back then the band wisely hid their elicit activities from Jimmy and me. I innocently pegged one guy who seemed to randomly show up backstage in different cities as just another hanger-on, though I should have been tipped off over breakfast one day in Boston when Recor was freaking out over money. He needed a large amount of cash for travel expenses, and the bank wouldn't give it to him. The dealer (whose name I'm omitting for obvious reasons) said, "Maybe I can help," and offered to let Recor write him a check for whatever cash he had on hand.

"Thanks," Recor said, laughing, "but there's no way you have enough."

"Well, how much do you need?"

"Ten grand."

We all watched in amazement as this guy pulled a roll of bills from his pocket, peeled off $10,000, and put the rest back.

"Will this do?" he asked.

Yeah, that'll do.

My first definitive evidence of cocaine use by the band came after a show someplace in the Midwest. At about one in the morning, I went on a run to an all-night burger place, and the dealer decided to join me. The only parking space available was on the left side of a one-way street. Entirely unpracticed at parking on that side of the road, I screwed it up pretty badly trying to get my car into the spot. Nobody ever fucking parallel parked on the left back in Alhambra. I was pulling in and out, again and again, when a cop knocked on my window, having mistakenly attributed my struggles to drunkenness. I showed him my ID and explained that I was performing in town. I even sang a bit of "Your Mama Don't Dance," and clarified that my issue was not inebriation but being a rookie at parallel parking on the left side of the road. The guy gave a nod, told us to have a good night, and took off. Catastrophe averted, though I didn't understand the size of the catastrophe until I turned toward the passenger seat and saw my man, ghost white and covered in sweat.

"I almost had to break and run, man," he croaked, pulling a *huge* bag of cocaine from his jacket pocket.

"Fuck, man," I yelled, "if you'd made a run for it, you'd have gotten shot and I would have ended up in jail!" I was pissed off. I kept my distance from the guy after that.

When the band figured out I'd caught on, they worried I'd fire them— or, worse, that I'd tell Jimmy and *he'd* fire them. I was hardly anti-drug. I'd done plenty of acid in my time. By the end of our run, though, we had at least one full-blown junkie in our midst, as evidenced by his tears when he watched his stash being thrown out of the pilot's window.

Sure enough, the authorities descended when the *Starship* reached the gate in Seattle. The lot of us ended up sitting for hours on the floor of a concrete room while they took the plane apart. They even removed the heels from our shoes. Luckily, there was nothing left to find. When they asked Recor if he had anything to declare, he pulled $250,000 from his satchel. The money was aboveboard; he'd been instructed to pick up cash payments for the Canada shows to hedge against a recent spate of bounced checks. Still, it was funny to see the customs guys' jaws drop at the site of it.

IT SEEMS LIKE in all the breakups I've ever had, with either of my wives or with Messina, the precipitating factor was that I'd outgrown whatever role I was in when the relationship started. With Jimmy, I'd begun as his student. He knew the music business and I didn't. I'd never done any of the things that were necessary to succeed, and he had. So I kept quiet, watched and learned.

Now that I was ready to stretch out in new directions, our relationship had evolved into something quite different. Moreover, I could tell that Jimmy was tired. I had to write songs and record them and tour behind the records; Messina had to do all of that plus produce the records *and* handle much of the business end of things. Looking back on it, it must have been a really tough time for him. Jimmy had been enduring marital problems that would soon lead to a split from Jenny, and having his band and his marriage come apart at once must have been devastating. I think that was a big reason he didn't pursue any solo projects for a few years following our split.

By 1976, we both needed a break.

The label released our final record, a greatest-hits retrospective called *Best of Friends*, in 1976. The title was Jimmy's idea. He thought it was an important image to present to the public. At one point it might even have been true, but by that time we'd evolved, like so many rock groups, into a primarily work-based relationship.

The motivation became clear to me about ten years later, when Jimmy approached me about a reunion tour. I was interested in bringing along a camera crew and interviewing everybody who'd been around in the early days for a documentary. Jimmy wanted no part of that. We had an image he'd worked hard to create, and he didn't want to disrupt it with the truth. That was the major difference between us. I thought reality was much more interesting than anything we might concoct, but he never wanted to let go of his control, even all those years later. "People *want* to believe we're best friends," he told me.

Well, we *weren't* best friends. We were two very different guys in a musical partnership who got along okay. We never even hung out together anymore. At the point of that proposed reunion tour I was at the peak of my solo career, and I'd have had to take a pay cut to do it. Without a documentary angle, I didn't have much interest. The Kenny-Jimmy dynamic had worked well when he called the shots and I agreed with whatever he said, but we were no longer those people. When I turned him down, he said to me, "Man, with all this therapy you do, you'd think that you could go on the road with me for a couple of months."

"Or," I replied, "maybe the therapy is to keep me from doing that."

That was basically it for us over the next twenty years. I'd occasionally invite Jimmy onstage to sing a couple of acoustic songs with me when I played in Santa Barbara or LA, but we really didn't see much of each other.

The public hears this excuse all the time, but it really was our creative differences that pushed me out of the cash machine of L&M. Sure, we had our rough moments and passionate disagreements, especially over the last couple of years, but even when I resented what I felt was a repressive regime, I never hated Jimmy. I was an aspiring soloist when we'd met back in 1970, and was still waiting patiently for that to happen. Loggins & Messina was born out of a compromise with Columbia Records, and I was naïve enough to believe I could hit it just as big when I went out on my own. Thank God no one hipped me to the reality that very few artists emerge from successful duos to ever reach similar heights. All I knew was that my music was calling, and I had to answer it.

CHAPTER 7

GOING SOLO

LEAVING THE MOST successful collaboration of my career—the *only* successful collaboration of my career—was a difficult choice, no matter how clearly it needed to be made. Jimmy handled our business decisions and our touring decisions and our set list decisions and our recording decisions and decisions I don't even remember. His guidance had been instrumental to the success of Loggins & Messina, especially early on, and there were no assurances I would be able to replicate that success on my own. I was downright scared. At least I had Columbia Records in my corner. Messina and I had separate deals, so contractually speaking I was already solo; the label simply extended my contract.

That was in stark contrast to the music itself. The first time I began to conceive of material beyond what I knew with L&M, we were working on *Native Sons*. I'd recently learned some new guitar chords, major 7s and 9s, which were far moodier than the first-position folk chords I'd grown up with. I used them to arrange the old Eddie Arnold country-blues classic "You Don't Know Me," and played it for Eva in the living room at Jimmy's ranch. It felt sexy to me, like a secret love letter. I decided then and there to put the song on my first solo album, whenever that might be. I never even showed it to Jimmy.

After that taste, I couldn't get enough. Every time I heard a chord I didn't recognize at a jam session or party, I'd ask the guitarist how he played it. And with each new chord, I seemed to get a new song. I spent the last year of Loggins & Messina writing like mad for my solo career: smooth jazz- and R&B-inflected pop, a synthesis of styles my collaborators and I made up as we went along. I didn't think of it in these terms back then, but we were literally inventing a new kind of pop music, some of which would end up on my 1977 record, *Celebrate Me Home*.

For me, the last year of collecting song ideas came to fruition when I met Phil Ramone. My A&R guy with Columbia, Michael Dilbeck, set us up shortly after Phil produced Paul Simon's *Still Crazy After All These Years*. Ramone was a true pro—part producer, part engineer, with an ear attuned to exactly the kind of sound I was looking for.

Then again, that sound was still an open question. It was only when I started calling my own shots that I began to learn what I wanted from the process—and, importantly, what I did not want. For example, I did not want to rehearse the shit out of my music before going into the studio, which is the only way I'd made records up to that point. With *Celebrate Me Home*, in fact, I wanted to record on the fly. I wrote the songs in advance, of course, but left the arrangements to whatever kind of magic could be conjured in the moment. Great players can do that, and I ended up working with some of the best.

Most of the group came courtesy of Phil, who started by hooking me up with pianist-arranger Bob James (writer of the theme to the TV show *Taxi*, and founding member of the jazz combo Fourplay). I met with Bob when he traveled out west for a tennis camp in Palm Springs, and we hit it off immediately. (It was the first meeting I ever took with somebody wearing tennis whites.) Instead of going home after his camp wrapped up, Bob drove up to my place in LA for a writing session. That's where we came up with the melody to the song "Celebrate Me Home." Some of it had already been floating around in my head as a medium-tempo pop tune in 4/4 time—something that would have fit in with Boz Scaggs's *Silk Degrees* album.

Phil's studio was in New York, but our first sessions were in Southern California. I'm still not sure why—maybe it was as a courtesy to me—but he and Bob came out for a couple of weeks to hunker down at the Burbank Studios with some local musicians. Among their ranks were L&M stalwarts Jon Clarke, Vince Denham, and George Hawkins, the bassist from the bar band in Ojai, whose lyricism was central to the vibe of the rhythm section. Those guys were perfect for my jazz-meets-pop concoction.

Before too long, we shifted to New York where most of Phil's regular players lived. That's when he introduced me to a couple of legends—jazz genius Steve Gadd on drums and the amazing Eric Gale on electric guitar. Bob shared keys duties with Richard Tee. Along with George Hawkins, who made the trip east with me, those musicians comprised the core of my new sound.

Ramone was a wonderful engineer, and consistently surprised me with his musical intuition. His first comment when Bob and I played him our sketch of "Celebrate Me Home"—all melody, no lyrics—was that it should be in 6/8 time. It felt like a gospel tune, he said, and when we tried it out on Bob's piano we instantly saw that he was right. But Phil didn't stop there.

"What do you call it?" he asked.

"I don't know," I said. "For now I'm calling it 'Celebrate Me Home,' but those are just placeholder words until I come up with something that makes more sense."

Phil did not hesitate.

"It makes *tons* of sense," he replied. "That sounds like what the guys on the block would say. Keep it." He sent me upstairs to his office to finish the lyrics then and there.

The room was hardly larger than a cubicle, with only a few photos on the walls for decoration. I started to scribble furiously in my notebook. It was early December in New York, I was feeling homesick, and the first thing I wrote were the words "Home for the holidays." At that point, the rest of the song just sort of spilled out. It amazes me that, based on nothing more than that opening line, "Celebrate" has been embraced as a Christmas classic. The heart of the song is true, and I think people can feel that.

The importance of the song for me hit home shortly after the album came out, when I had dinner at the New York home of Don Ellis, who would soon head Columbia Records' A&R department. We were talking about my upcoming tour, and it came up that "Celebrate Me Home" wasn't on my set list. Don's wife really liked the song and asked why it had been excluded.

"It's kind of slow," I explained. "I just don't know how it's going to fit into my act."

Mrs. Ellis quickly put me in my place.

"This will be an important song for you," she said. "It needs to be in your show."

I took her advice and put it in. It's been there ever since.

I HAVE TO LAUGH when I think about how little I actually knew going into the *Celebrate Me Home* sessions. Once I found myself with top musicians, I realized I had no idea how to approach them in the studio. How much should I suggest? When should I lead? When should I hold back and let them run with my ideas? Luckily, Bob led most of the sessions, which gave me freedom to watch and learn. I saw which players were the idea guys, which ones commanded the most respect, and who clicked with whom.

Initially, I was so caught up in executing my musical vision that I didn't know when to let these world-class players loose. I was dying to express myself after L&M, and too impatient to give the guys time to invent something for me. I ended up directing the musicians in such heavy-handed ways that I repeatedly stifled their creativity by imposing my ideas before they had a chance to explore their own.

The most prominent example of this came when James Taylor arrived to play guitar on "You Don't Know Me," that Eddie Arnold track I mentioned earlier. I wanted James on that song because he was the best acoustic guitar stylist out there, and I loved his way of reinterpreting classics. I was thrilled when he accepted my invitation to come down to Phil's midtown A&R Recording studio. When James pulled out his guitar, though, I wasn't savvy enough to just let him sit with the song a while and figure out how he might approach it. Unlike the other tracks on the album, I'd already been playing "You Don't Know Me" for more than a year, and was locked into my own arrangement—which I tried to teach him, one chord at a time. James is a better guitarist than me (times, like, a thousand), but he heard the song differently than I did, and struggled to keep up with my abundant instructions. We must have hammered at that thing for three hours, both of us growing more and more frustrated. We took a short break when James got a phone call in the control room from Carly Simon, his wife at the time. He spoke to her while the rest of us sat there, pretending not to eavesdrop. "Well, dear, I'm kind of busy right now," he said into the receiver. "I'm in the studio and . . . oh. Now? Well, what do you need?" He began to write a list: *milk, diapers, eggs*. "Okay," he continued. "Well, I'm going to be another hour or so. . . . Now? Okay."

James hung up the phone. "Sorry, fellas, gotta go." Just like that he was out the door. Only then did I realize how badly I'd blown it. The session might have grown so uncomfortable that James leveraged a fortuitous phone call to push the ejector button. Heck, Carly might not have said anything beyond "Have a nice night." If that was the case, I don't even blame him. I'd brought the guy in specifically because nobody plays acoustic guitar like James Taylor, then, through some combination of ego and insecurity, proceeded to tell him how to play.

After all of that, we didn't even have enough on tape to cut something together from different takes. The next day Eric Gale played the guitar part, accompanied by Bob on a Fender Rhodes electric piano. The version you hear on *Celebrate Me Home* is the three of us live in the studio. I love that version, but I still think about the one that got away.

Somehow, many of those early sessions never ended up quite as good as I'd hoped, and it took a while before I understood that the problem was usually me. Not much later in that same studio, Richard Tee, a respected elder on the New York scene, was leading a session in which we were working with a young drummer named Steve Jordan. Steve would go on to win a Grammy and an Emmy, and was so good that in 2021 he took Charlie Watts's place in the Rolling Stones, but back then he was still green. Come to think of it, we were both green.

I was in the vocal booth to sing live with the band, a technique common in the '70s to keep the singer's voice from bleeding into the instruments' mics, which allows for retakes and overdubs later. I never liked being in those little rooms, with only a small window in the door, which may have impacted what came next. Steve was in the drum booth across the room, also with a small window in his door, so we couldn't see each other at all while tracking. I was feeling more and more claustrophobic and impatient, and Steve wasn't giving me the groove I wanted to hear, so I began suggesting drum ideas to him. Trouble was, once I started I couldn't stop. My ideas came one after another like an extended drumroll, pummeling him until he was so tangled up that he could barely play. I didn't realize it, but in trying to get things moving I'd totally gridlocked the session. Thankfully, Tee recognized what was happening and wisely called a time-out to take Steve outside for a break.

They say that when you're a beginner, whether it's playing the drums or swinging a golf club, you *must* think about the task at hand to perform well. When you're an expert, the equation flips. When you play the drums like Steve Jordan, the *less* you think, the better you do. When you can really let go and stop thinking altogether? That's when cool stuff happens. You become the music. I had my guy about as far from that place as he could get.

I found out later that Richard's time-out involved another reason Steve might not have been able to keep up: "Kid, if you ever come stoned to another one of my sessions," he said, "you'll never work with me again!" Pep talk, New York style.

The lesson I learned that day—trust the talent of your players—took me a few years to fully absorb. Tommy Dowd, who I knew best from producing Derek and the Dominoes, once kicked me out of my own session—we were recording "This Is It"—after I kept telling the celebrated Brazilian percussionist Paulinho da Costa how to do his job. "I'm producing this song," Tommy snapped, "and there can only be one producer in this room at a time." Then he invited me to go get some air while he made my record. I spent the next hour pacing the studio lobby like an expectant father. When the control room door finally opened, I went in to hear what they'd been up to, and it turned out they'd done an excellent job without me. Imagine that. The thing is, percussion is a real weakness for me. I constantly hear rhythms in my head, and the need to transmit those thoughts to my drummer can be overwhelming. I've managed to settle the urge somewhat, in part because I've gotten to work with amazing pros like Tris Imboden and Harvey Mason. These days, I'll ask guys what they think, and only if their take is way off of my own idea will I begin to tailor it.

Over the years, my need to control the recording process has been balanced by my openness toward songwriting collaboration, especially when it comes to piano players. The first song I ever wrote with a keyboardist, "Rock and Roll Mood," off of the first Loggins & Messina record, was mostly happenstance. Michael Omartian had noodled a piano riff one day after practice that caught my attention. "Play that again," I said. We ended up making a song out of it right there. The process would become much more deliberate once I went solo.

First up was Bob James. Keyboard voicings are very different from those on guitar, and when I started imagining more complex chords I had no idea how to play, I realized that I needed people who could translate them into actual music. Bob would listen to me sing something, put his fingers on the keys and say, "Oh, you mean *this*?"

The irony is that, years later, I now have a bunch of tunes I can't play because I'm not a pianist and they're not written for guitar. "Celebrate Me Home" is one of them. Friends request it all the time, and I have to politely decline. (Remind me to learn that song someday.)

Bob was a good example of Phil's uncanny ability to stock the studio with the right players. The guitar roster on that album is fantastic, with amazing musicians like Eric Gale, Robben Ford, Dean Parks, Steve Kahn, Hugh McCracken, and Lee Ritenour, but my favorite guitar story involves a guy who provided only one solo on a single track. I still believe that the way I found him was orchestrated by fate.

We were at the studio in New York, and during a break I went to the front stoop to get some air. Somebody was already there when I opened the door, kicking back and watching the girls go by on a sunny December afternoon. I sat down beside him and we started to shoot the shit. I immediately liked his vibe. Seeing as how we were on the A&R steps, I asked if he was a musician.

"Yeah," he said. "Guitar." He'd just wrapped a session inside.

"Do you play electric?" I asked.

"Yeah."

My ears perked up. "Lead?" I already knew the answer.

"Sure," he said.

"Do you have your gear with you?"

"In the car."

That was all it took. I'd only just met the cat and had never heard him play, but I had him bring his rig into the studio. That's how I ended up recruiting a young Hiram Bullock, who within a few years would become one of the country's premiere jazz guitarists.

When Hiram appeared in the studio and started setting up, Phil looked at me incredulously.

"Who the fuck is this?" he said.

I could only smile. "I don't know," I said. "I just met him on the front porch."

Well, Hiram's solo on "Lady Luck" blew us both away. He was a true monster. Ramone liked him so much that a few months later he hired him to play on Billy Joel's *The Stranger* album. The only reason Hiram didn't play more for me on that record was that we already had Eric Gale, one of the great smooth jazz guitarists of his time. Eric is the only guy I've ever worked with who would tune his guitar *during* takes, waiting for a part where he could lay back, turn off his volume, and use the break to get into perfect tune. It sounds a bit OCD, which, if that's the case, paid off for every musician he's ever played with.

Being in New York to record, living at the Warwick Hotel, was exciting, though it eventually wore me down. I was just a few minutes' walk from the studio, through a neighborhood with an interesting mix of high-end boutiques and people sleeping on the sidewalk. One of the block's homeless guys actually died in a doorway during the East Coast winter while we were there. When I walked to work that morning he'd been alive. On my way home I watched the police take his body away. Only in New York.

BY THE END of my East Coast stay I was eager to return home to Eva and our little beach bungalow. We were a great match—she the cosmopolitan from Beverly Hills, me the starry-eyed wannabe from Alhambra. She knew so much more than I did about food, travel, and the finer things, and I ate her lessons up. I loved the home we made together so much that I used it for the *Celebrate Me Home* cover shoot. (That's Eva on the inner sleeve, standing in the background on the front porch.)

Eva brought comfortableness to my newly upscale lifestyle. She wasn't Jewish, but she turned me on to bagels, cream cheese, and lox, which we'd have for breakfast with champagne each Sunday. We laughed a lot together and really enjoyed each other's company. Everybody liked Eva.

One day we were smoking a joint while we watched the sunset from our front porch, and I played her an early version of "Why Do People Lie?" I didn't have any lyrics yet, so I kind of mumbled whatever came to mind. Eva surprised me when she said, "I love it—especially the words." She was high enough to have heard her own lyric in my cryptic primal tongue. I fished a pencil and some paper out of my pocket and handed it to her. "I have an idea," I said. "I'll sing it again, and you write down whatever you hear."

That was the start of our lyrical collaboration. As a songwriter, I like having somebody to bounce ideas off of, and Eva became the next logical person for me to work with. She was smart and creative, and wasn't intimidated when it came to putting her own twist on whatever I gave her. We ended up writing fifteen songs together over my first four solo albums, me on the melodies and her helping with lyrics.

I'VE BEEN SAYING for years that I don't recall *Celebrate Me Home* getting many good reviews, which makes for some amusing stories, even if it's not entirely true. It ended up selling close to a million copies in its first year and went platinum by 1980, so people must have liked it, but a

number of critics were turned off simply because the record was so different from Loggins & Messina. I don't mind thoughtful critiques, but I
want my work to be judged on its own merits—on what it is rather than
what it isn't. The loudest voices in the room seemed to be from the latter
camp, and it felt like I wasn't being given a fair chance.

What saved me was Stevie.

I'd met Stevie Nicks and the Fleetwood Mac crew at a couple of
Southern California arena festivals in August 1975, and they opened up
some shows for L&M later in that tour. Stevie and Lindsey Buckingham
had just joined the band, which was not yet nearly as popular as it would
soon become. Stevie and I didn't get to know each other well until later,
but we were close enough for me to lean on her for a favor.

At first, the *Celebrate Me Home* tour was going to involve the kinds of
venues I hadn't played in a long time with L&M: nightclubs and smaller
theaters. Then I got lucky. We'd put Fleetwood Mac on our bill in '75, and
they were happy to return the favor for their *Rumours* tour in 1977. Our
first set with them was at the Orange Bowl in Miami, in front of about
eighty thousand people. Talk about a rush.

That tour was instrumental in launching my solo career. *Rumors* was
released about two months before *Celebrate Me Home*, and within a month
sold more than ten million copies. It was No. 1 on the *Billboard* charts for
thirty-one weeks, during which time Fleetwood Mac regularly sold out
arenas and the occasional stadium. It was a seminal time for them. (It
was also a seminal time for Jimmy Recor, given that after the tour Mick
Fleetwood ran off with and eventually married his wife, Sara. Jimmy was
devastated. One day Sara was home with Jim in Sierra Madre, and the
next she went for a ride with Mick and never came back. The whole drama
played out in Stevie's song "Sara." Ironically, a few years later Jimmy ended
up managing Mick's and Stevie's bandmate Christine McVie.)

Fleetwood Mac had their own plane. As the opening act, my band
flew commercial. I was invited to travel with Fleetwood a couple of
times, but they used an old prop plane, which, frankly, was not my cup
of tea. Also, there was only enough space for me, not my musicians, so it
wasn't an invitation I sought out. Navigating airports alongside the general public usually worked fine, provided we didn't lose track of time at
an airport restaurant, fail to hear our boarding call, and miss our flight.

Which actually happened. It was the last flight to some midwestern city, and the only way for us to make it to the gig on time was to charter a jet for $10,000. It was way more than I made as Fleetwood's opening act, but I wasn't about to blow a plum gig by going AWOL. We arrived with about an hour to spare, raced to the arena, threw on our stage clothes, and got directly to business, offering apologies even as Fleetwood Mac's road manager, J.C., actively spurned us. He was an established asshole who'd been jerking us around throughout the tour, regularly reducing our sound checks for no apparent reason beyond the need to show he was in charge. Well, this time he had abundant reason to be pissed at us—I'm sure our late arrival threw their crew into a panic—but we'd made it to the stage well before curtain call. It didn't matter; the guy cut our set in half. Never mind that the decision shorted the fans and disrupted the headliner—J.C. always had something to prove. My band took the slight as motivation, and played a blistering (but short) set that the audience went nuts over. Honestly, J.C. was the only thing on the tour that was difficult.

Establishing myself as a solo act was the primary benefit of being on the *Rumours* tour, but it wasn't the only one. Stories about Fleetwood Mac's party excesses in the 1970s are legendary, and I'm here to tell you they're not exaggerated. There was cocaine *everywhere*. It was a social thing, a status symbol to the point that people wore little coke vials on chains around their necks, and record executives showed up backstage to offer toots all around. The band rented out entire floors of hotels, allowing only the right people off of the elevator and into the party. I remember walking down a hallway and seeing somebody ferrying an industrial-sized mayonnaise jar full of cocaine from room to room. In some cities we'd go to parties at local mansions, where rich fans got to mingle with rock stars by laying out sugar bowls filled with blow. Other times the entourage invaded local nightclubs, where we were treated like royalty. That whole tour was nothing but good-looking people dressed to the nines, snorting lines like the supply had no bottom.

I can't pretend that I didn't partake. It was almost impossible not to. Exploring that lifestyle, however, did teach me some things—about cocaine. At first snort, coke facilitates heartfelt communication, which I like. The initial rush dissipates quickly, though, at which point the drug's benefits—I still don't know exactly what they are—become less important than finding your next hit. I also learned that the first hit is always the best, so you end up spending the rest of the night chasing a feeling you're not going to recapture, until by four in the morning you wish you weren't alive. Then you have to pop a Quaalude or two just to fall asleep.

By the end of the tour, I'd decided that cocaine was not my drug. Acid and pot at least spurred my creativity, but cocaine didn't even do that much. Occasionally, coke even got in the way of a good time. I had a sexual situation interrupted when the girl I was with took a hit, got paranoid, and made a quick exit. I gave up the drug one night around three in the morning when I found myself sitting on my bed, alone and grinding-my-teeth anxious, and realized that I wasn't having any fun. I've barely touched the drug since then.

The other thing that sticks with me from the *Rumours* tour is the groupies. Not my own, necessarily, but Stevie's. She and I became fast friends, and though our relationship was never sexual, I often went out with her and her Stevie-ites, as I called them—hot young women who followed her wherever she went, all wearing a version of Stevie's signature diaphanous, flowing dresses. They were like a mama duck and her sexy ducklings, floating into clubs and parties together. The Stevie-ites gave the impression of a buffet table of delicious possibilities, though they weren't as available as it seemed. They were simply Stevie's traveling companions, there for her emotional support more than anything else.

Eva and I had an understanding that I would do my own thing on the road, and as long as she never found out about it, there would be no questions asked. It was the 1970s, and we were a with-it couple. "Just don't bring it home," she said. Unfortunately, neither of us understood that you *always* bring it home. There's no way to avoid that your heart has gone off with somebody else, if only for a night. We were too young to realize that a secret life is bound to make your real life suffer. Your partner can feel it when you lie about something, or even just hide it. It didn't matter that those affairs held no significance for me and were not in Eva's face. They eroded our relationship in ways that we continued to feel many years later.

I didn't recognize any of that at the time. On the road, the temptations were too intense. I always felt a sense of loyalty to Eva, though, and found myself drinking way too much in order to help rationalize my decisions. I was thrilled by the hunt, getting the attention of girls who wouldn't have glanced my way before I was famous. I was trying to fill a hole where self-esteem should have been. It was all so ludicrous and lonely, and the rush didn't last. No matter how amazing the conquest, it inevitably left me feeling bad about myself. Mike Love of the Beach Boys once counseled me by saying, "If you're going to fall, fall with an angel." Let's just say that I met a few angels in my time—but they didn't break the fall.

Toay, I see Eva as courageous. Any woman in a relationship with me had to be, because in my line of work women are constantly throwing themselves at you, and subtlety is not among their fortes. It takes a lot of self-confidence to know that you matter to your partner, regardless of how many women flirt with him.

It's a shame, all of it, because I really cared about Eva, and none of those women changed that. Hell, I married her and we had three amazing kids together. Over the years I have learned that it's far more fulfilling to be with somebody you love, who can stay present-tense with you, who you can talk to about your feelings and listen to hers, than to be with a string of strangers. These days I am a firm believer in techniques that enhance communication, and even provoke it, which I wish I'd had at my disposal back then. Growing older has helped in that regard, as I not only gain the wisdom of years but no longer feel the need to experience every sexy woman I meet. We can grow out of that place if we want to. At least I did.

CHAPTER 8

THIS IS IT

I WAS STANDING IN Michael McDonald's driveway, stock still and listening intently. I'd opened my car trunk to retrieve my guitar, but hadn't yet reached down to grab it. First, I had to listen to the music.

I was there for a writing session with a guy I'd never met but had long admired. Michael's front door was open on a warm winter's day, and he was inside at his grand piano, going over song fragments he wanted to show me. The tune that had me so transfixed was the melody to what would become "What a Fool Believes."

After a few moments, I grabbed my guitar and approached the house, but I didn't knock. I didn't want to interrupt that piano. Michael had worked things out only up to the bridge, and when he stopped, my mind kept going. I imagined the song's entire B section while standing on his concrete stoop. I rapped on the doorframe.

Michael got up to meet me, and I skipped right past the pleasantries. "What was that thing you were just playing?" I asked. They were the first words I'd ever said to the man.

Michael played along. "Just something I'm working on," he said, smiling. "I'm still trying to figure it out."

"Well," I said with a grin, "I think I know how the next part goes."

With that, we went to the Steinway. We still hadn't exchanged hellos. Michael replayed the part I'd just heard, including that signature piano intro, after which I hummed the melody of the song's first bridge (the words "She had a place in his life / He never made her think twice" would come later). Michael shifted back and forth from bright major chords to smoky, bluesy minors, lending depth to the composition. His left hand was nimble across the keys, always an octave or two below his right, like so much gospel music I'd heard. Listening to him was like going to church.

We spent the next twelve hours at that piano bench, batting ideas back and forth until nearly one in the morning, finishing almost the entire song while filling four cassette tapes with melodies and lyrics. I listened to our final version as I drove home that night, so excited that I barely slept. It was the best song I'd ever been a part of, and we both knew it.

I like to say that Michael and I were writing together before we ever met.

I first became aware of McDonald during the summer of 1977, when the Doobie Brothers released *Livin' on the Fault Line*. I listened the shit out of that album. I loved the group's new singer, who seemed to offer something unique in pop music, helping the Doobies evolve from guitar-centric rock to a smoother brand of blue-eyed soul. I was just beginning to recognize the benefits of collaborating with keyboardists, and *Fault Line* made me want to write with Michael. I knew Doobies bassist Tiran Porter from my days at Wingate, and he passed along the message that I was eager to meet. When word came back that Michael had actually been looking for *me* for precisely the same reason, I knew something good was about to happen.

I was incredibly fortunate that Michael had the best idea of his life just hovering over his keyboard, waiting for me to show up. That he hadn't already written "What a Fool Believes" by himself, or with anyone else, is nothing short of grace. Then again, everything we've written together since then has a certified Loggins-McDonald stamp on it. We really clicked together.

Michael and I each recorded our own versions, which we respectively released on our upcoming records—him with the Doobies and me on my second solo album, *Nightwatch*. That's when I learned that when you write with Michael, Michael *has* to play on the record. The keyboardist in my band, Brian Mann, was really good—he ended up on a bunch of my albums, and also on one of Michael's—but channeling McDonald just can't be done. Brian tried to mimic Michael's demo but couldn't come close. It wasn't his fault; I don't think many pianists, apart from Michael himself, could have done any better.

Michael plays in a style I've rarely seen, hands set apart like a stride-style ragtime player. His left hand focuses almost entirely on the bassline, while his right creates a counterpoint melody that supports the vocal.

A quick aside about playing with Michael. I started the song "Heart to Heart," from my *High Adventure* album in 1982, with pianist David Foster in New York. I already had some lyrics and much of the chorus melody, which is what Foz and I worked on. Once we locked things in, I realized the song needed some McDonald, so we saved the verses for him. I showed Mike what I'd worked up with Foz, and he instantly heard what we were after. As was typical for our writing sessions, I went to Michael's house in Encino and he sat down at his Fender Rhodes. Whenever he hit something I liked, he usually wouldn't know what I was talking about if I asked him to play it again. That's the nature of Michael's genius—he gets so hypnotized by the process that he almost never remembers what he's just played. That's why I always made sure to tape every moment of our writing sessions. "Heart to Heart" is the only time I've had two alpha-wolf songwriter-keyboardists collaborate on different parts of the same song, let alone doing it in different parts of the country. When the time came to record it, I was torn about who to bring into the studio. McDonald is gospel while Foster plays thumb to thumb, with thick, clustery chords that contain multitudes of voices. In the end, I stayed true to my resolution to always use Mike on stuff that we wrote together, yet Foster's section was so distinct that there was only one solution: use them both. David set up on an acoustic piano in an iso booth, with Michael in the main recording area on his Rhodes. The chemistry between those two guys makes the song one of my all-time favorites.

The Doobies' version of "What a Fool Believes" became one of the only non-disco songs to hit No. 1 in 1978, and won Grammy Awards for Song of the Year and Record of the Year. Truth is, I like their version better than my own, mostly because it features Michael McDonald.

That meeting began a decades-long partnership that saw Michael and me release our own versions of nearly everything we wrote together, eight or nine songs. The success of "What a Fool Believes," though, scared us. Winning a Grammy the first time out will do that. Worries about expectations for an encore—the old sophomore jinx—prevented us from booking another writing session, or even calling each other, for months. Eventually, I ran into him at a grocery store and laid it out. "Why don't we just write a shitty song together?" I said. "Let's get that out of the way so we can see what else is hiding in there."

Well, that didn't happen. The next song Michael and I wrote together was "This Is It," and it won another Grammy. The chemistry we had was now undeniable. It's *still* undeniable. Whenever Michael and I write together, we come up with something that's not like either of us, but exactly like both of us. It's difficult to explain, but there's a real synergy there, and we both recognize it.

"This Is It" started out differently than it eventually became. We hit on a couple of lines right off the top—"There have been times in my life / I've been wondering why" and "You think that maybe it's over / Only if you want it to be." Those were all the lyrics we had for a while, and as we sat with them, the phrase "maybe it's over" spoke to us as a relationship marker. We tried to write love-song lyrics, which felt forced. Nothing we came up with seemed right.

At that same time, my dad went into the hospital for major surgery. He'd been struggling with arterial blockage for years, and was sched-uled for a surgical procedure to increase blood flow to his heart. The guy was sixty-seven and at the wrong end of a series of strokes. He'd had too many punishing operations to fix the resulting complications, and for a guy prone to depression, this new development all but sank him. When I visited him the day before the surgery, he told me he was emotionally prepared to die on the operating table.

I wasn't fucking ready to hear that.

I suspect my dad was putting on a brave face for me, trying to make me feel like he was okay with dying, but I didn't understand that then. I grew angry.

"You have some say in this, ya know," I insisted. The intensity of my voice surprised me. "You have a choice about how this will to go. It doesn't have to be the end, unless you want it to be." I felt his despair, his fatigue over his fading health, yet I couldn't help but think that he hadn't fully committed to trying to live. Maybe it was selfish, but I was pissed at him for quitting.

The surgery was going to take several hours, so I intentionally scheduled a session with Michael during that time to help distract me. As I drove the twenty minutes to his house, I kept thinking about my dad and his chances. Was I right? Could he decide to live? If he did, would that influence the outcome? It had to, right? How could it not?

When I arrived, Michael and I went right to work on our song. The first time I sang through what we'd already written, the line "You think that maybe it's over / Only if you want it to be" was almost *exactly* what I'd said to my dad. I stopped playing.

"I know what the song is about," I told Michael. "It's not a love song. It's a *life* song."

I shared what had happened back at the hospital, and we started to write down lines reflecting that concept. Once we had a bead on the concept, lyrics started to fly. I sang whatever came to me as we ran through the melody, and when we reached the chorus I blurted out one simple line: "This is it." I hadn't used those words before, and was as surprised by them as Michael. He stopped playing. We stared at each other.

"'*This is it*'?" he said. "That's it?"

"Yep," I responded. "That says it all. What else could it be?"

To Michael, the phrase didn't offer the kind of tangible idea that choruses usually contain. I understood where he was coming from—it seemed almost too simple, too on the money. I was adamant, though. The line was perfect.

Mike quickly assented, and that was that. I always say that a song knows what it's about before I do, and that was certainly true in this case. This song was very much in charge, even rejecting our early attempts to turn it into a boy-girl relationship thing. Yes, it's still a love song, but it's so much more.

My dad's surgery took him past visiting hours, so I went to see him the next morning. He looked okay, and I played him the recording I'd made with Michael a day earlier. I was a little sensitive that he might take lines like "For once in your life, stand up and fight" as an indictment, but he didn't. Actually, he and I had a good cry over it.

Shortly after "This Is It" was released as a single, I got a letter from a teenage girl who had just emerged from her own life-or-death struggle with cancer. She explained how strongly she'd held on to that song during treatment, how it had become her anthem. That meant so much to me. The girl didn't know anything about the backstory, only that the lyrics were on the nose for her. Honestly, that letter was as impactful as the moment, a few months later, when "This Is It" won a Grammy for Best Male Pop Vocal Performance. I dedicated the award to my dad.

AROUND THE SAME TIME as my adventure in *Rumours*-land, I auditioned for *Hair*, the Milos Forman film adaptation of the Broadway musical. Weird, I know. I'd never considered acting before, but they called and I figured it couldn't hurt to check things out. They were looking for real rock 'n' roll singers to join the cast. It's been reported that Bruce Springsteen and a then-unknown Madonna were among the people they brought in to audition, but I don't think anyone's ever mentioned me.

I went to a sound stage someplace in Hollywood to meet Milos, and was led to a conference room. The director was sitting at the end of a long table, and I was asked to sit a couple of chairs down. He didn't say much directly to me, or anything at all, really. His assistant, however, kept circling the table with this quick, pitter-pat stride, and asked a series of questions, every one of them preceded by, "Milos wants to know . . ."

"Oh, Milos wants to know if you've ever acted before."

"Oh, Milos would like to know if you have any theater experience."

"Oh, Milos is interested in whether you enjoy musicals."

R. G. Loggins in Hollywood, lounging casually in white bucks like John Barrymore.

Me and Santa, circa 1954. I might have been asking for a new bow tie.

Brother Danny, the
James Dean of the family.

Senior year, San Gabriel
Mission High School, 1966.
I could barely contain
the suave.

OPPOSITE, BOTTOM: Family Christmas, 1971. From left:
Danny; his son Colin (from "Danny's Song"); me; Darla;
Mom; Dad; Danny's wife Sheila; Bob's wife Marilyn and
daughter Maria; Bob.

In the performance space of a long-forgotten SoCal guitar shop, 1968. I can place it because back then I never owned a guitar this nice.

Me and Jimmy in Murphys, California, on some downtime from our cover
shoot for *Sittin' In*.

Me and my Ovation, with L&M. Look how hard I'm concentrating to keep that thing from sliding off my lap. (Photo by Larry Hulst)

At the Crystal Palace Garden Party in London, 1972. Jimmy to my left, Al Garth to my right. (Michael Putland, Hulton Archive Collection, Getty Images)

Two Prince Charmings.

Santa Barbara County Bowl, 1975. That's Don Roberts, second-generation L&M member, behind me. I was reluctant to take off my shirt in public, so this must have been a really hot day. (Photo by Larry Hulst)

The river trip where brother Bob talked me down off a literal cliff. Pictured here are Bob (far left), Nathan East (just above Bob), Doug Ingoldsby (just next to Bob), and me and Jeff Bouchard to my immediate left. To everybody else in the boat: Sorry for keeping you anonymous.

Early-1980s photo session. Looks like I was ready to step onto the yacht.

A photo shoot at the Top Gun school in San Diego. It was kind of a theme for me that year.

In a studio somewhere, trying to become the next Nathan East. (Lester Cohen, Archive Photos Collection, Getty Images)

On the tour bus between someplace and someplace else.

Me and my mother. Yeah, my mama did dance.

Me and Graham Nash. We're teaching our children well.

My fortieth birthday. From left: my manager Larry Larson; David Foster with Eva in his lap; John Travolta. Not sure who the baby is.

Me, Julia, and baby Luke on his first day outside. He was born on the same day I won an Emmy for *This Island Earth*. We're taking them both for their first walk on the beach. (Photo by Carl Studna)

Me and my oldest three in Hawaii: Bella, Cody, and Crosby.

Me doing my best John the Baptist, a
look appropriate for much of the Julia era.
(Photo by Carl Studna)

Alaska, 2015. I was chosen to release
a rehabilitated bald eagle back into
the wild. It flew about a mile out over
the river, and then returned to swoop
low over our heads, as if to say thank
you. I chose to make that symbolic of
recovery from my recent divorce.

Family photo in Santa Barbara, Christmas, 2018. Top row, from left: Luke, Cody, me, Jordan (Bella's wife), Hana. Front row: Bella, Brooke (Crosby's wife), Crosby, and their daughter, Phifer.

My current band, 2020. Left to right: Scott Bernard on guitar, Dave Salinas on percussion, and Rick Cowling on bass. Not pictured: Carl Herrgesell on keyboard.

I hadn't done much acting, and never onstage. I enjoyed the small number of Broadway shows I'd attended, but was far from a theater aficionado.

After about thirty minutes of back-and-forth, Milos held up his hand.

"Can you dance?" he asked in his marvelous Czech accent. It was the first thing he'd said since I walked into the room.

"Not much," I told him. By that point I was eager to get the hell out of there.

"No matter," he said. And that was that. The guy stood up and gave me a wordless nod, and his assistant escorted me to the door.

I didn't get the gig, though by that point I no longer wanted it. Apparently, neither did Springsteen or Madonna. I thought the whole thing was cartoonish, Hollywood, and not at all me. It would have been an interesting challenge if they'd cast me, but I'm glad they didn't. Who knows where that kind of side trip would have taken me? Anyway, I already had my hands pretty damn full.

IT COULDA BEEN Melissa Manchester. Even all these years later I think about that.

Melissa and I wrote "Whenever I Call You Friend" together, and there was a reasonable expectation that she would sing it with me on the record. But as a wise man once said, when you get an offer from the most popular female singer on the planet to join you in the studio, you don't turn it down.

So Melissa was out and Stevie Nicks was in. Sorry, Melissa.

I came up with the song's beginnings in my dressing room before a show on the *Celebrate Me Home* tour, humming a capella into a tape recorder during vocal warm-ups. At that point, I didn't even know the chords to the song, let alone the lyrics or the chorus, but I was positive that I wanted to finish it with Michael McDonald. I could *hear* his voice on that thing. Problem was, when I sang it for him—just the melody, nothing else—he shook his head. "Sorry, man—I don't hear it," he said. "I don't think this one's for me."

I couldn't believe it. I was *positive* it was a hit idea, and rejection from a guy whose musical abilities I completely respected knocked me so thoroughly off center that I began to question my song sense. Could I have been that far off?

That lasted until I met up with Melissa a couple of weeks later. We'd been bumping into each other at various awards shows for years, and had finally arranged a meeting to see what we might collaborate on. I went to her house in the Valley and showed her a half dozen ideas I thought might be good to try out. She liked a few of them, and—lucky for me—wanted more. She asked if I had anything else. Based on McDonald's response, I was still so uncertain about "Whenever I Call You Friend" that I'd planned to keep to myself.

"Well, I do have a verse idea I've been cooking for about a month, but I'm not settled on it," I hedged. Then I hummed my small segment of the song.

"That's fantastic!" Melissa said as she ran to her piano bench. "What are the chords?"

I laughed. "I don't know, but there are a lot of them," I said. "It's definitely a piano song."

Melissa didn't miss a beat. She started filling in the gaps with her own musical sensibilities, and just like that the song started to take shape. As it did, I grew more and more reassured that it was a strong tune. I explained my lyric idea about how we rarely encounter the kinds of friends who last a lifetime. I was thinking in particular about Eva's relationship with her best friend from childhood, the kind of person you grow up with and never let go of.

We stayed up half the night until we had written enough to continue working on our own.

I took the cassette recording I'd made and headed home. I was pretty excited—and then it hit me. After I'd toured with Fleetwood Mac, Stevie Nicks offered to sing a duet with me, but I didn't have the right kind of song to take her up on the proposition—until now. Up to that moment I hadn't even thought of the song as a duet, but the lyrics naturally composed a dialogue between friends.

The next day I called to see if Stevie was still open to the idea, and we locked down a recording date. This was fucking awesome—and then it hit me again, in the opposite direction. In my excitement, I'd neglected to run Stevie by Melissa. Oops. Melissa was a fine singer herself, and even if we hadn't discussed her participation in recording the song, there was likely some level of expectation around it. There's no question that she would have done a fine job, but as a business decision Stevie was the right call.

Speaking of which, now I had to make another call: how to break the news to Melissa? I sat on the idea, trying to delay the inevitable. How difficult would that conversation be? Would Melissa try to put the kibosh on it? Would it fracture our relationship and maybe even scuttle the song?

So I decided on a different tack. I'd record it with Stevie first, and if it worked as well as I expected it to, it would be undeniable. Melissa would *have* to agree. Luckily, Melissa didn't hold it against me. As it turned out, recording with Stevie made sense to her, too, which I learned from an interview she did after the song hit No. 5 on the *Billboard* singles chart. I just wish I'd talked to her about this possibility when we'd first written the song.

There was another important lesson in that for me. From the time I conceived of "Whenever I Call You Friend," I knew it was strong, yet Michael's rejection had me questioning my own instincts. Melissa's affirmation showed me that it doesn't matter who does or doesn't like a song I'm writing; if I think something's there, I have to trust my instincts and pursue it. Period.

Stevie Nicks could sing damn near anything, though if I'm being completely honest I don't think "Whenever I Call You Friend" was exactly right for her. When she made her offer to work with me, I didn't fully understand how bluesy she was. It would have been smarter to write something for her, or better yet *with* her, but I knew "Whenever I Call You Friend" was terrific, so we made it work, recording in New York City during a break in Stevie's tour schedule. I was afraid it might be my only shot with her, so I pushed pretty hard. We were up half the night getting every nuance just so. To this day, Stevie jokes that I was a slave driver, though to her credit she was a total pro who also didn't want to give up until it was perfect. The process was difficult and exhilarating; we probably laughed as much as we sang that night.

I always say that I have Stevie and that song to thank for breaking me through as a solo artist. So many musicians emerge from duos or bands and immediately fall off the map; Stevie's generosity spared me from that. She even performed it live with me a couple of times, the most memorable show being my next hometown gig at the Santa Barbara Bowl, in front of family and friends. In the middle of the song, she stepped behind me and wrapped her scarf around my neck, which I hadn't realized when I took a step forward to sing and ended up with her scarf in my mouth, Stevie still holding either end like reins on a horse. There's a photo of that out there that still makes me laugh.

Passing on hits can happen to anyone, of course. A couple of years later, I was in the studio for my *High Adventure* album when Burt Bacharach and Carole Bayer Sager came in to show me a rough demo of "That's What Friends Are For." Burt said he'd written it specifically for me, and wanted me to use it on my upcoming album. I was gravitating toward more up-tempo rock material at the time, and just didn't hear it. The song, of course, went on to be the best-selling single of 1986 and won two Grammy Awards, including Song of the Year. I ran into Burt at the Grammys that year, and he smiled a little Cheshire Cat smile. "Remember that one?" he said. "You passed on it." I believe they were serving crow on the menu that night.

The idea of collaboration first came to me in high school, when I read a book about George S. Kaufman, the playwright credited with creating much of the Marx Brothers' act. He collaborated on a ton of Broadway plays, a detail that stuck with me for a long time. One had to have a certain kind of flexible personality to work like that. Getting along with idiosyncratic artists requires a relaxing of the ego. The finished piece has to be the reason for the exercise, not pride or money or anything but the vision of what might be. That truly started to make sense when I began writing in earnest with keyboardists who each brought something unique to my songs. When Bob James and I wrote "Celebrate Me Home," there was a lot of "Oh, not that one, try this one" and "Put that note in there." I'd stand over his shoulder while he sat at the piano, going so far as to peck at keys myself every now and again, saying things like, "I'm hearing these two notes in the next chord." Bob would then build what I was after. The part of the song where we leave the second verse and go into some strange bridge melody—"Come on mama / Come on daddy / Please . . . What you want from me?"—was just me following the free-form, stream-of-consciousness melody progression we'd been developing. Nothing in my musical history taught me to do that. Then again, many writers I've known remember every bit of music they've ever heard, and most of them draw from it all. It's in there, trying to sing to you if you'll let it.

I MET MICHAEL JACKSON at a listening party in Hollywood for *Off the Wall*, his first solo album for Epic Records. A lot of the guys he used on that record—David Foster, Greg Phillinganes, Paulinho da Costa—had also played with me. The party was nothing fancy, just a hotel ballroom with a good PA system. They played his album, and then some dance music, and everybody hit the floor. Eva and Michael cut quite a figure together on that dance floor, because she was aglow and he was only about half her height. Somewhere through the night, Michael and I found ourselves sitting at the same table, and I mentioned that I'd love for him to sing on my upcoming *Keep the Fire* record. Honestly, it was such an ambitious thought that I never figured he'd actually accept, so you can imagine how surprised I was when he said he'd love to do it. Michael wasn't yet the untouchable Neverland recluse of the 1990s; his solo career was only beginning, and he was really humble and down to earth, very shy and, of course, extremely talented.

I'd already worked up most of the songs for the album, and decided to bring him in for background vocals and choruses on a track called "Who's Right, Who's Wrong" that I'd written with Richard Page, later of Mr. Mister fame.

We cut it at a studio in Hollywood, with just me, Michael, and an engineer. Michael sang the choruses beautifully but conservatively. He was giving me a straight melody, and I wanted to hear more of his personality.

"Can you make it a little more . . . soulful?" I asked. It seemed strange to ask Michael Jackson to bring the soul, but he was giving a consummate studio performance, trying not to steal the show.

Michael smiled. "Oh," he said. "You want it *stinky*."

Yeah. Stinky.

So he made it stinky, adding a bunch of licks and classic MJ flourishes. He was typically great, but listening back to it now, it's clear to me that "Who's Right, Who's Wrong" wasn't the right song for him. It's jazzy, not funky, and Michael kind of got buried in the back. It's a good song, which is why I chose it, but instead of trying to squeeze Michael into it,

I should have tried to fit the song to him. I didn't know he was writing his own stuff, and, just like with Stevie Nicks on "Whenever I Call You Friend," I wish I'd written something with him instead—preferably something danceable.

Michael and I maintained a friendly relationship over the years. He was one of the most sensitive artists I've ever met, and he occasionally turned to me for business advice. He was the one who brought me into the "We Are the World" sessions (more on that in a bit), and he also called when he was looking for a personal manager for the Jackson 5 reunion. I turned him on to my guy, Larry Larson, who told me later that when he worked with Michael and his brothers, the financial numbers were so enormous that he'd frame all his concepts in terms of how many Rolls-Royces something was worth. Let's just say there were a lot of Rolls-Royces to go around for that family back then.

I MET MY BEST FRIEND, Jeff Bouchard, during my Loggins & Messina days. He walked up to me at a hotel in some forgotten city and said, "Hey, I just want to thank you because I love your music. I was going to see the show tonight but you're sold out, so I'll be sure to catch you next time through."

It was such a nice sentiment that I offered to get him into the arena, which I'm sure was his plan all along. Then I gave him a bit more.

"How well do you know this town?" I asked.

"I'm not from here, but I'm pretty familiar," he replied.

"Wanna hang later?" I asked. "Meet me after the show and let's have some fun."

That night I recruited Jeff as my tour guide—for the rest of our lives. He quickly became one of the primary people who got me into trouble, because he knew how to have a good time wherever we were. He was an amateur guitar player and singer, and we ended up hanging around together a lot, to the point that I let him sit in and sing background vocals at a few shows once I went solo. I was just giving my friend a thrill to be a pop star for a day and he loved it, even though his vocals weren't, let's say . . . perfect. His pitch was less than ideal, and the band wasn't thrilled. "You know, we rehearse for these shows," one of my guys told me one day, "and Jeff's pretty far out of tune." It didn't really matter—the sound crew ended up just turning down his mic in the mix. Still, I enjoyed the kick Jeff got from that kind of stuff. He'd smile onstage like a puppy in a convertible.

Jeff lived in Michigan, and when he came to town things usually turned into a party. One night during a trip to Santa Barbara, we were on the wrong end of too many lines of coke, and ended up back at my place in no shape to even consider sleeping. Just for the fun of it, I showed him a melody I was working on. My intention was to turn him on to what it's like to write a song, and before I knew it we were swapping lyric ideas. That's how it works with me; if you hang around long enough, we might just collaborate on something. In those days, it was kind of like friends working together on a crossword puzzle. The song in question is "Now and Then," from *Keep the Fire*. It's about my old friend and road manager Jimmy Recor, and Mick Fleetwood running off with his wife. I would introduce the song in concert by saying, "This is a ballad that I wrote for a friend. After his wife left him, I noticed that he kept talking about her in the present tense, as if she was still there—things like, 'She enjoys going for walks on the beach' and 'She likes scary movies.' I told him, 'Dude, the girl is gone. It's been a year. Let her go.' So I wrote this song for him. It's called 'Wake the Fuck Up.'"

Man, would the audience howl at that. When Kenny Loggins swears, everybody laughs. What the fuck, maybe I really *am* too nice.

I told that story every time we played "Now and Then" on the *Keep the Fire* tour, including an outdoor gig at the Boston Commons. Before the song was over, I noticed two policemen at the edge of the stage, arms folded and scowls on their faces. As I thought about it I realized, Holy shit, I just said "Wake the *fuck* up" in a conservative Catholic town. If there was a language law anywhere on my itinerary, Boston was a good bet to have it. I can't tell you how many random things can run through my mind during a performance.

It didn't help that Tim McCarthy, my road manager at the time, got my attention from the wings and pointed to the policemen with a worried look on his face. Goddamn, I must have been on to something with my suspicions. I didn't want to give them a chance to grab me in the middle of my set, so I spent the rest of the show avoiding stage left, where the cops were standing. I didn't even go backstage for my encore—I just ducked behind some amps for a couple of minutes until it was time to go back onstage.

When things finally wrapped I headed straight to Tim, and we immediately began to formulate an escape plan—until he burst into laughter. Like, huge belly laughs. Then I looked up and saw the cops. They were laughing, too. They'd been there because Tim had put them up to it, with instructions to look scary. There was no language law. They totally punked me, as well as the poor folks sitting stage left, who I never went close to all night long.

That was just one instance of many years' worth of pranks that went down on my stage. Sometimes I was in on them. Usually I wasn't.

I had something of a pranking history with my crews, dating back to the L&M days. At the end of a long tour, the final show was a designated free-for-all, where the crew could unleash their twisted brand of humor on whichever unfortunate band member they chose to target. This was hardly unique to me; lots of acts employ this venerable tradition.

One year, three or four crew guys came out naked and did a Radio City two-step across the stage while holding strategically placed pieces of cardboard. That sure caught the audience, and me, by surprise. Another time, they broke down the drum kit one piece at a time and removed it from the stage—while we were still playing. It was the last song of our set, and my drummer, Tris Imboden, valiantly did what he could to maintain the beat. Speaking of Tris, one year our stage set involved a clear Plexiglas floor for his riser that allowed us to light him from below. For the last show of one tour, the crew somehow got a stripper in there. The audience couldn't see her, but Tris sure had a view. I still don't know how, but he didn't miss a beat. Then again, he may have been a beat off. (Cue rim shot.)

With Loggins & Messina, Jimmy had a song called "Pretty Princess," which includes the lines: "A fireplace, a telephone / No word from him, she's all alone." When we played that song on the final stop of our *Native Sons* tour, the crew lowered a classic black Bakelite phone—you know, one of those heavy, rotary dial old-timey numbers—on a wire right over Jimmy's head. The lighting guy hit it with the spot and, on cue, it rang. *Rinnnng rinnnng.* I'm still not sure how they did that. The guy on the board announced over the PA: "Jimmy it's for you." It was hilarious, but after the show Jimmy went ballistic, dressing down the crew and banning any further practical joking. Jimmy was a very serious cat. At least the rest of us thought it was funny.

It's not like Jimmy was completely devoid of humor; he just didn't like to be the butt of the joke. Once, we opened up for Rod Stewart and the Faces at a giant arena gig in Southern California that also featured Fleetwood Mac and Peter Frampton. Rod had these huge clusters of white balloons strapped down backstage, to be released at some high-energy moment during his set. We'd just finished our own set, and before we retook the stage for our encore, Jimmy grabbed a crew kid and said, "I'll give you fifty bucks to let those balloons go right now."

The kid did it. We came onstage to thunderous applause and a zillion balloons. I heard that Rod put his fist through his trailer wall when he heard about it. I guess he really wanted those balloons.

THE RECORD ON WHICH "Whenever I Call You Friend" appeared, *Nightwatch*, saw me branching out even further from the leaps I'd taken with *Celebrate Me Home*. As a producer, Phil Ramone was a wizard, but during that stage of his life he was also deeply into cocaine, which made him erratic and nervous. He was having troubles at home (he'd get divorced shortly thereafter), and was really down about it. When he would slate recording pre-track tags like "This is mix 13 of 'Why Do People Lie,'" he'd constantly add things like, "I don't know why they fucking lie. I fucking hate that they lie." Every slate started with an I-hate-my-life/I-hate-my-wife kind of sentiment, and, to be honest, it was a downer. I loved Phil, and was grateful for how much he brought to *Celebrate Me Home*, but I just couldn't return to the studio with that kind of attitude. So I looked elsewhere for my next producer.

Bob James had been one of my closest collaborators. He was a funny guy, easy to be with, and a brilliant musician. Once, during a session for *Celebrate Me Home*, we played the board game Connect Four while he simultaneously corrected individual string parts as they were being played by an orchestra, and he *still* beat me every time. Bob and I laughed a lot during the making of that album, so I figured he was the logical choice to produce *Nightwatch*. He jumped right into the role.

Bob was very relaxed and let me be me, which is a great approach for some artists. When he suggested I make up an intro to "Whenever I Call You Friend," I just walked up to the mic and made up that whole a capella portion on the spot.

At that point in my career I was a musical loose cannon, crossing styles effortlessly, and could have used some direction in setting my course. Bob was a genius with smooth jazz, yet for some reason we didn't marry those sensibilities with the music I was doing. The only song on the album that approaches a true synthesis of our styles is "Angelique," which shows what *Nightwatch* might have been had we pooled our talents more intentionally. If we'd taken the time to craft an album's worth of that kind of music, it could have been stunning. Instead, he more or less left me to my own devices.

One of the most frustrating parts of making that record was that Bob was a quintessential family man, and left the studio at 5 P.M. every day. It was the first time I'd worked with a producer who actually kept sane hours. I went to New York to record with him, but didn't learn about this detail until I saw it in action: No matter where we were in the recording process on a given day, Bob packed it in at 5 P.M. sharp and went home to his wife and kids. I was consistently frustrated. I'd traveled three thousand miles to record the album, and I didn't want to spend nights in my hotel room instead of the studio. It was counterproductive and ended up costing me a lot of money, because I stayed in New York far longer than I would have otherwise, paying band and hotel costs all the while.

Now that I was integrating jazz into my music—stuff that people currently refer to as yacht rock—the entire city opened up. I was working with jazzers, and Eva and I would go to nightclubs where, at midnight or 1 A.M., I'd sometimes be invited up to sing with the band. It felt like an arrival of sorts. At that point, New York became one big party, chock-full of options. I was hardly a star in the jazz world the way I was in the pop world, but that didn't matter—music was calling, and I was right there to answer it.

CHAPTER 9

AT THE MOVIES

PRODUCER TOMMY DOWD once told me that success is like being on a moving train. Folks standing along the roadside can see you through the window as you roar by, but only for a moment. I was in that window with Loggins & Messina, and then again with singles like "This Is It" and "What a Fool Believes." Then my train moved on.

Actually, it moved on for a whole lot of us trying to make a living as rock musicians in the disco era. Those dance rhythms showed up and snuffed out not only careers but entire categories of pop music. Suddenly the Bee Gees, Donna Summer, and Chic were the only acts in the top 40. Go ahead, think about all the singers and bands who topped the charts in

1975, who by 1980 were never heard from again. Having a hard time coming up with names? That's because you don't remember them.

Unlike those guys, I survived. Thanks to the movies, my train did an unexpected U-turn and gave the public another look.

I'm probably best known for a trio of soundtrack hits: "I'm Alright," "Footloose," and "Danger Zone." Far from being a master plan by some genius strategist, that portion of my career unfolded one small step at a time. Before I knew it, instead of being Kenny Loggins, Hit-Song Guy, I was Kenny Loggins, Movie Guy, and the movies helped make the hits.

For the longest time, original pop songs weren't a staple of movie soundtracks. It wasn't until the Bee Gees sold twenty-five million copies of the *Saturday Night Fever* soundtrack between 1977 and 1980, helping vault the film to box-office gold, that movie studios began to notice the amazing opportunities provided by pop music. One might say that the brothers Gibb, while helping decimate the rock and pop landscape upon which I'd built my career, also helped seed the soundtrack landscape that brought my greatest success.

Then again, I'd been writing songs for movies since the 1970s, so when the moment arrived, I was ready for it.

When I was nine or ten years old, I devoured whatever soundtrack albums my brother Danny brought home. He might have been the James Dean of the family, but he also had a little George Gershwin in him. He loved movie music like "Lara's Theme" from *Dr. Zhivago*, and the scores from *A Patch of Blue*, *West Side Story*, *The Man Who Shot Liberty Valance*, and my absolute favorite, Miklos Rozsa's fabulous soundtrack for *King of Kings*. I would spread the stereo speakers as far apart as I could and pretend I was conducting the orchestra. I was especially struck by the many "themes" listed on the records. I thought that if I ever got the chance, I'd write a theme for every character.

The first movie I wrote for predated Loggins & Messina. I had just turned twenty-two and was working for Wingate when my boss introduced me to a bandleader named Don McGinness, who was putting together music for the Jackie Gleason film *How Do I Love Thee?* So one dark evening in the winter of 1970, I found myself nervously driving to Don's Hollywood home to write a movie theme. It was all so new and strange. Within a couple of hours we'd formulated a melody, and I went home elated. This was easier than I'd imagined. The next day I wrote some lyrics, and voilà, we had a song named after the film: *How Do I Love Thee*. Don heard it as the kind of harmony-heavy ballad the Association might sing, so two days later, we went into a studio to demo the tune with four male singers. That became a seminal moment for me, because I had to teach each guy his vocal part, singing them line by line. When I got to the lead vocalist, he complimented my voice and asked a question that should have occurred to me earlier: "You're really good—why aren't *you* singing this?" I hadn't even considered the possibility. I was thrilled to give it a try, and it came out great, with me on lead and the other four singing harmonies. I loved it, Bob loved it, everybody loved it—except for the movie's director, who passed on it for reasons I still don't understand. I can't say that I was heart-broken when the film bombed, losing the studio millions of dollars.

That was my first realization about how much of a crapshoot writing for the movies can be. There are an awful lot of chefs in that kitchen, and it's never a sure thing when it comes to creativity by committee.

Now that I'm thinking about movie soundtracks, I realize how often I was rejected early on. I was friendly with John Travolta in the late 1970s, and in 1979 he handed me a screenplay he was considering called *American Gigolo*. "Why don't you write a song for it?" he asked. The script opened with a tender love scene in which the lead character, a male prostitute, services an older woman. I figured I'd write something to counter that vibe, and ended up with a bump-and-grind shuffle called "Love Has Come of Age."

Well, John dropped out of the production at the last minute, they replaced him with Richard Gere, and I never heard from the producers again. I held on to the tune, though. It leads off *Keep the Fire*.

IT WASN'T ALL FAILURE, of course. I had a song in *A Star Is Born*—not the Oscar-winning film with Bradley Cooper and Lady Gaga, but Barbra Streisand's 1976 version. I was on the road with Loggins & Messina when I received word that Barbra was collecting music for a movie she was starring in alongside Kris Kristofferson. She was playing a singer, of course, and would handle the vocals herself. She wanted me to meet her at her house in Malibu to discuss it. By that point, I was already writing tunes for *Celebrate Me Home*, and my creative mind was going a million miles per minute. It seemed like an amazing opportunity.

Barbra had a comfortable way about her. She and her boyfriend, Jon Peters, took a liking to me right away. Conversation was easy, and before long we were singing ideas back and forth like old friends. Harmonizing with Barbra's amazing voice was an incredible rush. I showed her some of my ideas for *Celebrate Me Home*, and she showed me some other songs she was considering for the film, including something she'd co-written, "Evergreen," which would win her an Academy Award. Our lunch meeting extended through dinner, and then into a return call the next day.

There's an urban legend that I was up for Kristofferson's part, but the only thing that even came close was when Barbra asked whether I might be interested in appearing onscreen. She didn't offer anything specific, and I doubt she had a prominent role in mind. It didn't matter anyway because I turned her down. I'm just not comfortable on camera without a guitar in my hand or a band behind me. Acting was never my dream, and I didn't feel compelled to do it.

After our meetings, it was apparent that Barbra liked my idea for "I Believe in Love." I'd played her most of the melody, though the only lyric I had was the title phrase, "I believe in love," which I sang over and over again. I was a bit stumped on where to take it next, though, which is when I began to consider collaborating with a lyricist. I hit on Alan and Marilyn Bergman, who had written the lyrics to Barbra's signature hit, "The Way We Were," and were dialed in to her sensibilities. I'd never worked with them, but they had a great reputation and Barbra trusted them. She put us in touch.

I went to see the couple at their home in Beverly Hills, and left a cassette demo of my melody. I didn't hear what they came up with until I met them at Barbra's place a few days later, and Alan sang it for us. When Barbra said she loved it, I breathed a huge sigh of relief. She even invited me to her recording session, which surprised me since she's known for not wanting too many opinions in the studio. Still, I gave her one, suggesting that Jimmy Pankow and the horn section from the band Chicago might punch up the sound. She ended up bringing them in later for overdubs.

Barbra used the song in one of the movie's concert scenes, and while I liked the arrangement, I think they played it too fast. So I brought the tempo into a pocket I liked better, and recorded my own version for *Celebrate Me Home*.

"I Believe in Love" is a good song, and Barbara's version of *A Star Is Born* did well at the box office, but it didn't do much to move the needle on my soundtrack career, save for one thing: Jon Peters was more than Barbra Streisand's boyfriend. His experience with *Star* whetted his appetite for movie production, and before long he started his own company, a detail that would become vital to my future.

It started when Jon invited me to his office in Thousand Oaks for a private screening of his new movie, in hopes that I'd write a song for it. That movie was *Caddyshack*. It didn't yet have an ending or the gopher, but it was laugh-out-loud funny.

"You're gonna love what we do with this," Jon told me. "We have this puppet that comes up out of a golf hole and dances."

Now *that's* a stupid idea, I thought. Thankfully, I kept that opinion to myself. Shows what I know—people still love that fuckin' gopher. I know that I do.

I wanted to write every song I could for the movie. I even suggested taking over the entire soundtrack, but Jon wanted to feature a variety of artists. I did, however, get the lion's share of songs: an up-tempo interlude I called "Make the Move," plus "Mr. Night" and "Lead the Way." The latter was a melody I'd sung to Barbra for *A Star Is Born*, which I'd since rebuilt and jokingly called "Love Theme from Caddyshack."

My best-known song from that movie, of course, is "I'm Alright." It was inspired by the movie's opening scene, in which the main character, a teenage golf caddy named Danny, rides his bike through some featureless suburbs. The rough cut I saw featured a Bob Dylan song, "Gotta Serve Somebody," as the temporary backing track. That struck me as incongruous, and I couldn't help but wonder why they'd chosen it. Was director Harold Ramis trying to tell me something about this character? Dylan is the quintessential rebel, yet Danny was just a kid on a bike. He spends most of the movie trying to fit in with the country club scene, but by the end decides to thumb his nose at the whole idea and chooses another path for himself. That was when the light went on for me: Danny *was* a rebel. Ramis had clearly selected the Dylan song intentionally, foreshadowing the character's evolution, and I decided my song should have similar fuck-off undertones. What I came up with was a chorus that insisted, "Don't nobody worry about me." Instead of addressing the movie directly, I let the song's general message of rebellion do the heavy lifting.

I recorded a demo for Jon in a local Santa Barbara studio. We were on a schedule, so rather than take time to gather musicians I knew, I went with a local drummer and engineer, neither of whom I'd met. That was a lucky decision. The drummer was a basic rock guy, not nearly as skilled as the players in my New York sessions, but this inadvertently freed me up. He couldn't handle anything complex, so instead of spending time nailing down the difficult patterns I had in mind, I went with a simple foot-snare-foot-snare pattern I knew he could play. It was all downbeats—nothing cute or tricky, just gut-level rock that, against my better judgment, turned out to be the perfect groove for the song. More lastingly, the session's engineer was a guy named Terry Nelson, who impressed me so much that I made him my primary engineer for the next seven or eight years. He even produced *Leap of Faith* and my live album, *Outside: From the Redwoods*.

At the same time as I was writing "I'm Alright," Gerry Rafferty's band, Stealers Wheel, had a song on the radio called "Stuck in the Middle," which I always heard as Gerry doing a Bob Dylan impression. Well, if Rafferty could do Dylan, so could I. The director wanted a Dylan song, so I ended up giving him me doing Rafferty doing Dylan. When I got the demo home from the studio, I played it over and over. I couldn't stop smiling. I'd nailed it.

I recorded the final version with a bunch of my regular players, and one guy extra, which led to a decades-long beef. Eddie Money happened to be in the studio next to ours while we were recording, and I caught some snippets of his singing through an open door. Eddie had released a couple of albums by that point but hadn't yet hit it big, and that was the first time I'd heard him. He was a terrific singer, with a big, gruff voice that I thought would make a perfect contrast on "I'm Alright." I asked if he'd mind stepping into my studio, and twenty minutes later there he was singing the lines "Cannonball it right away" and "Man, you make me feel good." Unfortunately, when it came time to file the song credits I totally forgot to list him. Shit. When the error was pointed out to me, I did all I could to rectify things by acknowledging Eddie in as many interviews as I could. I even sent him a note of apology, but that wasn't enough for him. I'm still not sure what he wanted—it was never a financial thing—but he sure did disparage my name after that. I wish we'd had a chance to straighten things out between us, but I never saw him again before he passed away in 2019.

"I'm Alright" became a top-10 hit, and I was asked to perform it at that year's Grammy Awards in New York. (I ended up winning, but not for "I'm Alright," which was beaten out as Best Rock Vocal Performance by Billy Joel's *Glass Houses*. Instead, I took home Best Pop Vocal Performance for "This Is It.") The thing that sticks with me most about that ceremony isn't winning, which was nice, but the performance, which was . . . surreal.

I was about to go on vacation in Europe with Eva when the organizers called and asked if I wanted to play. They gave me the chance to bring my band along, but I was about to leave town and had no time for rehearsals. When I found out that the house band included Steve Gadd, Eric Gale, and the rest of Paul Simon's New York cats, I figured, well, that song is so simple that anybody can play it, and those guys can play circles around anybody. I'll just bring them up to speed at a pre-show rehearsal, I thought, and off to Europe we went.

I returned two days before the show, and was scheduled to go over "I'm Alright" with the band the day before the telecast. When I got to the rehearsal hall, though, the band wasn't prepared—no charts, no nothing. I don't think they'd even listened to the song. When we ran through it, they started swinging like it was some sort of jazz number. I guess that makes sense, because they're jazzers, but "I'm Alright" is one of my true rock numbers, and that's how I wanted it played. I ended up going over the song individually with each musician. I sang Eric Gale's guitar part to him, then did the same for Steve Kahn. I tried to get Gadd to play a simple rock 'n' roll beat, like on the record, but he couldn't help but swing it. That's how we spent most of our two-hour time allotment. I returned to my hotel room exhausted and shaken, terrified about going on national TV with a band that could not master my simple fucking song. Fuck! I guess it was *too* simple. I slept maybe two hours that night, tossing and turning until dawn. I did, however, hatch a plan. On the way to the theater I stopped at a liquor store and picked up a quart of tequila. If I can't make the song smarter, I figured, maybe I can make the musicians dumber. At the very least, I could get myself to the point where I didn't really give a shit. Maybe.

The Grammys were held at Radio City Music Hall, with its famous hydraulic stage. We were supposed to begin playing in the basement, then rise up to stage level mid-intro. We walked onto the set about ten minutes before we were supposed to start the song, which is when I made my move. I grabbed my bottle and took several laps around the set, singing each guy's part to him as he swigged. It was my version of a pep talk. We had to be loose, and tequila is a great lubricator. No jazz for us tonight, my friends. It's time to rock.

Well, the drunk part worked. By the time we went on, that bottle was empty and I had a hell of a buzz going.

Then, just before the stage ascended, I noticed a sound guy furiously messing with the microphones. I swear I saw him inexplicably switch the two up-front mics, exchanging the one I'd used at sound check with one of unknown origin from the other side of the stage. My heart skipped. Uh-oh, I thought. I was about to say something when the stage began to rise and the band began to play. Thanks to the tequila, the floor was already moving for me before it actually started to move.

We reached stage level just in time for me to step into the spotlight and sing the first line—"I'm alright / Don't nobody worry 'bout me"—to myself. I didn't hear *anything* in the house. Maybe it's just the stage monitors, I thought, and the audience can hear me. I looked into the front row and saw Dionne Warwick and Burt Bacharach, and gave Dionne a questioning look to see if she could hear anything. She shook her head no. So I backed off the microphone and signaled Steve Kahn to play a guitar solo. He looked at me like I was crazy, but started into some random licks while I ran to the edge of the stage and did my best cheerleader impression, getting the crowd to clap along and kill some time while the techs figured out what the hell was wrong. After what seemed like ten minutes, I went back and tried again—and got another head shake from Dionne. So I vamped some more. By that point, the crowd knew what was happening and was fully on my side. Finally, somebody swapped out the mic altogether, and on the third try my vocal was live. I guess the tequila did the trick for Gadd, because it was full speed ahead for him on the twos and fours: straight-ahead rock 'n' roll. What we ended up with wasn't exactly

"I'm Alright," but it was a whole lot better than the swing groove from rehearsal. They cut the entire clap-along intro out of the West Coast feed, but the whole crazy performance aired live on the East Coast.

As soon as we finished playing, I walked offstage and straight back to my seat in the audience next to Eva. I was drenched in sweat and stone-cold sober—whatever alcohol I'd consumed had completely evaporated through my pores. Almost as soon as I sat down, they announced the winner for Best Pop Vocal Performance (Male). I'd been so focused on "I'm Alright" that I hadn't really considered my chances, so you can imagine my surprise when I heard my name. I had nothing prepared, so I made up a speech on the spot, dedicating the award to my dad. It all goes to show that preparation sometimes has little bearing on how well things go. Those stage techs must have worked for days setting up a system that ultimately didn't work, but speaking from the heart about my father was one of the best moments of my night.

THE SOUNDTRACK SONG everyone remembers, of course, is "Foot-loose." My "Footloose" story doesn't start with *Footloose* the movie, however, but with another iconic film from the early 1980s: *Flashdance*.

Flashdance was set up perfectly for me. It was produced by Jerry Bruck-heimer, who I knew was a fan of "I'm Alright." The film's musical director was Phil Ramone, the producer on *Celebrate Me Home*. I was one of their first calls. When Jerry brought me to his Hollywood office and showed me a rough cut on his Moviola, I got excited. Back then, anything Bruck-heimer touched was gold. I'd loved my experience with *Caddyshack*, and was eager for another shot at a soundtrack.

What I came up with was the melody for a song I called "No Dancin' Allowed." Problem was, I was about to go on tour and wouldn't have time to record it properly for a couple of months. That didn't suit Jerry's time-line, so I regretfully had to withdraw.

Then fate intervened—if one chalks up poor stage management and my own clumsiness to fate.

One of the first stops on my itinerary was the sports arena at Brigham Young University in Salt Lake City. The stage was about ten feet off the gym floor and, before the lights hit it, completely in the dark. I was up there just before showtime, walking around to my normal entry spot from stage left. Well, there wasn't quite as much stage left as I expected and . . . let's just say that ever since, if it's dark onstage, I don't take a single step until someone shines a flashlight onto the floor.

Yep, I fell right off the side of that goddamn stage, and landed on my back atop some gear crates, breaking three ribs. I couldn't move, and nobody heard my calls for help because the room was so loud with the crowd chanting, "Keh-NEE, Keh-NEE, Keh-NEE!" In my memory it was quite the Shakespearean moment: the star dying as the audience screams his name.

I must have been down there for five minutes before somebody found me and I was helped back to the dressing room, and then via ambulance to the hospital. My lungs were badly bruised and exquisitely painful, but luckily they hadn't been punctured by my broken ribs. Needless to say, the show was canceled. Then the entire tour was canceled.

I was hospitalized for two days until it was safe to fly home. Even then I had to borrow a plane from one of the Osmonds (Donny, I think) because I couldn't sit up in a commercial jet. Once I got back to California, I crawled into bed and stayed there for weeks. (We did a make-up performance at BYU several months later, and I had three nurses escort me onto the stage. That went over pretty damn well.)

I managed my pain with a supply of Percodan prescribed by the doctor in Salt Lake City. Wow, did those pills work—maybe a little too well. I felt fine in no time at all, even though I was actually pretty far from fine. I knew I couldn't sustain a tour in my condition, but thanks to those painkillers I figured I could at least do a little studio work. So I called up Bruckheimer's office. "Guess what?" I said. "I'm available again!"

I went to an LA studio to record "No Dancin' Allowed" on Bruckheimer's dime. Unfortunately, Percodan and I produced the thing together. I was popping it around the clock, and it affected my judgment more than I realized. Without so much as a run-through, I ended up cutting the song in the wrong key and couldn't hit the high notes. There's no explanation for it beyond my inability to think straight. I should have either gone back and rerecorded it, or brought in some famous female vocalist to handle the high stuff and turned it into a duet. But I didn't do those things, or anything else. Once I saw how unsuited I was for the instrumentation we'd put down, I didn't end up recording a vocal track at all. Redoing the whole thing from scratch was too daunting; my injury had caught up with me and I was exhausted, so I just gave up. I still think of *Flashdance* as the one that got away.

That soundtrack ended up producing two No. 1 singles, and was the album that finally knocked Michael Jackson's *Thriller* from the top of the charts. And to think that for want of a sober co-producer I could have been part of it. Not that I'm complaining.

Lucky for me, *Caddyshack* was opening all kinds of doors, and it wasn't long before another soundtrack proposal landed on my desk. Dean Pitchford was a Broadway veteran who had won an Oscar for the theme song to *Fame*. He wanted to break into screenwriting, and was working on a script about a rural town that banned dancing. He called it *Cheek to Cheek*, a placeholder title designed to be so intentionally awful that nobody would fall in love with it and decide to make it permanent. Dean said that he, in addition to writing the script, wanted to direct the project's music, and asked me to help him with the score. He called my sound "uniquely American," and praised my material's relentlessly upbeat nature. He said he pictured me as the musical equivalent of the lead role.

That all sounded pretty good, but before I committed to a multi-song project, I figured it'd be best to give us both a little test to see how well we worked together. I gave Dean a cassette of a melody I'd been working on with Steve Perry to see what he could do with it. The words were just la-la-las, except for the chorus: "Don't fight it." Nothing in the verse set that up, and nothing else in the chorus completed the thought. I left all of that up to Dean. I figured that if I liked what he came up with, I'd be much more inclined to sign on to his movie project.

Well, I liked it so much that I ended up recording the song with Steve and used it as the lead track on my *High Adventure* album. "Don't Fight It" ended up nominated for a Grammy, which helped cement Dean's standing with the folks at Paramount when it came to entrusting him with their soundtrack.

By that point, Dean had written enough to show me what he was doing—the name *Cheek to Cheek* had by then been changed to

Footloose—and I grew enthusiastic. I was about to leave on tour, and told him that if he came to meet me on the road, we could make significant progress before I returned home.

That's when I cracked my ribs.

This threw off Dean's schedule. First, I was laid up and in no shape to work. Once I found my bearings, I dedicated myself to finishing "No Dancin' Allowed" for *Flashdance*. Dean and I had made some progress— we'd been trading ideas over the phone and via cassettes I kept sending him—but we wanted something in the can by the time I left for a winter tour of Asia. He said if he didn't come back with at least 80 percent of the title track for the execs at Paramount, they might make him look for somebody else to work with. By that point, we were limited to only a few days during a weekend engagement I had in South Lake Tahoe—some warm-up shows before I departed the continent. If we didn't get something done there, the work would have to wait for a couple of months, and I might be off the project entirely. So Dean booked a room in the hotel where I was playing, and we scheduled as much time together as we could.

Trouble was, Dean was already pulling twenty-hour days writing the screenplay and lining up musicians for the soundtrack, and the wear was beginning to show. He started to get sick before he left Los Angeles, and by the time he hit the snowy Sierras he found himself with a serious case of strep throat.

Dean knew the last thing I wanted on the eve of an international tour was to be exposed to a respiratory ailment, so he hid it from me, gobbling whatever medicine helped him appear healthy during our writing sessions. He must have used Chloraseptic spray by the gallon. I didn't learn that part until later, of course.

Somehow he pulled it off. For three consecutive days we spent hours together in his room, fully developing the song "Footloose." I was inspired by Mitch Ryder's "Devil with a Blue Dress," which had exactly the kind of groove I was looking for, and opening bars that are about as classic as rock 'n' roll gets. Dean helped integrate the script into our lyrics. I never would have thought of a line like "Kick off your Sunday shoes," but Dean knew that Ariel's father was a preacher—it was key to the movie's primary conflict—and that line became a great reference. Dean brought in a ton of ideas like that.

The part that lists all those names in rhymes—"Please, Louise," "Jack, get back," "Oowhee, Marie," "Whoa, Milo"—was inspired by Paul Simon's "50 Ways to Leave Your Lover," with its classic refrain: "Slip out the back, Jack / Make a new plan, Stan . . ." I always thought that was a fun lyrical trick, and it was only a small hop to "Please, Louise, pull me off of my knees."

By the time I left for Asia we'd finished everything but the bridge. Dean, finally able to let down his aura of invulnerability, went to a local emergency room to get treated before he returned home the following day. He really must have been in bad shape. His ploy worked, though; based on everything we'd done in Tahoe, Paramount execs agreed to his musical plan.

Initially, Dean wanted to use a demo of the song on set while they filmed. Many movies don't even use music during dance scenes, to give the editor maximum leeway when it comes to utilizing dialog; they make their cuts and music is dubbed in later. That's why so many dance scenes come off as awkward: the actors are just doing the zombie shuffle, moving to no background noise at all. In our movie, though, the plan was for them to dance to the actual song, which Dean and I thought would provide an excellent visual. At first I was going to cut a demo on the road using my touring band, but my injury put the kibosh on that, so Dean asked me what song he should use instead. Luckily, I had the perfect track: my tempo model was Chuck Berry's "Johnny B. Goode," and that's what they used on set. "Footloose" laid over it perfectly in post. (Actually, it wasn't as easy as I'd initially thought. "Johnny B. Goode" came out in 1958, before the use of click tracks. That meant that drummer Fred Below's sound, while classic, was not quite precise enough for our purposes. We needed every note exactly on the beat for us to match it up, which in the days before digital manipulation meant the film's music editors opened and closed the tape of the song by cutting pieces out or taping pieces in to ensure the beats were absolutely metronomic. It was painstaking and totally worthwhile.)

The last piece of the puzzle was put into place at my house in Sherman Oaks. Dean came over one rainy night shortly after I returned from Asia to nail down the bridge, which was the only part left. He arrived in the late afternoon, just in time for me to help feed the kids, and then hung out with Eva in the kitchen while I put them into the tub. Next, of course, was bedtime, so Dean waited around some more until they were asleep. Ordinarily, that would have been the time to get to work, but that night happened to be the final episode of *M*A*S*H*, which we ended up watching. Dean told me later he'd been nervous on the drive over about my reaction to the array of ideas he brought, but by the time we finally got down to writing, his anxiety had completely disappeared.

With the kids asleep nearby, we couldn't work in the living room, so I took Dean to my laundry room. I sat on the dryer with a guitar on my lap, and he pulled out his notebook. Outside it started to storm. I mean, the sky just opened up. It was like all of nature was conspiring to make this an epic evening. That laundry room was where we wrote the "First we got to turn you around" part and the "Ah, ah, ah, tonight I gotta cut loose, footloose" transition back to the chorus. Dean scribbled down the new lyrics on a printout of the ones we'd already written, turned on his tape recorder, and I sang the whole thing. With that, the writing was done.

We had some time before filming, so on my ensuing North American tour I worked out specific beats with my band during sound checks, which I viewed as de facto rehearsals. The opening guitar line is very much a twangy Duane Eddy influence. At first I had my stage guitarist, Buzzy Feiten, try it, but he couldn't get the phrasing I was after, so I ended up playing it myself. An avowed studio nerd, I went in the opposite direction for this one, grabbing my stage Stratocaster, plugging it into my stage amp, and cranking it up enough for a little raunch. It was exactly the sound I wanted. It came naturally, given that the style I was after was inspired by two of the first songs I ever learned to play—Eddy's "Rebel Rouser" and the aforementioned "Johnny B. Goode." To me, the opening lick to "Footloose" sounds incredibly familiar, even on first listen, like a classic rocker you can't quite recall.

Nathan East came up with the bass line within one or two takes, and it really brings the chorus home. As opposed to "Devil with a Blue Dress," in which the bass plays the root note over and over, Nathan played a Little Richard–style bass line, like "Good Golly Miss Molly" on steroids. The thing is, every chorus in the song is different because he was freeforming it off the top of his head, hauling ass at a hundred miles per hour. It quickly became clear that Nathan's bass line was the heart of the chorus, so I doubled it on guitar. That drove Buzzy crazy when we played it live, because every chorus features slightly different bass, and he had to learn each one of them. Why not simplify it and just pick the best one to repeat over and over? No way! That was the bass line. It *had* to be the bass line. That's Nathan's soul out there.

The groove of the song was inspired by David Bowie's "Modern Love," which was my favorite song to dance to that year. I slowed it down a little so my lyrics would sit on it better. It was a basic, gut-level, rock 'n' roll drum groove, which was exactly what I wanted.

Wow. Putting it all on paper shows just how many influences can go into a piece of music. Bowie, Mitch Ryder, Duane Eddy, Paul Simon, Chuck Berry, Little Richard—all in that one song. Those influences were part of my DNA, the rock of my youth, and it makes sense that they'd show up all at once. That's the history of rock 'n' roll: a constant gumbo in the making, alive and cooking.

CUTTING "FOOTLOOSE" WAS simultaneously easy and complicated. Because it was my road band in the studio, and because we had already run through the song so much, those guys knew every note inside and out. They nailed it in two takes—the first one to get the sound levels right, and the second one was *it*. (Years later my drummer, Tris Imboden, told me that as he was walking out of the studio with Nathan East he said, "Whew—that's the last time we'll ever have to hear *that*." Little did he know.)

Polishing the song was a bit more complex. For overdubs I brought in percussionist Paulinho da Costa, as well as a couple of synth players and two background singers. Even Tris, who'd initially played acoustic drums, came back and added that big Simmons electronic drum sound that's become so familiar in the breakdown. We eventually got up to 96 tracks, including guitar solos, hand claps, drum variations, and assorted instruments. That's a lot for any song at that time, let alone a simple rock 'n' roller. It's especially crazy considering that, in the age before digital recording, we had to link four 24-track tape decks together to get what we wanted. It was worth it. After the song came out, I was at a party with some of the Fleetwood Mac folks, and Lindsey Buckingham pulled me aside. "How the fuck did you get all that information onto that record?" he asked. I used a gigantic hamburger press.

Prior to hitting No. 1, "Footloose" was the beneficiary of a perfect marketing plan. The single was sent to radio stations six weeks before the movie opened, and man did that make an impact. *Footloose* the movie topped the box office for the first three weeks of its release. "Footloose" the song was an immediate hit on MTV, spent three weeks at No. 1, and reached the top 10 in seven countries besides the United States, hitting No. 1 in three of them. To this day, it's the most fun song in my show, the one guaranteed to make an audience get up and dance. It's almost Pavlovian: even folks in tuxedos and formal dresses at fancy benefit galas boogie to that one. They've been trained by the movie. They're not allowed to *not* dance. It's simply un-American.

I actually pitched Dean the idea of my doing every song on the record, but he explained that with so much ambient music in the film—songs coming out of car radios and juke boxes and the like—having one voice for all of it would ring false. We decided I'd do only two songs, the other one being "I'm Free (Heaven Help the Man)," which Dean assigned me once I returned from my Asia tour. Actually, he didn't even wait that long. I had a gig in Hawaii on the way home, and when I checked in to my hotel I found a faxed copy of his lyrics slipped under my door, waiting for me to write the music. A nineteen-year-old Richard Marx sang backup on the demo.

That one reached No. 22. Not bad for one album's work.

IN 1986, "DANGER ZONE" was a massive hit, the top single off a best-selling soundtrack from the year's top movie. It reached No. 2 on the *Billboard* charts. And I wasn't supposed to be the singer.

How I ended up on the song is the stuff of urban legend. I can't say positively who the original singer was supposed to be, but here's a list of possible candidates, in no particular order: (1) Kevin Cronin, the front man from REO Speedwagon, told me he'd been up for the gig but couldn't hit the high notes on musical director Giorgio Moroder's demo; (2) Mickey Thomas told me Starship was supposed to do it, but lawyers got in the way; (3) I heard Toto dropped out, and lawyers were blamed for that one, too; (4) and (5) both Bryan Adams and Corey Hart were supposedly approached and turned it down for their own reasons.

I don't know how much of that is true, but even if every detail is accurate I'm happy to be fifth or sixth runner-up given the success of the song. I actually *was* the producers' first choice for a song, but it wasn't "Danger Zone." By that point, soundtrack hits were coming rapid-fire for me, and I was included in what's known in Hollywood as a "cattle call"—an invitation for a bunch of top recording acts to come to a small theater on the Paramount lot to see a private screening of an early cut of *Top Gun*. The idea was that we'd each pitch songs for various scenes, and the producers would have a cornucopia from which to select. I went in with Peter Wolf (the composer-producer with whom I'd been working closely, not the J. Geils Band singer) to see what grabbed us.

The scene from the movie that immediately jumped out for everybody was the montage of jets taking off from the aircraft carrier. It was obvious to me that *everyone* was going to submit for it. Instead, Peter and I decided to zag and aimed at the beach volleyball scene, which we figured would have far less competition. Experience told me the most important thing was to get onto the soundtrack, at which point we might get the second or third single. If the movie became a hit, so could our song.

So Peter and I wrote "Playing with the Boys," and Giorgio loved it. So, it turned out, did gay men everywhere. It became a bit of a club hit, I think based mostly on the title. I didn't see that one coming.

I was in the studio recording "Playing with the Boys" when I got a call from Michael Dilbeck, my guy at Columbia, saying the singer they'd chosen for "Danger Zone" had dropped out at the last minute. (They never told me who it was. They also never said how Giorgio came to write the song himself rather than turning to anyone who'd attended that cattle call with me.) I'm not sure how they came up with my name after all those other guys (whoever they were), but I'm sure glad they did.

"Giorgio needs you to sing his song right away," Dilbeck told me. "He needs to dub the song into the movie in two days. Can you do it?"

"Is it up tempo?" I asked. My songwriting had been stuck in ballad hell for a year, and I desperately needed a driving song for my live show.

"Yeah," he said. "It's a rocker."

That's all I needed. I didn't even hear the song first; I figured that if Giorgio wrote it, it would be good. The next afternoon, Giorgio's lyricist, Tom Whitlock, came to my house and played me a demo. I felt like the song needed some depth, and rewrote a few chordal changes to add harmonic interest. I also added some lyrics and worked with Tom on the bridge. The only thing left undiscussed was song credit, which quickly became an elephant in the room.

I'd added enough to merit a writer's credit, I thought, but when I asked Giorgio about it he hesitated. It wasn't about my contribution—he admitted I'd done more than enough to put my name on it—but he and Tom needed only their names on this one, he said, same as the three other songs they'd written for the *Top Gun* soundtrack, because four was the minimum number that would qualify them for an Academy Award. If my name was included as co-writer, "Danger Zone" wouldn't count toward their goal. So we struck a deal: I let him keep my name off of the writer's credits in exchange for a bigger cut of the publishing. The arrangement led to a major headache for me later on, when Giorgio sold his catalog to Warner Bros. and I was omitted altogether. For decades, I didn't get paid anything for the publishing, which I noticed only after assessing my income sources for tax purposes. When my lawyer told Warners about it, they admirably not only made up the back pay but finally credited me as a co-writer, which is how it should have been all along.

The next day, I went to Giorgio's studio in Encino to record. I was deeply into Tina Turner's *Private Dancer* at the time, especially the song "What's Love Got to Do with It," which struck me as Tina doing her most Rod Stewart–like growl. So I approached "Danger Zone" as if it was a Tina song. If "I'm Alright" was me doing Gerry Rafferty doing Bob Dylan, "Danger Zone" was me doing Tina Turner doing Rod Stewart. (Who didn't want to do Tina Turner in those days?)

Giorgio had already rerecorded the changes I'd implemented onto the backing track he'd put together, and everything was ready to rock when I showed up in the studio. I played one of Tina's songs from *Private Dancer*, "Can't Stand the Rain," to show Giorgio what I was after vocally. He loved it, and thought it was a great direction for our track. I really Tina-fied that thing, going so far as to affect my pronunciation of words like "DAYN-ger

ZOH-ahn." I'd never sung like that before, putting my voice into such a straight-ahead rock mode.

The song turned out great, the movie was a hit, and the video (helmed by the movie's director, Tony Scott) was hugely popular. Ultimately, "Danger Zone" didn't quite top "Footloose" on the singles charts, but the soundtrack did spend five weeks atop the album charts. It made me the first male solo artist to chart three top-10 singles off of three different soundtracks.

AFTER THE SUCCESS of those three movie hits, I ended up fielding a ton of offers. I did songs for a couple of Sylvester Stallone films, including "Meet Me Halfway" (also written by Giorgio Moroder and Tom Whitlock) for the arm-wrestling movie *Over the Top*, and a duet with Gladys Knight for *Rocky IV* called "Double or Nothing."

In 1988, Jon Peters asked me to write the theme song for *Caddyshack II*. I did, and "Nobody's Fool" hit No. 8 on the charts, making me the first male solo artist with top-10 singles from four different soundtracks. I've been told many times it was the best thing about that movie.

"Nobody's Fool" was so popular, in fact, that I was asked to perform it from the steps of the Old Mission Santa Barbara for live broadcast in Japan. What I hadn't considered was that, to account for the time difference, I'd be playing at four in the morning. To the chagrin of the neighbors, me and a TV crew that must have had seventy-five people in it ended up doing the song again and again in preparation to go live. To make matters worse, I wasn't even playing but lip-synching. Pajama-clad residents started showing up at the mission steps at about four-thirty, shouting at the producers to shut things down. Before long, the police were there, too. (One of the cops described the angry crowd as a "lynch mob" for the press.) We were finally live when the police arrived, and my manager, Larry Larson, held them at bay, talking them into waiting just a minute or two more until we wrapped. I keep thinking how punk rock it would have been to get dragged off the stage in the middle of a live broadcast, and how funny it would have been for the singing to continue, given that I wasn't actually singing. Either way, now I will never be able to run for mayor of Santa Barbara. Thank God.

That moment would have served as a fitting cap to my soundtrack work, but movie songs kept rolling in. I teamed with Michael McDonald to write and perform "She's Dangerous" for the Sean Connery movie *The Presidio*. It's a really good song, and I'm still not sure why they rejected it. It's the rare tune in which I pulled Michael into my groove rather than adjusting to his—the song is much more "Footloose" than "What a Fool Believes"—and the result might have been too different for the producers to get their heads around. Then again, it was 1988 and maybe they figured our run was over. That happens in pop music—your sound will be hot and all of a sudden it's not. "She's Dangerous" might just have arrived too late.

The thing those last tunes have in common is that, unlike "I'm Alright," "Footloose," or "Danger Zone," they all showed up on one of my albums—the same album, in fact: 1988's *Back to Avalon*. Why didn't those other hits appear on my records? Well, for the latter two, Columbia had an agreement to release Paramount's soundtracks, with the studio participating in ownership and publishing rights. For the *Back to Avalon* tunes there was no accompanying movie soundtrack album to get in the way, so I got to use them myself. I wish Columbia had included me in their negotiations with Paramount, but they didn't, and I didn't have the clout to fight for use of my songs. I can only imagine what kind of difference that might have made for sales.

In 1996, I recorded "For the First Time" for the George Clooney–Michelle Pfeiffer movie *One Fine Day*. The song was brought to me by Don Ienner, the president of Columbia Records, and soon thereafter we learned that Rod Stewart also wanted to do it. I'm not sure what kind of sway Rod had, but we both ended up recording versions of it. They picked mine, but only barely. The director was so set against using pop music in his film that he put the song at the end of the closing credits, so it played only after everybody had left the theater. Nonetheless, "For the First Time" ended up as No. 1 on the Adult Contemporary chart, was nominated for an Academy Award, and I got to perform it at the Oscars.

For all of that, the soundtrack song that was most fun for me also had the smallest chart impact. It was the title track for a hastily constructed movie from the comedy studio Funny Or Die, made during the presidential campaign in 2016—a fifty-minute sendup called *The Art of the Deal*, starring Johnny Depp as Donald Trump. The Funny Or Die writers composed the basic song, and I added some lyric lines (e.g., "We shall over-comb") and new chords here and there. We also shot a video in which I wore a star-spangled headband and shirt. How'd they end up picking me? I really don't know, but I was happy to serve.

PEOPLE CONSTANTLY ASK me why music isn't as important in today's movies as it was when they made *Footloose* and *Top Gun*. When I started, rock 'n' roll songs were a soundtrack novelty. In 1967, Simon and Garfunkel did "Mrs. Robinson" for *The Graduate*. In 1971, Isaac Hayes came out with that classic soundtrack for *Shaft*. Bob Dylan did *Pat Garrett & Billy the Kid* in 1973. Those were the beginnings. With the notable exception of *Saturday Night Fever*, not much had changed a decade later. By the time *Caddyshack* came out, audiences were finally being primed to accept pop songs as an integral part of the movie experience.

The other part of the equation is that songs nowadays are rarely written for the movie in which they appear. It's almost all existing material that doesn't fully capture the emotional content of a given scene. The songs don't live on because they don't establish a connection with the audience.

I think it's consequential that every one of my hit soundtrack tunes was written specifically for its film, and fit its movie better than some off-the-rack pop song. Ultimately, quality soundtrack work possesses a synergy in which the song lifts the movie, and the movie lifts the song. Putting rock songs into movies was hardly a new idea when I started, but for some reason filmmakers hadn't given the idea nearly enough credibility.

They say success is 10 percent luck and 90 percent preparation. Fortunately, I was ready when the opportunity showed itself, and that made all the difference in my career.

CHAPTER 10

LET'S START GIVING

I WAS SITTING AROUND the house in Santa Barbara one day in 1985 when the telephone rang. Okay, so that's a pretty dull beginning to a story. When I picked it up, though, a high, familiar voice greeted me.

"Kenny?"

It was Michael Jackson. The story just got better, right?

As previously discussed, I'd met Michael during the release of *Off the Wall*, and we'd been in loose touch ever since.

"What's up, Michael?" I asked.

"I'm getting some musicians together for a special session," he said. I didn't even need details. I was in.

As it happened, the session in question was for "We Are the World"—the record that Michael, Lionel Richie, and Quincy Jones were spearheading to raise money for famine relief in Africa. I'd never met Quincy, but he'd once called me up to tell me how much he loved my song "The More We Try," which, okay, was extremely flattering, and also confirmed he was familiar with my work. So I had that going for me, which was nice.

He and Michael both wanted me to join. Cool.

The recording was scheduled for just after the American Music Awards (at LA's Shrine Auditorium) to capitalize on all the stars who'd come to town. I was at the show—Sheila E. and I presented Favorite Pop or Rock Single (won by Bruce Springsteen for "Dancing in the Dark")—hanging out in a dressing room with Huey Lewis when somebody came in and asked if he was going to Michael's session. I think they enlisted him there on the spot.

Michael was nominated for three awards that night, but never showed; he was across town at A&M Studios, prerecording chorus parts for "We Are the World" and getting ready for the well-heeled crowd that was about to show up. Lionel decided to pull double duty and attend the AMAs, mostly because he was the show's host. Also, he won six of the twenty-seven awards, and performed three songs before darting from the auditorium as soon as the curtain fell to race through Los Angeles and help coordinate "We Are the World." Talk about a busy evening.

The participants—those of us who weren't recruited that evening, anyway—had all been sent a cassette demo of the song, with vocals by Michael and Lionel, to familiarize ourselves with the tune. Accompanying it was a letter from Quincy explaining the situation and telling us where to go for the recording session, except the address had been blacked out after a late-breaking decision to keep that information close to the vest. The last thing anybody wanted was a throng of fans blocking the entrance. During the AMAs somebody must have given the location to the various drivers, who after the show ferried us ten miles from downtown to Hollywood. The A&M Studios complex had been built by Charlie Chaplin in 1917 to film movies, and now forty-five of the world's biggest pop stars were descending on it to do something unique for all of us.

Security was tight. I saw Columbia VP Ron Oberman—the guy who called the shots on my records—across the parking lot, and heard later that the only way he could get in was to volunteer as valet. Wow.

The musicians were led through Studio A's double doors, above which was taped Quincy's handwritten sign: "Leave your ego at the door." Everybody else—family members, friends, managers, bandmates, *everybody*—was taken to the Chaplain Stage, a huge room used for filming wide indoor scenes, including *Soul Train*. Nobody except the singers and production crew were allowed into the actual recording studio.

I was one of the first to arrive, and was shocked when A-listers began pouring into the room. I hadn't realized just how big the session was going to be. I had to continually remind myself that I wasn't crashing somebody's Hollywood party—I'd been invited to this. I circled the room, greeting familiar faces—Michael, Lionel, Steve Perry, Darryl Hall, Huey Lewis, Lindsey Buckingham, the Pointers—and introducing myself to folks I'd never met.

Risers filled the long end of the studio. Each performer was allotted a spot, our names written on pieces of tape indicating where we'd stand. There was more tape with additional names on the floor in the middle of the room, which we'd soon learn were for solos to be recorded later that night. Not everyone got one, so I was especially excited when I saw my name in blue ink, right between Springsteen and Steve Perry. I felt a rush of satisfaction. This was gonna be fun.

At 10:30 p.m., after about an hour of mingling, Lionel asked us to find our places. I was on the top row on the left side of the risers, which gave me a great view of the surreal scene taking shape below. It was like a dream in which everyone you see looks like somebody famous, only this time they actually were.

Before we started, Bob Geldof—the singer of the Boomtown Rats and the founder of the England-based Band Aid campaign, on which much of USA for Africa was modeled—stood at a wheeled podium in front of the group and gave a short speech reminding us why we were all there. It was grounding and inspirational, and spotlighted the bigger purpose the evening served.

When he finished, Quincy took over and told us how things would go down. First, the entire chorus would record the main melody and counterpoint vocals, and then the soloists would take their turns. To keep things simple, he told us not to harmonize and to hit the same octave as Michael's guide track. When he said, "Anyone who can't sing up that high, just lay out on this one," I smiled. Singing up that high was kind of my thing.

The demo we'd been sent was played over the monitors, and I could tell from looking around that not everybody had listened to it. (I had. And I liked it. With such a diverse group of musicians, some people were bound to quibble with whatever was presented, but I thought Michael and Lionel wrote a good tune with a strong chorus. Any qualms from others were quickly dropped in the spirit of why we were all there.) The song was catchy and simple, and it took only one or two run-throughs for everyone to sing it with gusto.

At one point, Paul Simon, who was on the riser below me, looked around and said, "Wooo, if a bomb drops on this room, John Denver's back on top." That cracked us all up.

The group vocal stuff took several hours—not bad for an on-the-fly recording without any rehearsal, but a long time when you consider that we didn't start until close to midnight. Sometime after three in the morning we gathered for a group picture for the album cover, and then Quincy invited the selected soloists to the center of the room. There was a lot of talent there, and it was a huge honor to be placed on that front line.

Quincy and Lionel explained to us that small groups of vocalists would take turns singing around the same mic, stepping up for our lines and back when we finished. It was then that it hit me: I hadn't perceived myself as a member of this particular club, yet there I was, among Michael and Springsteen and Stevie Freaking Wonder. I was starstruck and a bit intimidated. I really wanted to make a good showing and would have been mostly happy to just not embarrass myself. As we ran through our lines, it became clear that each soloist had his or her own style and sound, and I figured that as long as I stayed true to my voice, everything would work out fine.

One guy who wasn't on the front line, or anywhere, was Prince. He never showed, leaving a vacant spot on the floor near the piece of tape with his name written on it. We all just kind of stared at it. I got an inkling of what might happen when Michael sidled over and put his arm around me. "Who should I put up there instead of Prince?" he asked. To me, the answer was easy. "Huey Lewis has a great voice," I said. Within minutes, Michael, Huey, and Quincy were off to one side of the room, Michael singing Prince's part and Huey echoing it back with his typical panache. You're welcome, Huey.

Finally, at what must have been four in the morning, it was time to record. We all did multiple takes. I sang my line—"We are the ones who make a brighter day, so let's start giving . . ."—three times. The highlight of my night came after the first one, when Stevie enthused, "Yeah, man!" Fuck, it was the highlight of my *life*.

Somewhere along the line we all sang an impromptu "Day O" for Harry Belafonte. Somewhere else, they brought in burgers. One of our breaks became an autograph-fest, with each artist collecting signatures from everybody else on their sheet music. Unfortunately, the pen I handed people was a red Sharpie, and after all these years many of my signatures have faded into practically invisible ink.

We finally filed out after eight in the morning. I was exhausted, but felt a happy pride in knowing that I'd just been part of something historic.

ONE THING BOB GELDOF mentioned during his speech to the "We Are the World" group was an idea for a multi-continent concert to raise money for famine relief. About five months later it happened. Live Aid consisted of simultaneous sold-out shows at Wembley Stadium in London and John F. Kennedy Stadium in Philadelphia. The broadcast drew upward of two billion people.

I received word at the last minute that they wanted me to perform. I was in the middle of a tour, and caught a lucky break when I didn't have a show scheduled for that day. Travel was quickly arranged for me and my band, not to mention our gear and our roadies, from Houston, where I'd just played, to Philadelphia.

JFK Stadium held more than ninety thousand people. It was packed, and the day was so hot they repeatedly sprayed down the crowd with fire hoses. A split rotating stage allowed one act to set up behind a screen while somebody else performed. Bill Graham was in charge of everything, and he was a guy you did *not* fuck around with. He was notorious for keeping things running on time; shows at his venues in San Francisco were known for starting not even one minute late. At Live Aid, Graham was constantly moving people on and off the stage like a freaking dervish. Almost nobody got a sound check, me included.

I went on after Tom Petty. My band and I were there to play one song: "Footloose." I guess that's all you get when you have one No. 1 to your credit, which at that point was barely a year old. We could play that thing in our sleep, so even in front of that many people there weren't many nerves involved.

Chevy Chase was doing the introductions. Just before I went on I heard him ask Graham, "What should I say?" The promoter responded with one line: "Call him Mr. Footloose." So that's what Chevy did. Like I said, you do what Mr. Graham tells you to do.

It was hardly a standard show. Our guitars weren't in tune and one of the keyboards didn't work at all. When we tried to take a moment to correct things, Graham started screaming, "Get on! Keep the show going! I'm going to unplug you!" As I said on the MTV interview shortly thereafter, our lack of sound check made it feel like playing a high school dance.

Backstage, there was very little of the love vibe that Quincy, Lionel, and Michael had fostered in Hollywood. Hell, none of those guys was even in Philadelphia that day. Every star seemed to be surrounded by an entourage and security team. I hardly interacted with anybody until shortly after my set, when someone from the telecast asked if I wanted to help out, and I was shuffled into a control-room trailer.

I ended up doing about two hours' worth of announcing for the TV broadcast. They wanted pop stars to read from fundraising scripts and occasionally comment on whatever was happening onstage. Teddy Pendergrass's set came during my time in the booth, and I did the best I could with it. It was Teddy's emotional return to the stage after a car crash three years earlier left him paralyzed from the chest down. He was in a wheelchair and came out to a heartfelt introduction by Ashford & Simpson. It was a really moving moment.

For the closer, they gathered a bunch of us together onstage for a rendition of "We Are the World." The main thing I remember is Patti LaBelle's voice; she flat-out soul-screamed into her microphone. It was overwhelmingly loud. There must have been a dozen mics onstage, and the sound folks were probably freaking out trying to figure out which one she was using so they could turn it down. They never did find it, and she screamed all the way into the fadeout. She left no air in the song for the rest of us to breathe. I was kind of annoyed in the moment, but in retrospect it's hilarious.

I couldn't stick around afterward because I had to get to Nashville for a gig the next night at the Grand Ole Opry. I heard there was a bit of bacchanalia at some of the stars' hotels, but between "We Are the World" and the excitement of Live Aid, I don't feel like I missed out on too much.

THE MID-1980S WERE also my prime MTV video era, and boy did I have some good ones. "Heartlight," from my *High Adventure* album in '82, utilizes everything the early 1980s had to offer: lots of neon, a set with a rainy windowpane, copious fog, a drummer (Tris Imboden) wearing a Panama hat and a tank-top undershirt with suspenders, and a keyboard player with an undone bowtie. Everything is perfect, up to and including my own purple blazer with the sleeves rolled up. Fantastic. (Tris wore the same hat for the faux-live "Swear Your Love" video, probably because we shot both of them on the same day, with the same director. It was like a discount-store version of video shoots: come in, get a bunch of stuff on tape, and get out by ten. That was a long day; I'd eaten some bad sushi the night before, and was vomiting pretty much up till call time. My doctor gave me something for my stomach and a shot of morphine for the pain. I persevered.)

When I first heard about the concept for MTV—a channel running nothing but music videos?—I thought it was great, a new horizon for record promotion. Early on, budgets were low (just look at "Heartlight" and "Swear Your Love"), but within a couple of years videos had turned into major productions.

The whole medium created strife for artists, forcing constant negotiation with their record labels to convince them extra expense was warranted. *If we just had a video, this song would go to the top of the charts.* That actually helped determine how committed they were to your record: if the label was stingy with your video budget, you knew you had bigger problems on your hands.

Once the cost of videos soared into the hundreds of thousands of dollars—more than the records themselves—labels started to count that money as an advance against royalties, forcing the artists to share in the cost. That was a deal killer for those not moving millions of units.

My peak 1980s look might have come in my "I'll Be There" video, in which I wore an oversized salmon-colored suit with huge shoulders. My hair was short compared to my L&M days, but it had never been bigger thanks to gallons of hairspray. El DeBarge was in that video, too, and brought a strong '80s game of his own.

My wildest video was for "Vox Humana," set in an art gallery featuring a bunch of paintings that come to life—all of me. Rather trippy, by 1980s standards. I created a mock band for the shoot, with Nathan East's brother Marcel on bass, Marilyn Martin (a friend of my guitar player, who would later have a hit of her own) on keys, and Tris on drums, this time wearing a beret. Why a fake band? I have no better answer than that I wanted a different look and the '80s were weird.

For the "Keep the Fire" video we pretended to play live onstage, and used so much smoke that you literally can't see a single person in some of the wide shots. "Heart to Heart" opens with a wistful little boy in pajamas clutching a teddy bear on the front steps of his house, before he wanders off into yet more fog. We did like fog machines back then. I play an architect in that one, or maybe an artist. Who knows? Certainly not the director.

Videos were so slipshod in those days that when we shot "This Is It," rather than getting Mike McDonald onto the soundstage, I lip-synched both of our parts. Makes perfect sense, right? It was all about trying to capture the MTV audience as cheaply as possible. Michael was on the road at the time, and the show must go on.

A lot of the videos—and I made many—blend into each other in my memory. I didn't even appear in two of my biggest videos—"I'm Alright," from *Caddyshack*, and "Footloose"—both of which featured wall-to-wall clips from their respective movies. "Footloose" was basically just a trailer for the film, and garnered some controversy because it was so slick and got so much MTV play that other labels couldn't afford to compete with it. They called it a movie ad. Well, that's exactly what it was—a free promo that played dozens of times each day. It was brilliant, exactly what the studio had hoped for.

My other video from the *Footloose* soundtrack, "I'm Free (Heaven Help the Man)," was a big production number. We shot all night long, and it was exhausting. Unfortunately, it was one of those videos in which I had to semi-act. Not good. The female lead was played by a young Virginia Madsen in one of her first ever screen roles. The director took the song title literally, and set up a scenario in which I escape from prison to find my old lady. (My old lady actually looks like she's about thirteen in the bedroom shoot. Maybe that's why my character was in jail.) We spent the rest of the video running from the police.

It was all ridiculous. Fun, but ridiculous.

IN THE EARLY 1980S, Eva and I became friends with John Travolta and Marilu Henner. This was when Marilu was starring in *Taxi*. (I somehow never connected the dots that one of my closest collaborators, Bob James, wrote the theme song for that show.) Only in Hollywood would my wife end up as one of her best friends.

John took a liking to my kids, Crosby and Cody, who were five and four at the time. He had his pilot's license, and a couple of times he flew us down to Anaheim in his Cessna Citation so we could all go to Disneyland, which was one of his favorite things to do. My kids knew him as Johnny the Pilot; they had no clue about his movies. One day John came over with a videotape of *Grease* and said, "I think it's time the kids see what I do for a living." Crosby asked which movie he'd brought. "That's *my* movie," John said. Crosby looked at me, confused, and said, "Johnny the Pilot made a movie?"

Once, Johnny the Pilot even flew the adults up to San Francisco for a night. We went to dinner at Ghirardelli Square, and ended up dancing alone in a hotel bar to keep the paparazzi away.

Eva, like nearly every woman in the country, found John attractive. I didn't imagine anything would come of it, so there was nothing to be concerned about, until John called me one day and confessed that he was attracted to my wife. Not only that, he said, things started to heat up one evening when I'd been on the road, although they didn't get sexual. Travolta told me he hadn't slept with Carly Simon until after she'd broken up with James Taylor, and he wouldn't do that to me while Eva and I were married. I didn't ask for any details. I got the feeling that he and Marilu were only loosely together, and that John had a large palette of lovers. I was not interested in watching my wife become one of them, and cut off the relationship. Strangely, I never let myself talk to Eva about that. Years later, she would balk at John's way of assuming she would just fall at his feet the way he'd portrayed in his story to me. "I think he forgot that I might have a say in it, too," she laughed.

THE SEEDS OF divorce can take years to grow. Those weeds might seem like they sprout overnight, but they don't. We water them with silent resentments, unexpressed anger and pain, and, worst of all, secrets. Eva and I had been married for twelve years, and the relationship turned into frozen stares and power battles. I felt like I was starving to death emotionally, and I suspected that Eva was, too. After all those years, we found ourselves in a classic loveless marriage, an argument that nobody wins.

I take most, if not all, of the blame. I'd spent years living a double life on the road. That Eva had tacitly approved of it makes no difference; that secret version of me, which she didn't understand because I never let her understand it, was probably freaking her out. She felt our remoteness from each other, and she was lonely and sad. Rather than confront it, she withdrew, which I used to rationalize that it was okay to have more affairs. One behavior fed the other, and it all started with our foolish agreement.

We spent five or six years in couples therapy, which brought us no closer together. In fact, it seemed mostly to underline our differences, and may have even made us more distant. Things came to a head for me during one session when the therapist looked at me and said, "You have to make up your mind what kind of woman you want to be with. Eva is one kind of woman. If that's who you want, then you must try and make this work. If that's not who you want, then you guys need to let it go."

That was the first moment I actually considered a reality in which I wasn't always working, working, working to make our relationship stable. You do this, I'll do that. By that point there was so much negotiation and so little heart. To my mind, a combative marriage, or even just a loveless one, teaches your children things about love that won't serve them when they get older. I finally considered doing the thing my father never let himself do: leave.

That thought occurred to me late one night as I sat alone on a beach in the Bahamas. I was there for a gig and couldn't stop contrasting the beauty of my surroundings with the ugliness of my marriage. I called Eva the next morning and suggested a separation. I expected dramatics, but she received the idea matter-of-factly, with (I hoped) maybe a touch of relief. She'd been thinking the same thing, she said. Just like that, we found ourselves talking through the logistics of lives apart.

I moved into a friend's guest house in Montecito, and we began the process of giving each other space.

CHAPTER 11

TRUST LOVE

I WAS ON A SOLO TRIP up the coast, staying in a small redwood cabin at the rear of Deetjen's Big Sur Inn amid some of the most amazing seaside forests you'll ever encounter. It was 1991; Eva and I had been split for a couple of months, a period we'd framed as a "trial separation"—a time to breathe and see if there was any chance for reconciliation. Trouble was, I'd recently noticed a strong attraction to another woman and was trying to figure out what it meant. I was forty years old. What if this was just a mid-life crisis, one of those temporary-insanity things? Maybe I would come to my senses and realize everything I'd be losing.

Some soul searching was in order, and for me, Big Sur was the place to do it.

I'd recently bought a book about Native American ceremonies, one of which involved drawing a large circle on the ground and placing items of personal importance at points north, south, east, and west. Author Lynn V. Andrews called it the "sacred medicine wheel." On my third night in the forest, a full moon emerged and I was inspired to act.

I spent the day thinking about where to do it—in the woods? at the beach?—and by dinnertime, I realized that something was missing from my plan. I was at the inn's restaurant and impulsively called my waiter over. "Do you know where I can get some psychedelic mushrooms?" I asked. I'd had positive experiences with MDMA, plus all those acid trips as a college student in the hills outside of Pasadena, but had somehow never tried magic mushrooms. An all-natural journey seemed like just the thing.

The waiter raised an eyebrow and said, "Let me make a call." A few minutes later, he returned and quietly told me about a local mountain woman who might be able to set me up. Her name was Clovis. He slipped a scrap of paper with her phone number into my hand.

After dinner I called Clovis, and she gave me directions to her place—no easy thing in the rural mountains where not every road has a name. It took about thirty minutes in the dark, across lots of switchbacks. The directions were detailed, but more than once I had to guess which way to go.

I finally worked my way up a dirt road to the top of the mountain, which is where I found Clovis's cabin, with its amazing view of the moonlit ocean below. As I pulled up, I could make out the figure of a woman on the front porch. She might have been in her fifties, or maybe her seventies; it was impossible to tell. Her salt-and-pepper hair was piled into a nest atop her head. She came out to greet me. "You made it," she said, chuckling in a soft, gravelly voice. "You've passed the first test." I assumed she was teasing, though on a night like this I couldn't be sure.

Clovis walked with a bit of a stoop as she led me through the front door and into her tiny kitchen. The cabin was lit mostly by candles, very small and extremely cozy. As I sat down at her wooden kitchen table, she reached to a high shelf and pulled down a mason jar half filled with dried mushrooms. "Somebody left this here a while back," she said with a smile. "Help yourself."

I looked at the jar and realized I didn't know a thing about the stuff inside it. "How much should I take?" I asked. "I've never done mushrooms."

"I haven't either," she laughed. "Take as much as you want."

So I grabbed a handful and munched them one at a time. They tasted like cardboard with overtones of potting soil. I washed the powdery residue down with a cup of herbal tea that Clovis handed me. "Yum," I said sarcastically.

Then I told her why I was there—my crossroads and the pending decisions in front of me. I mentioned the ceremony I wanted to create. Clovis knew the perfect spot for it, she said, and gave me directions to her favorite beach: down the hill, right on the highway, then take the first right toward the ocean. "Drive for a couple of miles to the end of the road, then walk through the trees for about five minutes," she said. "When ya can't go any further, you're there." She grinned at her own joke.

I figured I'd better make the drive before the psilocybin kicked in, so I grabbed one more mushroom—"for good measure," I said. When I asked how much Clovis wanted for my snack, she turned me down flat.

About twenty minutes later I pulled into Pfeiffer Beach at Big Sur. I could hear the waves rumbling through the darkness, and hiked through the moonlit scrub pines and sage toward the water. It was all I could have hoped for. The beach was small by the standards I'd grown up with in Southern California, maybe a hundred yards long, and was unlike anything I'd ever seen. The rising moon gave the low cliffs behind me a silver-blue, otherworldly quality. A great rock arch sat in the water directly before me. I found a stick and, following instructions from the book, drew my circle in the deep sand near the cliffs, about four feet across, with a horizontal line and a vertical line intersecting in the center. I laid out my items—photographs of my wife and children, my journal and pen, a crystal that my new romantic interest had given me, and an exquisite Native American flute made from tree roots, which I'd bought earlier that day, representing music. I felt like a feather in the wind, ready for wherever this breeze might take me, surrendered and divinely guided.

I knelt in the circle and read prayers in each direction, then added one of my own. As I shivered in the cool ocean breeze, I watched the sand begin to swirl around me and began to feel a tingle of heat, pure energy moving from my tailbone up through my spine. I closed my eyes to focus on it, and before I knew what was happening, those mushrooms snuck right up on me. I became intensely aware of the moon, huge and directly above me. Was it closer now? The energy surged to the top of my head, then burst through, emerging from my spine like Jack's beanstalk growing up into the sky. It was like a huge snake made of turquoise, coral, and bone beads, coiling ever upward, loop upon loop. Unsure whether my eyes were open or closed, I observed, fascinated and unafraid, as it attached itself to the full moon. I was the watcher and the participant, totally involved and totally at peace. I was very, very high, and completely immersed.

I stayed on the beach for what seemed like hours, awash in feelings of love and connection. Kneeling in the sand at the center of the circle, I occasionally felt the bead snake undulate, part of me yet distinctly separate. It shivered there in space for a long while, me at one end, the moon at the other. Eventually, after eons and eras, it descended from the sky, and slowly wound its way back into my body. As it did, I began to notice of the sound of waves crashing behind me and the salt-wind in my face, as if my outer awareness had been turned back on. The vision finally disappeared and I realized that my ceremony was complete.

Fully back in my body, I loaded the ceremonial items into my backpack and walked barefoot to the car. By the time I got there I was totally clear-headed, completely straight. Looking at the clock, I saw that I had only been on the beach for forty minutes. It was one hell of a hallucination, but I still didn't have the clear message I'd been hoping for.

The next day at my rented cabin, sunrise brought a foggy Big Sur morning—a perfect day to light a fire and write. As I settled into my chair, I was drawn to a melody I'd started a week earlier. I began grabbing lyrics from the ether, and it didn't take long to realize that I was writing about my possible new romance. Here was the clarity I'd been looking for. My heart was totally open to this awareness of love.

The words I wrote that night would become the song "Sweet Reunion": "In the moment I first saw you / I could swear that we had met / The look in your eyes was so familiar / Where and when, I forget." Noticing that several artists had left drawings and poetry behind as mementos for the inn, I wrote out a copy of the words and left it on the table. The next time I visited, I found it framed and hanging on the wall.

When I returned home, I could see only one choice. I had to follow my heart.

WHEN I MET Julia Cooper-Fries in 1984, our relationship was strictly professional, and it would stay that way for six years. Given that we started dating shortly after I broke up with Eva, some people assumed we had been intimate earlier than that, but it wasn't until I was single again, and so was Julia, that we finally became romantic.

I'd initially met her as the result of digestive troubles brought on by the stress of my career. I'd been dealing with pressure by falling deep into my long-term affair with tequila, which I sometimes augmented with cocaine, after which I'd have to even out with a downer if I wanted to sleep at night. Not only was such a pace unsustainable, but it soon led to a pre-ulcerous condition that left me with persistent gut pain. My doctor suggested a treatment I'd never heard of called colon hydrotherapy. Colonics.

I was in such discomfort that I was willing to try anything. At his recommendation, I went to an alternative health-care collective on the east side of Santa Barbara. It was there, in a tiny office toward the back, that I first encountered Julia. The room was barely big enough to fit her massage table. When I lay down, my extended frame reached both walls.

Julia was twenty-nine but looked ten years younger, bright-eyed and petite, the quintessential California girl. When she was younger, she'd modeled for the Wilhelmina agency and did on-camera work as a TV weather girl in Tokyo, but had since turned her back on all of that. Now she took a natural, hippy approach to beauty: no makeup, long, flowing skirts, her light-brown hair tied into a knot atop her head. Julia was different from anyone I'd ever met, having lived her entire life outside of societal norms. She said her grandparents were Romanian gypsy Jews, and she really tried to embody that—at least the free-spirited gypsy part of it.

Julia grew up suffering liver and kidney issues, and was so sensitive to environmental toxins that a single bite of pesticide-sprayed food could make her sick. (She was the only person I'd ever seen bring her own Tupperware-packed food to restaurants.) Being in a room where the cabinets had been glued together with the wrong adhesives, or the rugs were sprayed with moth repellant, might land her in bed for days. Her doctor said she was allergic to the twentieth century.

To counter all of this, Julia experimented with diet and colonics, which is how she became a colon therapist herself. Her seeking didn't stop there. She moved to Boston, into the home of the founder of the wheatgrass movement in the United States. She dove into self-betterment programs like EST, meditation, and yoga. Later, she lived at the Oregon ranch of Bhagwan Shree Rajneesh, wearing the orange robes of the Rajneeshpuram. ("Wasn't he the crazy guru who owned like a dozen Rolls-Royces?" I asked. She replied coolly: "Oh, I would never follow a guru who wasn't crazy!")

Pertinent to me, Julia also studied something called the Fischer-Hoffman Process, an alternative form of talk therapy. Robert Hoffman was a former tailor who claimed to have channeled the spirit of deceased Swedish psychiatrist Siegfried Fischer in formulating his self-betterment program. It's a detail that illustrates the outer edges of the process—and Julia's life. She grew so enamored with the system that she became a skilled practitioner of it.

I'd long since appreciated the benefits of talk therapy, and Julia's explanation of Fischer-Hoffman sparked my curiosity. It seemed like an interesting approach to self-exploration, and after a few colonic sessions I decided to try it out. During that first encounter, I may have been staring at Julia a little too intently, the way I might have with a woman I was interested in pursuing backstage. It was pure reflex, nothing I intended to follow up on—she was married, and so was I—but Julia caught it. "Honey," she said, "there'd be too many people in the bed." She was right, and I appreciated her all the more for saying it. That our relationship would remain platonic was just fine with me. Free from the possibility of sex, I was able to open up to her about things I barely wanted to acknowledge to myself. One by one, she learned all of my secrets: my affairs, my lies, my rationalizations. When she asked, "How does that make you feel?"— it was a go-to question for her—I was frequently at a loss about how to answer. At one point, I even yelled, "What the hell does that mean? I have no idea how I'm supposed to feel!" Well, she said, that was what we were going to figure out.

My Fischer-Hoffman encounters with Julia were intense and deep, and basically came down to one principle: many of our insecurities aren't our own but are learned over time, presented to us by family members. I began to recognize which of the negative voices in my head belonged not to me, but to my mom, my dad, or to Danny. Julia's emotional-release work brought some perspective. I'd write down my various traits on index cards, then channel my feelings about them while punching a pillow. I'd scream at my mother and I'd scream at my father, setting loose anger that had been holed up for years and years. Inside the pillow was a smaller pillow, representing my mom or dad as a child, which I removed before I began. Once the screaming was over, after I'd pushed myself to exhaustion, I talked to the little pillow, using nurturing sentiments like, "I know the version of you I'm screaming at isn't how you were born. It comes from what was done to you, and the things you learned." The goal was to turn my anger into forgiveness and compassion for those who'd taught me my negative traits, and for myself.

With Julia, the Fischer-Hoffman work went hand-in-hand with colonics, which are such an intimate therapy that people tend to share their life stories as they're being administered. I sure did. Julia told me emotions are stored in the gut, and when people release from their liver and colon, whatever feelings they have locked up inside emerge in unexpected ways. This is what led her to Fischer-Hoffman in the first place: her colonic clients kept presenting her with fertile emotional territory, and she wanted to develop some therapeutic chops that would help them move in more ways than one. Integrating her Fischer-Hoffman work was a logical step, and she soon found it worked in both directions—releasing anger could create physical releases as well.

Whenever I got a colonic I'd talk about something that was troubling me. When I hit a place of awareness—"Oh, I never thought of that"—my entire system would move. *Everything* opened up. There were times when I went in depressed, and as soon as my liver released I felt much lighter. It makes you wonder how much of your emotional state is directly tied to your gut.

FOR THE NEXT six years, I saw Julia every couple of weeks when I wasn't on the road or in the studio. During that time, I found myself increasingly able to identify my feelings, and started to notice everything I was burying when it came to my marriage. Eva was very bright, and I tended to lose our arguments because I couldn't keep up with her intellect. She always had just the right retort, the perfect comeback. When I complained about this to Julia during one of our counseling sessions, she suggested I not overthink things. "Just say how you feel," she told me. "You can't argue with a feeling."

So I tried it. During my next squabble with Eva, I told her: "That just doesn't feel right to me."

Her response was instinctive. "If you're going to talk about feelings," she said, turning to leave the room, "this conversation is over." I realized I was speaking a new language now—one in which Eva wasn't conversant, and didn't want to be.

I ended up doing a lot of talk-therapy with Julia, and a fair number of colonics. Conversation with her was comfortable, and I appreciated her insight into my emotional world. As the years went by, we'd occasionally do our sessions (therapy, not colonics) while out on walks instead of in her office. Julia took it a step further one day when she asked me to join her and a girlfriend for a hike in the Santa Barbara foothills. That was strange. It was clearly not an appointment—more like three friends going for a hike. Midway up the hill, Julia mentioned that she'd just had her yearly meeting with her astrologer. "He told me that I'd be in a new relationship this year," she said. "I told him that would be a surprise to my husband." She paused for a moment to let the sentiment settle. "So my astrologer said, 'Your husband? Oh, *that's* over.'"

The idea sat me down, literally. I had to take a moment on a boulder by the trail to catch my breath. I let the women walk on ahead, then, without even realizing what I was doing, heard myself say, "It ain't me!" I was *not* going to be Julia's next relationship. No fuckin' way. I was surprised by the intensity of my response. She'd never suggested that it *was* me. Why was I so adamant about this? I gathered myself and caught up with them, making sure not to bring up the astrologer again.

A few weeks later, I went to my friend Pam's birthday party at a restaurant in Santa Barbara. I'd just separated from Eva, and was still getting used to going out on my own. Julia was the last person I expected to encounter, but when I walked in the door, there she was. As I watched her from across the room, I felt a sudden magnetic attraction unlike anything I'd experienced in her office. She seemed equally delighted to see me. We pulled two chairs close together and ended up talking for the next couple of hours. The connection was electric. That was where I learned she'd actually left her husband, just like the astrologer said. The same attraction she'd shot down during our very first meeting now seemed free to express itself, and I could swear that she felt it, too.

We didn't do anything more than talk that night, but it sure got me thinking. Eva and I had framed our separation as a trial period, a chance to consider who we were to ourselves and each other. I honestly had no idea what I wanted. That's what led me to Big Sur for my mushroom ceremony—to try and figure out the details of my life.

When I returned to Santa Barbara after that epic trip, I asked Julia out.

Our first date started with dinner, and ended with us being inseparable for years to come. The relationship became a deeply spiritual experience for me, something made of destiny. It was different than anything I'd known. Nothing about Julia was "normal," and I absorbed as much of her as I could, gleefully deferring my middle-class values to her idiosyncratic lifestyle. She was tapped into a way of being I wanted access to. In Julia's eyes, anything was possible.

After only a couple of weeks, I decided to mix things up further. "Let's go to Hawaii," I said. Some friends had recently returned from Maui, and called the town where they'd stayed, Hana, the most romantic place on earth. The fact that Hana had only a couple of small hotels, both usually booked months in advance, didn't faze me. My travel agent called around and found that one of them had just processed a cancellation. They could take us immediately. "What are the chances?" he said. In my mind, they were 100 percent. As Julia liked to say, we had our angels working overtime for us.

Hana was lush and beautiful. We spent a month there, hiking, swimming, laying, and loving. On one of the first days of our trip, we found ourselves sunning on a rock near a remote waterfall, when I noticed I'd been withdrawing somewhat from our closeness. This relationship was intense, and I was feeling it. A voice inside my head said, Just open up to her about what you're scared of.

So I did. I began to recite my doubts, my unspoken monsters.

"Love is an illusion."

"She could be anyone."

"I'm not ready for a relationship."

"Julia is crazy."

As I spoke each of them, it felt like I released it into the wind. Julia was empathetic and understanding, open to whatever I said. Rather than push me away, she held me closer. We decided that telling and hearing the truth was the key to keeping our hearts open and the love flowing. That was the beginning.

Soon, we committed our entire relationship to telling the truth. Whenever a feeling occurred to me that I might normally try to hide or ignore, I forced myself to allow it and talk about it. At first it felt like I was confessing things that would make Julia run away—but she never ran. Usually, she'd just smile and say, "Is that all?" At that, we could feel our love for each other replacing whatever fear might have existed. We called it "courageous communication," and it became vital for us. We were determined to be completely unguarded with each other about everything.

We came to see ourselves as pioneers in a new world of "conscious relationship," where we'd notice the things we said and did that enhanced our connection, while remaining aware of the things that diminished it. I trusted my intuition, and hers, viewing our connection as some sort of divine gift, as if we were being rewarded for our bravery.

AFTER TWO YEARS of intense closeness, Julia and I decided to get married, though we weren't even sure we would call the ceremony a "wedding." It would be based on commitment, of course, but the proceedings we envisioned were far from usual wedding fare. The way we saw it, our enduring promise was to each other's emotional and spiritual development. I viewed "till death do us part" as trying to control the future. What if our respective growth led us in different directions? If we were committed to *forever*, what then? Instead, Julia and I dedicated ourselves to concepts like *listen to your heart* and *trust love*. Rather than ascribe the mystical quality of our relationship to religion, Julia and I came to refer to the godly presence surrounding us as Spirit, which we viewed as a force that loves you and wants you to have love in your life.

Boy, did our wedding embrace those ideals. It happened deep in the Big Sur forest, at a spot selected by Clovis, the woman who'd given me those mushrooms way back when, with whom I'd since grown quite close. We decided the wedding should embody our highest aspirations as a couple. The purest representation of what we were trying to achieve was to strip away every layer of pretense, even our clothes. That's right, we were gonna get married in the buff, with literally nothing to hide from each other or the people around us. I think it's similar to what John and Yoko hit upon in *Two Virgins*: this is who I am, no artifice attached. We would be starting our lives over, together, naked as babies. It's the opposite of a bride going to the altar in her mother's wedding dress, which, like it or not, is a metaphorical statement about love and marriage inherited from previous generations. We didn't want that. We didn't want *anything* that bowed to the past. Your promises are to the things you believe in, to your futures together, not what you're told to promise. Julia and I wanted to reinvent the entire institution of marriage, and this was our first step.

Also, we requested that everybody in the wedding party join us in the nude. That spurred a few of our guests to drop out, including my brother Bob. As it turned out, he didn't have any reason to worry—the day was so cold and damp that we all ended up adding layers, not removing them. We were making it up as we went along anyway—I figured that Spirit would understand.

Then again, the fog and light rain made the hike into Clovis's secret glen feel especially mystical. The ceremony took place in a forty-foot clearing between stands of redwoods that sheltered us from falling raindrops, as did the large hand-made chuppah representing Julia's Jewish roots. We stood inside a circle of hand-painted silk banners I'd commissioned, which gave a medieval quality to the gathering. Each one bore images of runes and spirit animals, selected to represent the seven families in attendance. We also had a banner for the group as a whole, adorned with a painting of a unicorn, symbolizing the magical unknown.

Trying to shed societal conceptions, Julia and I put a twist on the traditional ring exchange: instead of giving them to each other, we threw them into a nearby river. Well, Julia threw hers, but I'd somehow misplaced mine in the days before the wedding, leading me to consider whether it might be a sign that our alternative ceremony wasn't quite alternative enough. To me, wedding rings symbolized ownership, which is why I wanted to throw them away. This ritual was intended to represent setting each other free, the ultimate expression of love. To that end, we'd actually exchanged our rings several weeks earlier so we might grow attached to them and imbue them with meaning. It'd be too easy to throw away something we'd only just received. There's no power in that symbol.

I guess I never quite embraced my ring the way I'd intended, which is probably why I lost it so easily. Instead, I brought along something I really did not want to part with: the first gift I'd ever received from Julia— the large, clear crystal I'd used in my Native American ceremony on the beach. Instead of throwing it into the water, I dug a hole in the dirt with my hands, placed the crystal inside, and covered it up.

We'd asked everybody to bring an object symbolizing who they were, which they wouldn't mind leaving behind as a marker of our enchanted day. Clovis brought two melted coins she'd retrieved from the ashes after her house burned down years earlier. They were the only objects that had survived. Other people brought poems and childhood photos.

I recited vows I'd written, things like, "I will tell the truth always, all ways" and "I will express my fear, but I won't let it lead," and "I promise to trust love." Julia responded with sentiments like, "I let go of the ancient chains of limitation" and "I let go of the nos, the can'ts, the won'ts, and open to Yes, Yes, Yes!" She recited a few lines from Rumi, we took a moment to absorb the emotion from those surrounding us, and like that we were married.

JULIA HAD ALWAYS wanted children, and because she didn't have any with her first husband, she was eager to get started with me. In 1993, Lukas was born in our home, and four years later we welcomed our daughter, Hana Aluna, also at home.

During our kids' early years, I was frequently on tour. Instead of seeing my work as something that came between me and my family, Julia recognized it as an essential facet of who I was. She would explain my absences to the kids by saying that "Daddy is going hunting and gathering"—a metaphor in which I headed onto the road to kill a woolly mammoth for food. "When he comes back home," she told them, "we'll all celebrate."

My coming and going became a natural part of their lives, and reminded me of my own father being gone a lot for his sales job with the jewelry company. Danny and I had joked that Dad was Willy Loman, but looking back on it I see—wait a minute—so was *I*. I may have had a glamorous rock 'n' roll lifestyle, but I was really just a salesman, going town to town to sell this year's album.

In that way, my second marriage did not diminish my career. Which is not to say it had no effect. With Julia, I began to examine myself and my place in the world in new ways, eventually falling so deep into our total-honesty lifestyle that I decided to confront the mask I'd used since high school to hide my insecurity: I shaved my beard. It was a public proclamation: *This is me, folks, like it or not.* I did not want to be blackmailed for the rest of my life by a decision I made when I was eighteen.

I liked my new look. Julia liked it. My kids? Not so much. Our newborn, Hana, would cry whenever I picked her up because she didn't know who I was—and she wasn't the only one. My fans were not shy about letting me know their feelings about my face. I kept thinking of a warning my manager gave me early on: If you start your career clean shaven you can always grow a beard later, but if you start off with a beard you'll never be able to lose it. I'm living proof.

I ended up clean faced for a few years, until I realized that by confronting my self-esteem issue head-on, I'd completely let it go. I no longer felt that I *had* to have a beard, which ultimately allowed me to grow it back. I've had it ever since. (I'd like to say that there's some profound symbolism there, but truth is, I just hate shaving.)

IN 1993, I got the devastating news that my brother Bob had passed away. He was fifty-one years old and in great shape, and collapsed on the jogging track at a high school near his home just south of Santa Cruz, felled by a massive heart attack. When his wife, Marilyn, called to tell me, I couldn't even muster a response. I went completely blank.

Bobby and Marilyn had three daughters: Maria, Katie, and Nicole. Maybe he was dealt a bad hand, given that our father had died of arterial blockage almost a decade earlier. There were differences, though. Dad was a Montana-bred meat-and-potatoes guy, while Bob was an uber-fit vegetarian. He did everything he could to overcome his genes. It wasn't enough.

Bobby had studied advertising in college, and after spending a year in the mailroom at an LA insurance company, he decided to become an optometrist. He was a zealous athlete, preceding me on the basketball team at San Gabriel Mission High, then playing four years at Cal Poly Pomona. He was so dedicated to basketball that after busting up one of his fingers in high school, he got it set to match the curvature of the ball so it wouldn't affect his dribbling. Now that's love.

Bobby and I were very different people. He was disciplined and humble, believing unerringly in the value of hard work, and was soft-spoken unless provoked. He held a lot inside, and when he blew, it was volcanic. (Once, when he was my Babe Ruth League coach, he chased an umpire up the third base line with a bat after a game-losing call.) Bobby had none of my show-biz aspirations; he was completely content being a small-town doctor. In fact, when my career began to take off, Bob worried about me ascending too quickly. He'd built his career on the principle of hard work, and he was concerned that my success might have come too easily. I still remember a quote from Cyril Connolly that Bobby fed me early in my career: "Whom the gods wish to destroy, they first call promising." I could easily have taken that as critical, but I knew he meant it as protective counsel. He was worried that I'd lose my perspective amid the Hollywood success machine, which, of course, I did from time to time.

Bobby was always a fan of my music, going so far as to ask me to write a song for the birth of his first daughter. (I wish I'd recorded that song, "You, Me and Maria," with L&M, but for some reason I never presented it to Messina.) Bob always came to my shows when I was in town, and he loved to introduce me to his friends. I never felt any jealousy from him, and there was no mistaking his pride.

In the early days of mourning after Bob passed, I kept thinking about a two-week river trip we'd taken down the Grand Canyon in 1983. It was after I'd recorded "Footloose" but before the song came out, and Bob was part of a big group I put together to run the Colorado River, some of the best rapids in North America. Nathan East was there from my band, and Don Felder was there from the Eagles. Danny was in Europe at the time, but Bobby was eager to join us. We brought a handful of guitars and ended up finding an amazing natural amphitheater along the river that made us sound like we were playing in Carnegie Hall. Of course we broke out "Watching the River Run." Bob sat next to me, front and center, singing along at the top of his lungs. I'd never seen him so happy.

Bob's role as protective big brother never shone more clearly than during that trip. A few of us decided to hike up a steep cliff-side trail to some Anasazi ruins at the top of the canyon wall. The path was formidable, and about halfway up I made the mistake of looking across the canyon's expanse. Instantly, the far wall moved in on me like a zoom-in shot in some movie. Just as suddenly, it receded into the distance, then ping-ponged back and forth like that for several terrifying moments. At first dizzy, then nauseous, I dropped onto my belly in a full-blown panic attack, and began to hyperventilate. I couldn't slow my heart down. I was convinced I was going to die on that trail, a hundred feet above the canyon floor.

It was Bobby who talked me down, figuratively and literally. With his encouragement, I started to crawl down the trail, inches at a time, Bob crouching beside me, offering quiet reassurances all the while. At first I stayed on my stomach like a giant lizard, and eventually found the nerve to scoot on my butt. After a while I was able to regain my feet, at which point Bobby reminded me that I only had to take one step at a time. That's how I made it the rest of the way down. Bobby's encouragement was so effective that when we explored a side canyon the next day, not only did I hike to the top, but I kept on going up the side of a twenty-foot waterfall. Standing on that majestic perch, I looked down toward Bobby, we exchanged knowing smiles, and I jumped into the pool below. Thanks to his help that day, I've never had a height-induced attack like that again.

Even though Danny and I shared a connection in our love of music, I always felt that Bobby understood me better. Maybe it's because we were born on the same day, seven years apart.

I flew to Aptos for Bobby's memorial service, which was held at a local gym to accommodate the crowd. Without telling me, his wife Marilyn decided to play my song "Celebrate Me Home." That hit me hard. When I'd written the song, "home" to me meant "heaven," though I'd never told that to anyone. Hearing it for the first time the way I'd intended it, let alone at my own brother's funeral, made it more impactful than I ever imagined.

Today when I face a particularly challenging task, I still tell myself, *Just one step at a time.* I think of Bobby every time.

CHAPTER 12

LEAP OF FAITH

I CAME UP AS an album-oriented musician. With Loggins & Messina and then solo through the 1980s, that's how I wanted it. Album-oriented artists tend to have lengthier careers than our singles-cutting counterparts, and my own longevity was bearing that out.

Then came "I'm Alright," "Footloose," and "Danger Zone"—soundtrack hits that never appeared on my own albums—and almost before I realized it I was a singles guy. This first became clear to me while I was putting together my first record after the runaway success of "Footloose." Some label execs gave the rough tracks a listen, and one of them literally told me: "We want another 'Footloose' but we don't hear anything that sounds like 'Footloose.'" Okay. So I dug through my idea tapes, where I'd hummed potential song snippets to build out later, and found the cassette on which I first imagined "Footloose." The concept just before it included a verse and a pretty decent groove, I thought, so I sat with it a while, came up with a chorus and some more verses, and pieced it all together. That song was "Vox Humana," the first track on my 1985 album of the same name.

It's a good song, and it became a turntable hit with lots of radio play, but for whatever reason it never sold through. The song peaked at No. 29 and the album topped out at No. 41, a startling decline from my previous effort, *High Adventure*, especially considering that "Footloose" came out between the two.

The more I thought about it, the less I liked the idea of chasing radio. "Vox Humana" was supposed to be "Footloose, Part II," just like the time, back in my L&M days, when "My Music" was supposed to be "Your Mama Don't Dance, Part II." In both cases I had little personal connection to the songs, so it's no wonder audiences reacted similarly. I had known back in the '70s that "My Music" would be a mistake, so why was I trying to repeat the formula? I like "Vox Humana," but it's a pop tune that didn't mean anything to me. When it failed to hit, what was I left with?

It didn't help that my next two hit singles, "Danger Zone" and "Meet Me Halfway," were written by Giorgio Moroder and Tom Whitlock for use in movies. Sure, I helped out considerably on both, but they were never my songs. That's when I noticed that the people around me—my manager, my agent, certainly the label—were consistently asking me to record other people's music. I guess that was the formula for my recent hits.

Well, I didn't want to continue down that rabbit hole. When people start to run your career based on you as a commodity, then you lose touch with your art. I had ideas to express, and while the "Danger Zone" paycheck was nice, it wasn't what I was after. By the end of the '80s I felt like I was barely involved in my own music anymore.

Even the first appearance of bona fide soundtrack hits on one of my own albums *Back to Avalon*—"Nobody's Fool" (from *Caddyshack 2*, which hit No. 8 and spent more than three months on the *Billboard* charts) and "Meet Me Halfway" (from *Over the Top*; No. 11, six months on the charts)—didn't help. That record peaked at No. 69, by far the worst showing of my career. It didn't even go gold.

Things got so bad that the label wanted me to do a bunch of Dianne Warren songs. Nothing against Dianne; she was a hit factory back then, and wrote a lot of great songs for movies. She just wasn't *me*. I was forty years old and tired of recording songs aimed at chart position and singles sales, sick of chasing the formula that had brought me so much success. I wanted to make the music I wanted to hear.

That's why, when I went into the studio in 1988 to begin recording what would become *Leap of Faith*, the first thing I did was tape a sign to the wall with two words on it: "Fuck radio." This thing had to stand on its own, apart from the demands of the pop charts. In my mind, anything that remotely fit the hit-single formula had no place in my studio. Fuck radio.

Part of my passion stemmed from the fact that, unlike my recent albums before it, *Leap of Faith* came from an intensely personal place. The record opens with the breakup of my first marriage and ends with the hope and excitement of what would become my second. It's a death-rebirth process, the stuff of mythology and romance. I'm writing so much about it here because I think it's the best work I've ever done, and I want to tell you why.

I went into the project feeling like my house was crumbling around me. My marriage to Eva was coming apart, and my songs reflected that. In fact, our split began with one of them. It happened just before the christening of our third child, Isabella. I wanted to write a song to perform at the ceremony, and started it the same way I did so many songs, by pacing the floor and singing freestyle into a tape recorder. What I ended up with floored me.

I did it for you and the boys
Because love should teach you joy
And not the imitation
That your mama and daddy tried to show you

That came out spontaneously, and really knocked my wind out. This wasn't a christening song; it was a divorce song, an open letter to my children to explain why, as I wrote, "Daddy doesn't live here anymore." I hadn't even let myself become aware that my marriage was so close to dissolution. My parents taught me to stick things out, to do the honorable thing just like they had done. Eva and I had three kids together who were at the front of my mind.

When I realized what I'd written, tears came to my eyes. At first I couldn't even look at the tape. When I got home I put it in a basket and tried to forget it was there. Before long, though, I realized that while I might be able to ignore the song, I couldn't ignore the feelings that led to it. The divide between me and Eva was just too big. It took about a year before I brought myself to finish it. That's when I found the tape and flew to Canada to meet David Foster. When we sat down at his piano and went through it, his first question was, "Is this happening to you?"

It was all still raw and I was not ready to talk about it, so I lied and said it was fictional. I couldn't bring myself to be that revealing. Rather than using the names of my kids, I even created a character named Amanda in the lyrics to carry the burden.

We finished the song in one night. It's called "The Real Thing," and it was only the beginning of what was to come on *Leap of Faith*. By the time the record came out, I was on my way to being divorced.

Of course, nothing is ever so concrete. The decision to leave your partner, the mother of your children, is fraught in so many ways. In those big moments, we're often of two minds: part of us wants to hold on to the status quo, and part of us wants to blow it all up. At least that's the way it was for me. The song "Now or Never," for example, is about my confusion around our split, wondering if we shouldn't try harder to make it work: more therapy, more talking. Eva and I had been to years' worth of couples counseling by that point, and had long since stopped finding new ways to communicate with each other. At some point, you have to face reality. That reckoning is all over *Leap of Faith*.

Sometimes I feel like my songs talk to me, trying to get my attention. *Leap of Faith* was very much that kind of record. I intimately understood the impetus behind every track. At one point, a reporter asked me about the album in contrast to my soundtrack work, and I told him I was scoring the movie of my life.

I like that answer.

BEFORE THE TRUCK got stolen with all of my gear and master tapes while heading from Los Angeles to Santa Barbara—the story I tell at the beginning of this book—a lot had happened. I began recording *Leap of Faith* in Hollywood with producer David Kirshenbaum. I'd never worked with him before, but he was coming off of notable production stints with Tracy Chapman and Joe Jackson, and I really liked what he'd done. I hired him based on his track record and one interview. It didn't take long for me to question my decision.

In the studio, David was distracted and remote. It seemed like he spent most of his time inputting recipes from a binder into a computer. Hell, if he'd gone on to write a cookbook, at least there'd be an explanation, but instead I felt like I was in charge of the whole process. After maybe a month, I told David it wasn't working out. Letting him go actually didn't change much since I was producing the record myself anyway. Tommy Dowd had once kicked me out of my own studio because I had too many ideas. This time, those ideas were running the show.

Musically, *Leap of Faith* is a really rhythmic record. Take the song "If You Believe," which I wrote as a gospel tune and cut with Herman Matthews on the drums. Herman plays amazing backside R&B grooves, and gave me an Al Green–type thing that worked really well. Every time the chorus kicked in, though, I felt let down, and tried hard to figure out why that was. When I looked at the Pro Tools waveform for the drum parts, I saw that Herman's backbeats were *really* far behind the two and the four. That's a feature, not a bug—one of the things that makes Herman such a great drummer. He calls that aspect of his groove "the hump," and it was perfect for the song's verses, but not so much for the choruses. For those, I wanted a drummer who hit hard and kept the backbeats on the nose.

John Robinson, the drummer from Rufus and Chaka Khan, was one of David Foster's main guys—a powerful player with big, loud grooves. I had him come in and lay down the choruses. It gives "If You Believe" a completely different vibe, driving forward in a classic-rock way. Just like that, the song opened up. So that's what I used on the record: Herman on the verses, and J.R. on the choruses. It worked amazingly well.

As we progressed through the album, I paid close attention to the outside stuff I was listening to—in particular, the way some Windham Hill artists, as well as pianists like Michael Whalen and Benjamin Dowling, would repeat segments over and over again, creating a hypnotic, trance-like effect before the song gradually evolved into something different. The secret was in the space they used, I thought; not a one of those tunes was limited to a sub-four-minute runtime to fit into a pop radio format. I wanted some of that.

In "Too Early for the Sun," for example, the B-section after the first verse—"I've never been so afraid that love is just a dream / And darlin' I'll awake and you'll be gone"—is such a mesmerizing cycle that I decided to hang out there for a while. Instead of limiting it to the usual four bars, that section runs twelve bars the first time through, and even longer on the next pass. I asked Mavis Staples to sing on it with me, and we spent three hours in the studio experimenting with her vocal parts. When we hit that B-section the second time, we devoted extra space to let Mavis's husky voice take the song to an even more soulful place.

When Columbia was looking for a fourth single, that's the song Bobby Colomby suggested. It was more than eight minutes long, though, so he requested that I edit it to a radio-friendly length. I tried, really, but couldn't find a way to shorten it and maintain the song's integrity, so I turned him down. Maybe I should have just recut it, but I was touring by then and didn't have time to go back to the studio. Besides, breaking out of the old song form is where I was at emotionally and spiritually at that stage of my life. Reinventing my music was an extension of reinventing myself, and it felt good not to be trapped by any parameters. It felt like rebirth.

THE MOST POPULAR TRACK from *Leap of Faith*, not to mention my own favorite song, is "Conviction of the Heart." I wrote the song with guitarist Guy Thomas, who came up with the melody and the first two verses. It was about a man's feeling of disconnection from the world around him, the key sentiment being "I've never given love / With any conviction of the heart."

The night after Guy and I wrote the third verse together, the chorus came to me in a dream: "One with the earth / One with the sky / One with everything in life." The paradox in the lyrics was underscored by how different they and the melody were from the song we'd started the day before, but I knew it all belonged together. When Guy and I connected the pieces, it was like magic—the chorus took the song to an emotional climax we didn't even know was missing. It gave the song and its lead character a sense of homecoming. It was more than a chorus. It was anthemic.

It took me years to figure out how those segments connected, but I finally did.

"Conviction of the Heart" is about the main character's realization that he's detached from himself and everything around him. What came through in my dream was that until you achieve connectedness with the rest of the world, you are alone, and in that aloneness you suffer. That's the chorus: "One with the earth, one with everything in life." It's like a ceremony, a prayer. The character evolves past the false belief that he is alone, and embraces his kinship with the rest of the planet.

Ultimately, "Conviction of the Heart" is a riddle, asking whether we care enough to make the changes necessary for the earth to survive. It's the only song I've ever written in which I point my finger so prominently outward.

I originally cut the song in a studio on Maui, with Guy and Steve Wood on keyboards. We didn't use a click track because I wanted the song to breathe, to move in and out of tempo according to the emotion of the moment. I sang the lead vocal live. The more I listened to it, though, the more I realized the tune needed drums. Trouble was, the rhythm was so varied and organic that it was almost impossible for a drummer to play along. So back home I recut the song entirely with local musicians, every part laid down completely in time. Everything was perfect. The new version glistened . . . which itself became a problem.

We'd polished the emotion right out of it. So I tossed the new take, and reconsidered the Maui version. The more I thought about it, the more I realized there was one drummer who might be able to handle the task. Tris Imboden had been a full-time member of my band for more than a decade until he left to join the group Chicago, and knew my tempo quirks better than anyone. I sent him the Maui rough track, and about a week later he showed up at my LA studio, sat down at his kit, and matched all of the speed-ups and slow-downs exactly as we'd played them, overdubbing to a track with no time signature at all *on his first try*. Tris understood inherently where I wanted to lean forward and where I wanted to lay back. I thought it was impossible, and he made it look easy.

Once I decided to keep the original version, I began to overdub. I wanted a unique sound, so for the first verse we mic'd the holes of a hollow-body electric guitar, which we ran through a small amp in the corner of the room with barely any volume. The combination of the two sounds—acoustic strings and faint amplification—is tight and percussive, just what I was looking for.

Actually, finding sounds we'd never heard before quickly became a hallmark of the project, eventually leading my engineer, Terry Nelson, to coin the motto "Take more time! Spend more money!"

Was he ever right. We used our budget to discover sounds from top-flight musicians like drummer Herman Matthews, sax player Marc Russo, and guitarists David Lindley and Guy Thomas. We were burning through my advance, but wasn't that what it was for? I've always considered my advances like subsidies to acquire raw materials—the canvas and colors—for my art. Out of everything I'd ever recorded, this was the album I *had* to make. I was going to do it right.

In 1995, I performed "Conviction of the Heart" on Earth Day at the National Mall in Washington, DC, where Al Gore called it "the unofficial anthem of the environmental movement." I loved that, because to me the environmental movement is actually a spiritual movement viewed through a political lens. Connectedness to the earth is the basis for our caring. Why should you give a shit about a polar bear or a rainforest somewhere far away? Compassion helps, and so does empathy, but until you firmly understand that *your* survival depends on *their* survival, you can't commit yourself to the environmental movement with any sort of conviction.

There's one more story about "Conviction of the Heart," though it didn't play out until a couple of years later. It started when Guy Thomas called me up with a warning. He'd just heard the new single from Garth Brooks, "Standing Outside the Fire," which became a massive hit, reaching No. 3 on *Billboard*'s country charts. The album it appeared on had already sold five million copies.

"I think we've been ripped off," he said.

I tracked down the song and gave it a listen. Damn if Guy wasn't right. The song seemed nearly identical to "Conviction of the Heart."

Guy wanted to sue Garth, but I took a different path. I figured that if I talked to him first and he realized our song had been so influential for him, we could reach an understanding without need for lawyers. So I gave him a call. When I mentioned his song's similarity to my own, his response was not what I expected.

Garth told me that "Standing Outside the Fire" was definitely influenced by "Conviction of the Heart," that he loved my song, that I did a great job, and that he'd wanted to write a song just like it.

I guess he expected a response along the lines of, "Well, thank you, I'm flattered." Though he might disagree, what I'd heard was an admission.

"I guess that makes me an invisible collaborator on your song, right?" I said. "It's like we were there, singing those lines to you." I suggested he consider giving a percentage to Guy and me.

Garth didn't like that idea at all. His tone grew steely and defensive. He told me that he wasn't one to cut his song into little pieces, and that he sure wasn't going to split up "Standing Outside the Fire."

I tried reason. "You just said that your song was influenced by mine," I said. "Some of your melodic lines are clearly from my song."

That was about as far as the conversation went. Garth said his lawyer would handle matters from there. Okay. So Guy and I sued him for $5 million.

It took about two years for the case to go to trial. We listed Guy as the plaintiff, because I didn't want the press to get hold of the fact that Kenny Loggins was suing Garth Brooks. That meant it was Guy in court, not me. Garth actually showed up in the courtroom with an acoustic guitar, ready to play the song live for the judge. Before he could, though—before the proceeding even got underway—the judge called Guy and Garth into his chambers. When they emerged, Garth was ready to settle.

What was said in that room is not part of the public record, but the key factor is intent. If a songwriter inadvertently comes up with something similar to somebody else's work, he or she would likely be found innocent of theft. That's not what happened here. According to Guy, the judge said something along the lines of, "Garth, you don't want to walk into that courtroom," and then gave him a list of reasons why it might not end well for him. The agreement we reached stipulated that we could not disclose the specifics of the deal, although Garth had to admit to settling the suit. Afterward, he said publicly something like "Sometimes you just have to pay to get people off of your back." I let that one go. I haven't seen him since.

Honestly, I didn't expect we'd get as far as we did. I mean, money and power have considerable sway, and the questions about how much of my song was in his, or how much it just served as an influence, and how much any of that is worth are all complicated issues. Lord knows that I wear my own influences on my sleeve, and have talked about many of them at length. I don't hide having taken the opening riff of "Footloose" from "Devil with a Blue Dress." Then again, you can't copyright a two-chord progression.

Rock 'n' roll is a derivative, ever-evolving art form, with one song leading organically to another. Even the Beatles had their early rock influences, but they never outright stole other writers' melodies. There's a big difference between influence and plagiarism.

THE SIXTH TRACK on *Leap of Faith*, the ballad "I Would Do Anything," features Sheryl Crow singing a boy-girl duet with me. That seems like a big deal in retrospect—Sheryl has since won nine Grammys and sold tens of millions of albums—but at the time she was just an LA studio vocalist with a soulful, Bonnie Raitt kind of quality. I was impressed by the versatility of her voice, and ended up directing her to sing with a sweet innocence, like Kate Bush did on Peter Gabriel's "Don't Give Up." It might be the only time you'll hear Sheryl sound like that: quiet, accessible, and extremely vulnerable. I wanted us to sound like two people who had surrendered control in their love affair, which is how I was feeling with Julia. I wanted it to be an extremely honest song, admitting fear while expressing love. It worked so well that a few of my friends and even my kids asked if the female voice was Julia. It was that intimate.

Early on, Bobby Colomby and Terry Nelson believed "I Would Do Anything" had hit potential, and even considered it as the album's first single. When I listened to it, though, it felt too . . . normal. I thought the voices, mine and Sheryl's, got lost amid the instrumentation when they should have been the essence of the song, so I stripped away the drums and gave it a simpler, almost acoustic approach. Now I could *feel* the words as they were sung. Instantly, the tune felt courageous and raw. Of course, it no longer sounded like a hit single (sure enough, it was never released that way), but it was exactly the song I wanted to play for my new lover. Perfect.

I'D LONG ADMIRED the unique guitar style of Will Ackerman, the founder of Windham Hill Records, and thought his sound would be ideal for *Leap of Faith*. Before going into the studio I traveled to Kauai to meet with him. As the scion of an alternative label focusing on instrumental acoustic music—stuff that would come to be known as New Age—he was understandably wary of working with the dude from "Danger Zone." Will had never collaborated with somebody in the pop world before, and he didn't even pick up a guitar when we met at his house in Hanalei. I explained the spirit of the record I was making—which had everything to do with the transformation in my life and nothing to do with the *Billboard* charts—and he said he would think about it. It wasn't until after I'd left that he agreed to give it a shot.

A month later we met again, this time at his other home in Mill Valley, just across the Golden Gate Bridge from San Francisco. There, we wrote two songs together: "My Father's House" and the melody for "Will of the Wind." When it came time to record the latter, I improvised lyrics live while Will played. What you hear on the record is the first or second take of the song. The entire process flowed just that smoothly.

Every song on the album has stories like that. I won't get into them all here, but breaking down the title track might help illustrate the level of attention we embraced. "Leap of Faith" was one of the first songs we recorded, and on the initial master it was just me, guitarist Guy Thomas, and Randy Jackson on bass. (Randy would eventually become my A&R guy with Columbia, starting with my very next album.)

We were recording in Hollywood, and Julia recommended I rent a small apartment in Santa Monica to save me the three-hour round-trip drive from Santa Barbara each day. We didn't have kids yet, so it made a ton of sense. I didn't know at the time I'd be using that apartment five days a week for a full year.

My first night there I woke at sunrise from a dream of primal music, like the score to some ancient tribal ritual. I sang what I remembered into my tape recorder—vocal versions of a kalimba groove, a fretless bassline, a throng of drums, and synths, all playing counterpoint lines to each other. Then I raced to the studio to add all of those ideas to our master recording. They were in direct contrast to the mellow R&B vibe of the stuff we'd recorded the previous day, and they changed everything. *This* was the intention of the song, the soundtrack to the ceremony in which the lead character takes his leap of faith.

At the time, I was deeply influenced by Peter Gabriel's then-recent explorations into African music; his *Last Temptation* album was a touchstone for me when it came to stepping outside the pop form. Terry and I spent days recording percussion for "Leap of Faith," calling in Bill Summers and Munyungo Jackson, two of the top session players in LA, who brought my dream to life with rhythm instruments like okonkolo, batá, and udu. I did my part, too. Returning to the studio for an evening session after dinner one night, Terry and I found the entrance to the studio blocked by a metal shopping cart half filled with empty booze bottles. I was about to clear it out of the way when inspiration hit. We dragged it into the studio, and Terry set up mics all around the room, including a couple thirty feet off the ground, way up in the corners. Then I hit that thing with a baseball bat like it was some sort of piñata, creating a backbeat like we'd never heard before, an exploding sound with a cool, natural delay . . . and an interesting odor.

I also played a "buddy case"—a term we made up for the huge equipment containers used to transport instruments—by thumping it with my hands for a mega kick-drum sound.

Terry and I were so devoted to rhythm that we even went out to the studio's gravel parking lot and recorded me walking toward him, then manipulated the sound so it started off as a normal gait and gradually became the song's groove. I thought it would be a mysterious way to catch the listener's attention.

Later I brought in Hiram Bullock (more time! more money!), the young guitar master I'd met on the studio steps in New York while recording *Celebrate Me Home*. Something about this project made me embrace my various influences from over the years, and Hiram was certainly that. Knowing he was a strong singer, I set up a microphone and had him sing at the same time he played his solo. Over the years, I've discovered that technique leads jazz guitarists to play simpler and more melodically, and Hiram's solo on "Leap" is a great example of that. It's composited from three takes, though you'd swear it's one piece because it flows so beautifully.

You can also hear Smokey Robinson toward the end of the tune, trading scats with me as the song fades out. He happened to be in LA for a gig, and accepted my invitation to come by the studio. Well, Smokey nailed it, but his voice is so unique that I had to mix it low because it was diverting attention from the hypnotic spell of the song. In that way, "Leap of Faith" was just like the rest of the record. I was so deep into my new love affair, so under the influence of Julia, that I could feel every note viscerally, which gives the record a distinctly sensual quality.

I got so invested in leaving the traditional song form that I decided to not even sing the second chorus of "Leap," leaving a blank space where the vocals would have gone, and letting the track carry the groove. Bobby Colomby called the decision brave—which might have been code for "crazy"—for a song that could have been radio friendly if we'd wanted it to be. But I was totally focused on the vibe, the emotional effect of the music, and felt that surprising listeners with unusual choices would keep them off balance and more willing to go on my ride with me.

Did I sabotage my commerciality with decisions like that? Possibly, but that wasn't the point. By 1990, commercial radio had become utterly predictable. When Bobby first signed on as my A&R man, he said something that stuck with me: "If you want to stand out from the crowd, be willing to give listeners something they haven't heard yet. Don't copy. Be the innovator, and if you hit, you own that sound. Then everyone else is imitating you." When I thought about the albums I loved, the magic always came down to the artist's vision. I hadn't always felt that way about my own records, but I did now. I wanted to be courageous, and felt that such courage would be rewarded. Ultimately, it was.

I consider *Leap of Faith* to be my best work because of the continuity of its emotion. It's certainly the album to which I am most connected. The people who "get" it, whose devotion to the record rivals my own, are like a community unto themselves. I call them the "Leapers." If you're among their ranks, you know who you are. It's a bit of an exclusive club, like a secret society but without the handshake.

Say it with me now: "Fuck radio."

CHAPTER 13

"POOH," PART II

IN THE WAKE of *Leap of Faith* I did a couple of noteworthy gigs. One of them helped usher a president into the White House.

It was early 1993, and Bill Clinton had just been elected. My friend David Pack, who I'd met when he was Michael McDonald's lead guitarist, had been hired by the Democratic National Committee as musical director for the Arkansas Ball, the biggest of several parties being held around Washington, DC, on Inauguration Day. He asked me to be a headliner. I'd voted for Clinton, so it was an honor and an obvious thrill to accept. David put together an all-star band of his dozen favorite studio players, musicians like Nathan East and Greg Phillinganes. We were going to perform four songs, and had one rehearsal the night before the gala to get them down. I was on tour, though, and would arrive in town on the day of the event, so I sent over some live recordings for the band to study.

With twelve thousand people attending, the ball was held at the Washington Convention Center. I was onstage when the newly elected president made his entrance more or less right next to me. That much I'd been prepped for. What I did not expect was for him to pick up a saxophone almost immediately and play along on "Your Mama Don't Dance." ("What key are we in?" he asked Pack. "B-flat, Mr. President," David said. And we were off.) I must admit, jamming on "Mama" with the president of the United States was not something I ever anticipated would end up on my résumé. I'm happy to report that POTUS handled his horn with aplomb.

After Bill put down the sax, he and Hillary had their first dance to "Biggest Part of Me" by Pack's band, Ambrosia, which led directly into a medley with "Celebrate Me Home." As soon as my song started, the first couple abruptly stopped dancing, waved to the crowd, and descended from the stage to shake some hands. I recognize that the happy couple would likely have stopped dancing anyway—they had people to meet and multiple balls to attend—but I was shocked when our incredible drummer, Steve Ferrone, started playing my 6/8, waltz-time song in 4/4. Meanwhile, other members of the band were playing it in 3/4, turning it from a waltz into a car crash. I don't know how anyone could dance to that. I desperately signaled Steve to change the timing, but couldn't get my point across. He knew something was wrong; I could see the panic in his eyes. It's not like Steve didn't have the chops; he's really a great drummer. He just started in on the wrong time signature on a song we clearly hadn't rehearsed enough.

I think that rhythm snafu is what led me to gradually believe the Clintons stopped dancing because my song was so messed up. In fact, I've talked over and over again in interviews about how they just bailed on "Celebrate," with the punchline being that Bill was enough of a musician to recognize a disaster when he saw one. When I finally saw the clip many years later, though, I finally realized the song had nothing to do with their decision. So I forgive you, Steve, for my imagined tale of woe.

MY OTHER MAJOR gig in the wake of *Leap of Faith* took place in Santa Cruz. My manager, Denzyl Feigelson, hit upon the idea of doing an unplugged concert to prominently showcase *Leap of Faith*.

He sold PBS on the idea of filming and broadcasting it. I thought performing in the redwood forests of Santa Cruz would be a good twist. My brother Bobby had lived up there, and I'd always been astounded by the region's natural beauty.

As it turned out, finding the glen of my dreams was not easy. I needed a place that could hold hundreds of people, with parking and facilities, accessible enough to build a stage and bring in generators. Even with PBS money behind us, that was an expensive proposition. I flew up to Santa Cruz to scout locations with the producer, the director, and Denzyl, but the more we looked at potential sites, the less likely it seemed that such a place existed. One site had perfect geography but was too remote to truck in our gear. Another had great access but didn't feel like it was in the woods.

The more we searched, the more frustrated we became. We spent a day wandering around the gorgeous forests above UC Santa Cruz, crossing off one possibility after another. We were trudging back to our rental car in defeat when it finally happened. After walking through a stand of pine trees, we accidentally found ourselves in the university's outdoor Shakespearean theater. It was perfect: a small outdoor stage built right into a gorgeous redwood grove, just like I'd imagined. We immediately booked it for three days that summer.

Still bolstered by the magic of *Leap of Faith*, I decided this would be no ordinary show. I wanted the concert to be acoustic and unplugged, which would let me get at the album's songs from a new perspective. For me, part of making the event special included a special audience, and I hit upon the idea of inviting each attendee individually. With PBS funding, I didn't need tickets as a source of revenue, so I gave away every spot for free— with a catch. I ran a notice in the *Santa Cruz Sentinel* soliciting people to fax in leap-of-faith stories from their own lives. I wanted my audience to connect on the deepest level. We had five hundred tickets to distribute, and the response was overwhelming. I hired a couple of college kids to go through all the submissions, and they showed me anything they thought was cool. I have to say, those letters were amazing, from real people with real stories. That audience became the first of my legion of "Leapers."

Because we were taping the show for TV broadcast, we ended up doing two shows on back-to-back days, and two takes of each song, between which the production team would change camera setups (which made the final cut seem like they had twice as many lenses). This gave us five to ten minutes of downtime between songs, so while they messed with the video equipment I sent my mic into the audience and people shared their leap-of-faith accounts. One guy had ridden his bike across the country after suffering a traumatic brain injury to establish a national bike lane. Another woman told about her bravery in escaping an abusive relationship. The stories were emotional, and so inspirational. Julia and our first baby, Luke, were in the audience, as were members of Bob's family. To the chagrin of my PBS producer, I even shared some of the spiritual and psychological concepts I'd been exploring with Julia. The show was unlike anything I'd done or seen.

Since we were playing acoustically, I had to replicate my songs without synthesizers, which wasn't easy. I rearranged a lot of them, and assembled a fourteen-man band, many members of which played multiple instruments, plus a ten-person choir, plus another seven-person choir from a local Baptist church to fill out the sound. (The only instrument I hedged on was our pump organ, which is such an unreliable and musically inconsistent instrument that I used a sample on a synth hidden inside the body of an actual pump organ.)

Musically, I lined up a bunch of surprises. I had five or six drummers march in from the trees playing the intro of "I'm Alright." One of them was Steve Croes, a Los Angeles session man whose song "March of the Red Beans" was a longtime zydeco favorite of mine. I asked whether he might give "I'm Alright" a similar vibe, and he did—which included calling in Louisiana slide-guitar legend Sonny Landreth for some authentic Cajun flavor. Steve also turned me on to many of the amazing musicians in what would be the largest, most talented band I've ever worked with live, including Chicago-based harmonica wizard Howard Levy and Ed Mann on vibes.

I dueted with Michael McDonald on "What a Fool Believes," and didn't even introduce him—he just walked onstage singing the first bridge:

"She had a place in his life . . ." The audience went nuts. Shanice, who'd recently scored a couple of massive R&B hits, handled female vocals on "I Would Do Anything" and "Love Will Follow."

My regular drummer, Herman Matthews, wasn't available because he'd taken a gig with Tower of Power, so I brought in Alvino Bennett, one of LA's great session guys. Trouble was, because I wanted this to be a unique reinvention of my music, I was changing arrangements on the fly during rehearsals, and I threw a lot of ideas at him in a very short period of time. Anyone who's performed with me knows I'm exacting when it comes to my ideas, but Alvino was not one for note-taking and kept forgetting my instructions. We rehearsed for about two weeks, and he never seemed to play what I'd asked him to play the day before, approaching my directions as if they were arbitrary. I guess he figured I would forget about them overnight. Eventually, I couldn't wait any longer for him to catch up with the band. About a week before the show, I learned that Herman would be returning from his Tower of Power gig on the same day as the first redwoods concert. So I flew him directly to Santa Cruz to sit in on four songs that Alvino never quite mastered, which Herman already knew inside and out because I maintained the regular show arrangements on them.

Whether Alvino was upset that I brought in a ringer was secondary; I wanted his focus on the new arrangements, which Herman hadn't seen. Herman's presence actually kept Alvino from being overwhelmed. I also made sure that Alvino wrote down the new parts, and he ended up crushing on them. In fact, I ran into him a few years later, when he was drumming for Dave Mason, and he pulled me aside for a chat. "Man, working with you was the most educational thing in my career," he told me. "That's where I learned how to take notes and rehearse from them." I couldn't help but smile.

Ultimately, all that preparation for a pair of performances was a great experience. The first night ended up being something of a dress rehearsal, because almost everything we took for the recording, which in addition to the PBS special was released as my *Outside: From the Redwoods* album, came from the second show, which was off the charts. It was a thrill to work with the band, the audience was truly special, and the location was beyond compare. The program was nominated for an Emmy, and is easily my favorite recorded television performance.

LEAP OF FAITH was so successful, and Don Ienner loved it so much, that he wanted me to make another album just like it. That would have been great, commercially speaking. Instead, I made a children's record.

I was searching for ideas of what I might do next when Julia got pregnant. I've painted a picture of myself as a somewhat absent father, but my times at home between tours are the source of my most precious memories. When my third child, Bella, was a baby, it was my job to put her to bed at night. I even bought a rocking chair to make it official. While giving her a bottle I'd sing whatever came to mind, and the more we rocked the more songs I ended up singing. These were adult songs that worked perfectly as lullabies, like John Lennon's "Love," "St. Judy's Comet" by Paul Simon, and "The Last Unicorn" by Jimmy Webb. Hmmm, I thought one night, Why doesn't someone make a children's record with songs like these, that parents can love, too?

I revisited those thoughts when Julia was pregnant with Luke. (It might have started with the realization that, oh shit, I'm going to have to listen to Barney a zillion more times.) Then it hit me. The person to make that children's record should be *me*. I already had the repertoire, plus, of course, my own song about Winnie-the-Pooh. Why hadn't I thought of this before?

I'd come up with "House at Pooh Corner" as an eighteen-year-old, and so many things had changed since then. If I was going to make this record, I wanted to write something that spoke to my experience as a parent, so I wrote a new third verse:

It's hard to explain
How a few precious things
Seem to follow throughout all our lives.
After all's said and done
I was watching my son
Sleeping there with my bear by his side.
So I tucked him in, kissed him
And as I was goin'
I'd swear that old bear whispered
"Boy, welcome home."

I called the new version "Return to Pooh Corner."

Coming out with a children's record in the middle of the most creatively fertile period of my career was irregular, to say the least, but my romance with Julia had inspired me to question old beliefs and be more courageous in my artistic expression. I realized that I had to pursue this. So I told Ienner what I envisioned for my follow-up to *Leap of Faith*.

He hated the idea. Don said a children's record would be the end of my career, and if I insisted on making it then Columbia would not be involved. I'd have to pause my contract with the label, he said, and get it released on my own. Luckily, I didn't have to look far.

Columbia's parent company, the CBS Records Group, had been purchased by Sony in 1988. As it happened, Sony had a kids-centric label called Sony Wonder. I knew one of the A&R people there, Becky Mancuso-Winding, who'd been the music supervisor for *Footloose*. It turns out that Becky was on precisely the same page as me: she'd been spearheading a collection of special releases called the Family Artist Series—albums geared toward parents and children alike—which would one day include Johnny Cash, Tony Bennett, John Denver, and Keb' Mo'. Mine was the first album of the bunch. Since I saw my new "Pooh" track as the cornerstone to the album, I called my new CD *Return to Pooh Corner* as well.

At first I thought I'd just pick out the material and sing it. In that way I was in alignment with Ienner, viewing this less as a major project than as a side trip. I got David Pack, who I'd just worked with at the Clinton inaugural ball, to co-produce with me. The more I got into arranging the songs, however, the more I began to realize this was something special, a quality record for a niche that didn't yet exist. David Crosby and Graham Nash came in to sing on an old folk tune called "All the Pretty Little Ponies," for which I wrote a bridge and a new verse. I revisited the song I'd written for my second son, "Cody's Song," which had first appeared on *Leap of Faith*, simplifying it by removing orchestration in favor of a stripped-down approach. I even got Gene Wilder to recreate some of his Willy Wonka dialog for "Pure Imagination." The deeper we got into it, the clearer it was that this album was killer. It had all the production value of my Columbia records, only with much simpler arrangements, relying more on acoustic instruments like mandolin, harmonica, and accordion and less on synths and strings. Becky loved it.

"House at Pooh Corner" had never been released as a single for L&M, so we made my remake the first single. It spent fourteen weeks on the *Billboard* Adult Contemporary singles chart.

When the album came out, I went to New York for promotion and was exuberantly received by all the radio and TV folks I met. They were really excited to talk about why I made *Return*, how I recorded it, and why I selected those particular songs. I hadn't felt that kind of warm, fuzzy embrace for any of my previous records. The response was so overwhelming, in fact, that I called Becky from the back of the limo that was ferrying me from station to station.

"In your wildest dreams, what do you think this record can sell?" I asked.

Becky thought for a moment and said, "Well, we're shipping fifty thousand, but I think we might be able to do a hundred thousand." A big smile crossed my face.

"Becky, go back to bed and dream a bigger dream," I said. "I think we have a million seller here, maybe the biggest album of my career."

Well, *Return to Pooh Corner* did go platinum, marking one million sales. And, yeah, it's my best-selling record ever. Sorry, Donnie.

Since that time, kids' music has taken on an increasingly prominent position in my catalog. Six years later I released a follow-up, *More Songs from Pooh Corner*, featuring a duet with Olivia Newton-John on Paul Williams's "Flying Dreams," Alison Krauss on the Lennon-McCartney song "Goodnight," and the return of my old pal from L&M, Jon Clarke, on a variety of woodwinds and horns. This time I included a song for my daughter called "Hana Aluna Lullaby," which I wrote with Barry Flanagan, half of a Hawaiian duo called Hapa. (I had sung backup on one of their songs, "Ku'u Lei Awapuhi," which went to No. 1 on the Hawaiian charts.)

Just because I made a follow-up to *Return to Pooh Corner*, of course, doesn't mean it sold nearly as well. About a week after I delivered *More Songs* to Becky, Sony Wonder was sold to Nickelodeon. It was part of a larger strategy, as Nickelodeon dropped its record division and transitioned strictly to video, completely orphaning my brand new release, which came out almost entirely without promotion. It was like it saw the light of day from inside a coffin, even though I'd just had a million-selling children's record.

Still, the idea of my making children's records remained popular. In 2009, I was contacted by the new president of Walt Disney Records, David Agnew, about doing something similar for them. "I put my daughter to bed every night with *Return to Pooh Corner*," he said. "I think it's brilliant, and I'd love for you to make something like it for Disney." The catch, he said, was that he wanted an up-tempo record, not lullabies. I had to think on that one. Lullabies are easy lifting compared to dance music that'd satisfy a cross-generational audience. The more I thought about it, though, the more I recognized the abundance of pop songs that could work really well for young children, like Paul McCartney's "All Together Now" from *Yellow Submarine* and Dave Mason's "You Can All Join In" from Traffic's second album. Kids would love those songs, I thought, and parents would be grabbed by the nostalgia factor.

I recorded those two—Mason joined me in the studio for his tune—for the album I'd call *All Join In*, plus songs like Randy Newman's "You've Got a Friend in Me" (for which we mic'd a tap dancer's feet for the percussion) and the old Del-Vikings hit "Come Go with Me" (which features eleven-year-old Hana and some of her friends singing backup). I also recorded Hana jumping rope to serve as percussion on the Feist song, "1234."

I reunited with Jimmy Messina (as well as John McEuen, the banjo player from the Nitty Gritty Dirt Band) on the Beatles song "Two of Us." I also revisited a song I'd written as a teenager for my dog Moose. Once called "Moose Is a Good Dog," it was recast as "Moose 'n' Me" for *All Join In*. Cody sings lead on that one.

I thought the album was great, but one thing neither Agnew nor I had counted on was that I was at an in-between age in my life: young parents hadn't grown up with my music, and my ingrained fan base wasn't yet at grandparent age. We did a test release on QVC, for which I went into their TV studio in West Chester, Pennsylvania, and played a couple of songs with my band (and also stood around patiently while they peddled blouses and birdfeeders). It was a viable strategy at the time, with musicians like James Taylor and Neil Diamond making similar forays. I don't know how it went for them, but it was a disaster for me. Not only did it fail to impact sales, but the response was so dispiriting that Disney postponed the album's release.

That was significant, because before it came out the company cleaned house of many of its execs, including my champion, David Agnew. None of the new guard seemed interested in my album; it quietly came out in 2009 and was left to wither on the vine. Finally, in about 2015, I was given back the masters. *All Join In* is now available on my website.

The fact that *All Join In* failed to reach the masses was actually not nearly as problematic for me as the fact that *Return to Pooh Corner* sold like gangbusters all those years earlier. Don Ienner missed out on what's now north of two million copies sold because he wanted me to keep writing white R&B, and once I was ready to return to pop songs I met a lot of resistance from him. I suspect he was pissed at me for not doing what he wanted me to do initially, and then being so successful at it. Of course, by the time I released my next record, *The Unimaginable Life*—which I saw as *Leap of Faith, Part II*—it was six years later and a lot had changed in radio and at Columbia. For one thing, Bobby Colomby had departed.

I was now without a champion at the label. I felt stranded and alone.

LEAP OF FAITH had been inspired by falling in love. My next adult-oriented record was about *being* in love. *The Unimaginable Life* emerged from my journaling during my early days with Julia. We were in Hawaii when we started to truly fall for each other, and there was a magical quality to everything that happened. I thought it would make an interesting book someday, and started taking notes. Eventually, it did become a book. And an album.

The idea for the book was to combine my journal notes with Julia's to document our combined experience of what we were learning about love and relationship. To be completely transparent with a partner was an entirely new way of being for me. This kind of emotional freedom had been unimaginable to me previously, which is where the title came from. Julia went along with the idea because she trusted my vision.

People misjudged the book as if I was preaching about how great our love affair was, but it wasn't *I'm Okay and You're Not*. I always saw the book as a simple love story, which is reflected in its subtitle, *Lessons Learned on the Path of Love*. It's about how to be present and transparent in relationship, which I'd never been. I really thought (extremely naively, I must admit) that I'd discovered the keys out of hell, and was eager to share them. I thought people would go, "Wow, I never thought of that, thank you." I never realized they wouldn't want a new perspective.

To me, the book is an exploration of "conscious relationship" in which you become aware of your motives and who you are, a relationship where you hide no part of yourself because there's nothing to hide. The advantage to Julia having been my therapist is that over our years of counseling, I'd already revealed the facets of my personality that I considered shameful—never once thinking that we'd one day be in a romantic relationship—and the fact that she loved me anyway was liberating. I no longer needed to feel that some part of me was unlovable. As I wrote in my song "The Art of Letting Go," "Life is nothing without love / Love is nothing without freedom." I'd discovered during my marriage to Eva that the more secrets I held from a partner, the more distance I created, so being completely transparent with Julia allowed my heart to stay open. We were totally honest with each other, and had deep communication all of the time.

When it came to the music, *The Unimaginable Life* album didn't have the same iconic message of death and rebirth that so fueled *Leap of Faith*. The music I was writing leaned even more heavily toward R&B, and I wanted a producer who could enhance that. That's why I brought in John Barnes, a highly respected synclavier/synth player, who I'd worked with on *Leap*, to guide me. Hoping that proximity would help our collaboration, I invited him to live in my guest house while we developed each song.

At least that's what I expected would happen. Instead, John used up a lot of my initial budget, while offering what I felt was almost no creative input. I was hoping he would at least come up with some grooves and maybe basic keyboard sounds to get us started, but he came up with very little for months on end. I'd go out to the guest house to check on his progress, and he rarely had anything ready. All I recall were some skeletal arrangements and the occasional drum part. It became clear to me that he was either in a dry spot creatively or he just wasn't into it.

When we went into the studio, I wasn't happy with the sounds we got. John kept saying, "We'll fix it later," which was not a way I'd ever worked, and was difficult for me to believe. This was the late-1990s, and live drums were sounding lamer and lamer to me. Synth drums were bigger and more interesting, and you could pick from a sound library, an option we'd never had before.

For me, the technology was simultaneously exciting and confusing. I wanted to use it, but I didn't know where to start. I needed people who knew what they were doing to harness that power, but what John ended up giving me were very expensive session musicians who did the same kinds of things I'd always done. To have almost nothing prepared, and then to go into the studio with all these high-end people who expected me to tell them how the songs were supposed to go was extremely frustrating. I kept thinking, What is he doing? John Barnes should be leading this session.

Enter Randy Jackson. When I found myself struggling with John, I reached out to Columbia Records for help and was informed that Randy was my new A&R man—the guy responsible for shepherding the record through to release while trying to keep it on budget. Randy had played bass on "Leap of Faith," and he blew away everybody in that studio. He was already a friend, and I was relieved to learn he'd be the guy at my back. (This was all before he went on to *American Idol* fame, of course.)

During our first conversation about *The Unimaginable Life*, I expressed my misgivings to Randy about what was happening with Barnes. "I'll be right there," he told me. The next day he drove up from LA, assessed the damage, and fired John.

After that, Randy stuck around and co-produced the rest of the record with me. By that point, I was way out of budget. I think part of his motivation may have been a desire for me to wrap things up financially, and I was fine with that. I'd been writing the book and the album at the same time, and had already submitted the manuscript to the publisher, who was designing a marketing plan that included both book and record. Problem was, there was no record. With Randy's help, I managed to bring the album home in time for a simultaneous release, which, based on my experience making *Leap*, was just short of a miracle.

In order to hit my deadline, I actually had four different rooms at the same recording studio going at once, each with an engineer working on a different track, plus a Pro Tools expert tweaking things in his own small space. We were recording vocals in one room and horn parts in another, while mixing tracks down the hall. I jumped between each session, trying to keep tabs on it all. It was a month of money flying out the door, although it would have needed to be spent eventually had I been able to record at a saner pace. Mostly it just made me crazy trying to do four months' worth of work in four weeks' time.

At the end of all of that, I learned that Columbia had never intended to release the record in conjunction with the book. As far as I could tell, they'd never even talked to the publisher about it. The book and record ended up being released about a month apart from each other in 1997.

In my mind, the *Unimaginable Life* album was the soundtrack to the book Julia and I had written. To me, record and book alike were love stories, written by the lovers. Because they were so intertwined, I included two tracks of Julia reading her poems from the book on the album, one at the beginning and one at the end. Since there was no marketing effort to connect the two, few of my fans seemed to understand that move. Instead, it looked as if I was arbitrarily dragging my wife into my music. Years earlier, my brother had warned me never to do that, pointing to examples of musicians like Sly Stone and John Lennon, who'd brought their wives into their creative process. Yet there's a reason they did, just like there was a reason that Paul McCartney started writing songs with Linda once the Beatles split up. Those women were an important part of their creative inspirations, but the rest of the world didn't want to know about it. Well, Julia was a full collaborator on the book, and that was all the justification I needed.

In the end, I think the six years it took me to come out with *The Unimaginable Life* stripped away whatever kind of momentum *Leap of Faith* had built. I didn't know it at the time, but that was the beginning of the end of my time on the pop charts.

PROBABLY THE BEST-KNOWN song off of *The Unimaginable Life* is "This Island Earth," which I wrote for a nature television production of the same name. After the producers heard it, they asked me to narrate the show as well. The song won an Emmy, and so did the program.

The moment that sticks with me about that song came early in the process, before I'd even finished writing it. I'd been invited to Oahu, to a dolphin rehabilitation facility called EarthTrust, which included a gigantic tank and an underwater control room with a viewing window, where they could record the dolphins' sounds and movements to try and decipher their language. The facility also included underwater speakers so the scientists could play things for the dolphins, too. When I visited, what they played was . . . me.

They'd received minimal response from the dolphins to recorded music, and wanted to see what would happen when somebody played live. I had my guitar with me, and set up in front of the window and played what I'd written so far of "This Island Earth." I started timidly, noodling on verse ideas, and felt like a pied piper when four baby dolphins came over to the window. They hovered not ten feet away while their parents swam around the tank. When I reached the chorus I dropped more deeply into a groove, and just like that the babies were joined by all of the other dolphins, about a dozen in all, who stared at me collectively through the window. Something about my voice, my focused expression, or maybe even the song itself caught their attention. It was suddenly a command performance. Such is fame, eh? I guess those dolphins knew a groove when they heard one.

We were all blown away by the interspecies communication. As I was discussing it over dinner that night with my manager, Denzyl Feigelson, it suddenly dawned on me: speakers had been positioned around the tank, and sound is omnipresent under water. How did the dolphins know the sound was coming from me? What if they were responding to something that wasn't the sound at all, but some sort of visual element? Maybe when I hit the groove of the chorus, my energy field shifted. Maybe my aura changed color or size, a light show that caught the older dolphins by surprise? I wonder if the EarthTrust people have figured that one out yet.

AS A WAY to promote *The Unimaginable Life* book, the publisher got me onto *The Tonight Show*, which I remember mostly because Jay Leno said to me, on the air, "So what, your wife is a colon therapist? She does high colonics? That brings a whole new meaning to the 'House at Pooh Corner.'"

I replied, "Well, the advantage was that she knew I was full of shit from the very beginning." I don't think I was supposed to say that on TV.

Neither the book nor the record were well received. Many reviewers had difficulty with the spiritual message of the book. MTV's resident music critic, Kurt Loder, actually ripped pages from it while talking about how much he hated the thing. He enlisted Keith Richards and Marilyn Manson to join him. I guess they decided it was pick-on-Kenny day. My son Crosby, in eighth grade at the time, came home from school in tears. He'd been hearing about it all day. "Nobody else's dad gets made fun of on MTV!" he cried.

People say you have to have a thick skin in my business, but there's no such thing. I write songs based on feelings, and you can't just turn that off. I'm not going to change who I am or how I write because of responses like that. As Tommy Dowd said, one minute you're in the window of public attention and the next minute you're not; the train has moved on. If you take your good reviews too seriously, you'll give too much weight to your bad ones. Either way, popular opinion can have almost nothing to do with your work. One minute you're huge and the next you're not. That's pop culture. If you hang around long enough, you just might get back in, and that's cool, too, but it's not as seductive for me as it used to be.

THE YEARS FOLLOWING *The Unimaginable Life* involved a Christmas album, *December*, which was never promoted or even made it into record stores, and became the lowest-charting album of my career. When my next release, *More Songs from Pooh Corner*, got buried under Sony Wonder's sale to Nickelodeon, things were officially a mess. They got even messier with my next effort.

I was about four songs into what would become *It's About Time*—days after my fiftieth birthday, no less—when I got word that Columbia was dropping me from the label. I sort of saw it coming, given my recent track record, but the way they went about it shocked me. My manager told me he'd received the news from the secretary to a lower VP. No direct call from anybody whose opinion actually mattered saying, "Thanks for all the hits, dude, but we have to move on." No gold watch, no nothing. I'd made millions of dollars for Columbia and was stunned by how they chose to end things. I'm not sure what I was expecting when the time came, but it sure wasn't that.

I don't fault the label for whatever business decisions they made, but their management style showed me less humanity than I'd seen during Clive Davis's time at the helm. I believe that Clive would have called me personally to deliver that kind of news.

I didn't have much time to consider any of that. I was left with a half-finished album, no budget to move forward, and a sudden midlife crisis that would take the better part of a year to work through.

To that point, I'd paid for the record with advance money from the label, same as always. By dropping me early in the making of it, though, they no longer had to pay that out. Without financing, my producer, Tommy Sims, dropped out, and I brought the master tapes from Nashville back to Santa Barbara.

The project sat untouched for the better part of a year. I found myself completely adrift at age fifty. I didn't even know whether I should keep recording. Was there a marketplace for somebody like me? I actually deliberated finding another line of work, although I had no idea what that might be. I was depressed to the point of inaction, and must have been really difficult to live with. Finally, Julia encouraged me to finish the record using our savings. That decision made a huge difference in my emotional reality. Getting back to work was exactly what I needed. I ended up doing some terrific collaborations with Michael McDonald, Richard Marx, and Clint Black.

When you make a record on your own, though, at least in those days, there was no way to promote it without money behind you. I ended up with an album that very few people have heard because the only place it got released was through my website. Only my most hardcore fans know *It's About Time* even exists.

Despite the lack of commercial success, I did come to realize that things actually get better when you become a legacy act. At fifty, I was just old. At sixty, I was somehow cool. By seventy, I was an icon. My records might not have moved like they once did, but I was still selling out theaters across the country, for as many dates as I wanted to book. I performed "Footloose" with Blake Shelton at the Country Music Awards, and sat down for an hour's interview with Dan Rather. I actually found myself doing more TV than I'd done in years. Maybe there was a future for me in this business after all.

CHAPTER 14

APART/TOGETHER

HERE'S ONE REASON why my marriage to Julia didn't work: I fell in love with her when she was my therapist, and that kind of relationship flows in only one direction. I knew nothing about her and she knew everything about me. Upon that blank canvas I came to project a level of perfection— something I've since discovered is common between therapists and their patients—which is precisely why romantic relationships of this kind are discouraged. In fact, Julia could have lost her license for it, if she'd had a license to begin with. Fischer-Hoffman was outside of that realm.

There are so many levels to this. Yes, Julia was my crazy guru, and I was the classic acolyte. In that kind of relationship, the guru knows everything and the follower knows nothing. To learn, you must surrender. No wonder I fell so hard. This was the person who'd taught me that no part of my personality was unlovable. I put her in charge of our reality and bought in fully, growing so absorbed in her lessons that I completely lost track of who I was. My friends saw it and they didn't like it, but I wasn't about to let them talk me out of being in love.

It takes a while, but one day you realize you've grown, and that maybe you don't agree with everything the person you've chosen to share your life with says. Maybe you're learning enough to become your own guru. That's how that sort of relationship is supposed to go. Trouble is, the guru is always more comfortable as leader than as partner, and the more I questioned Julia's leadership, the more distant she became.

I still loved her, but our values were increasingly at odds. Her idiosyncrasies, once so captivating, were becoming tangible problems. Julia found my need for a more normal home life—things like dinner with the kids at a table, a somewhat stable day-to-day schedule, even my request to put on some makeup and maybe fix her hair now and then—to be oppressive. We made our home in upscale Montecito, and the closer we got to a suburban family lifestyle, the further Julia was torn from her gypsy self-image. Part of her wanted to run away, to be "a free spirit," she said. But she'd also always wanted children, and we had two wonderful young ones at home. That free spirit was tearing her in two. Sometimes the traits that most attract us at the beginning of a love affair are the very things that come between us later on.

Something had to give.

To be fair, I'd pulled an unassuming hippie girl into my celebrity lifestyle, which was very complicated and overwhelming at times. In my world things went a thousand miles per hour, and you'd better be ready to rock and roll. Ultimately, my celebrity was larger than her life. For example, when I sfirst uggested we write a book about our first few years together, I forgot to mention she'd have to do a promotional tour that included multiple TV appearances. I never warned her that her life was about to become very public. She saw it as a huge interruption.

In my view, Julia panicked when she began to lose control of our relationship, or maybe she was just overwhelmed. This was not the life she thought she'd signed up for. A squadron of assistants was hired, whose primary job seemed to be agreeing with her every decision. It seemed like Julia effectively built a wall of kindred opinions, a sphere of her own reality, around her. At points we had a rotation of four maids and five nannies on the payroll, less to watch the kids, I thought, than to keep her company and nod eagerly at whatever she said.

George Carlin used to say the problem with women is men, and I found that to be true. I felt Julia was also running from her own demons, which long predated my presence in her life. As our relationship matured—as I gained a voice of my own—I found myself increasingly shouldering the male role that had so frightened her. It wasn't what I did, but what I represented. There is no compromise for somebody who sees the "straight" world as the enemy, and when I stopped buying in fully to her perspective, I became a stand-in for the world.

Like I said, there's a lot here to unpack.

The reason I'm writing about the end of my relationship with Julia more so than the end of my relationship with Eva is that, between our book and the *Unimaginable Life* record, we were so very public together. My marriage to Eva was our business; my marriage to Julia became everybody's business.

Our romantic relationship lasted fourteen years, a union based on complete transparency until, all of a sudden, it wasn't. We'd always been able to work things all the way out, talking through every detail until we were both satisfied. I never imagined we'd get to a place where Julia believed her fears more than she trusted us. She thought that our love could heal each other's childhood trauma, but it turned out that's an inside job—work you have to do yourself.

When a relationship is built solely upon being in love, should things shift there's nothing remaining to hold it together. It's still remarkable to me that we wrote a book about how to make love last, and within a few years we were separated. I was not emotionally prepared for that.

As I wrote in *The Unimaginable Life*, "Spirit gives us nothing we're not ready for," but that was being put to the test. It really came home when Julia called me into the backyard, sat down on a bench, and asked for a divorce.

I was completely blindsided. I felt like I'd been fired from my marriage.

With Eva, I did the leaving. With Julia, I was the one left and still very much in love when we split. Initially, our affair had been the lightning bolt that triggered me awake and moved me into a spiritual awareness that I still appreciate all these years later. I know now that the love we experience comes from inside ourselves; what fucked me up was the belief that Julia was the source of my love.

When she left it was as if she took my love with her. I came apart entirely.

LOSING JULIA MADE me question everything we believed. As a matter of self-preservation, I had to fully disconnect from the belief system we had built—to throw it all up into the air and see what came back to me. It was a process that my therapist, Myrna, referred to as "reconstellating my inner cosmology." I had to own who I still was and discard the parts of myself that were really Julia's. It was an arduous climb back to who I had been, or who I was becoming in the aftermath of the breakup. The turmoil took an especially heavy toll early on. I couldn't sleep for more than three hours at a time, and was so fully consumed with anger and grief that I barely ate, living mostly on protein-powder shakes. I dropped a ton of weight from an already thin frame, getting down to about 150 pounds, my weight in high school. Find a picture of me in concert in 2005; I look more like a prisoner of war than a rock star. Things grew so dire that online rumors began spreading that I was sick with AIDS or cancer. I wasn't, of course. At least I had that much going for me.

A good friend, Susan Pelfrey, came over each morning to make breakfast and encourage me to eat. She also taught me to reframe my fears, so that instead of saying, "I can't do this" I would say, "*Up until now* I've had trouble doing this." She drove me crazy with that shit, but it helped rebuild my fucked-up self-esteem. But I needed more than that to keep functioning as a father of five children, two of them very young, let alone maintaining my status as a touring musician. Enter modern medicine.

The glue my doctor used to keep me together was benzodiazepine. Benzos are popular nerve-calming drugs, and over the first post-divorce years I became acquainted with every member of their family: klonopin, Ativan, Valium. My search for the right formula was focused. My doctor tried to tell me the entire suite of benzos is highly addictive, and getting off of them can be a nightmare, but I'd never been addicted to anything and had no clue how difficult detox would be. I figured I'd just use the drugs for a little while to get back on my feet, then taper off whenever I wanted to. Well, I found out that while benzos are really good at calming the nerves, should you miss a dose your anxiety will come back tenfold. Once you're hooked, you have to keep taking them or you will suffer. And getting off of them is torture. You get the shakes, you get nauseous, you get panic attacks. It creates the very thing you're taking it for—anxiety—only worse than it had been. Way worse. That's the most insidious part

I managed to kick the habit using Wellbutrin—an SSRI used primarily for depression, which my doctor occasionally utilized for benzo detox. That helped me ease off the Ativan, and within a few weeks I was able to live without it.

Another thing that helped came about a month after the split, when I was pulled back to reality by Jimmy Messina, who called to remind me about his benefit concert in Santa Ynez, which I'd long since agreed to play. I was struggling with my state of mind, but figured the diversion might do me some good. Rusty Young and Richie Furay, both from Poco, were there. Getting to sing "Kind Woman," Richie's song from his stint in Buffalo Springfield with Jimmy, was a dream come true for me. How many times had I played that tune with Dougie in the San Gabriel Mountains back in college? It was exactly what I needed. I became absorbed by the old harmonies, and the kinship Jimmy and I had felt in the early days of L&M. After the show, Messina pulled me aside. He saw how poorly I was doing.

"Hey, brother, I recognize that look in your eyes," he said. "I went through a rough time with my divorce, too." Then he suggested a remedy: a short reunion tour. "At the very least," he said, "it'll give you something else to put your mind on."

The more I thought about it, the more sense it made. Focusing on music would allow me to spend at least some time outside of my own head. We set to putting a band together and booked forty dates for a summer tour. It was the first time Loggins & Messina had performed in almost three decades.

Jimmy knew what he was talking about. Being on the road eased the pain of the divorce. I didn't think as much about my arguments with Julia, at least in part because I was now thinking about my arguments with

Jimmy. I'd developed considerably as a musician since our split in 1976, and now had my own approach to the craft. So, of course, did Messina. I saw the reunion as an opportunity to correct a few things; for example, the tempos of some of our L&M originals had always seemed nervous and fast to me, and I wanted to slow them down. I figured that the audience, made up largely of the same people we'd left back in '76, might appreciate something that swung a little harder. I wanted to *feel* songs like "Didn't I Know You When" and "Back to Georgia," so I worked with our rhythm section— bassist Shem von Schroeck and drummer Steve Di Stanislao—to make some subtle changes. I occasionally altered the key of songs we'd recorded decades earlier, back when those high notes didn't seem quite so stratospheric. It wasn't like I was rewriting our classic tunes, but I discovered that Jimmy had a hard time accepting any of the tweaks I made. It seemed as though he felt our songs had been handed down to us on Moses's tablets, and everything about them was sacrosanct. He tried to be very patient with me, but I could tell that my numerous changes were starting to get to him.

One day before rehearsal, Jimmy pulled me aside. "Kenny," he said calmly, "the band has been complaining about your behavior."

I was taken aback, not from the criticism but from the idea that such a thing might exist in the first place. I hadn't noticed any tension at all.

"A couple of the guys told me that they're thinking about quitting," Jimmy continued. "I'm really concerned. You're changing the arrangements almost every day, and they can't keep up. It's too erratic. And your temper has been freaking them out."

I had to take a deep breath at that one. My temper? I couldn't even recall losing my temper. What the hell was going on? I'd been using rehearsals to relieve the emotional pain from my divorce, but it wasn't until Jimmy spoke up that I realized my inner rage might be showing up in misplaced, unconscious ways. Maybe I *had* been acting erratically, and I wasn't letting myself see how it affected those around me. I thanked Jimmy for the input, and promised to rein myself in. As soon as rehearsal started, I apologized to everybody in the band.

My manager, Steve Moire, gave me a different perspective.

"Kenny, you don't need to reinvent Loggins & Messina," he explained. "You have other places to put your creative energy, but this is Jimmy's primary outlet. It's been many years since he's had something like this.

Change what absolutely has to be changed, and leave the rest alone. Get through it, keep the peace, make some money, and have a good time."

Starting that day, I took Steve's advice. I backed way off, and let Messina take the reins. It felt good, up until Jimmy started acting as if no time had passed and he was still the man in charge. He began to dictate policy just like he'd done in the 1970s. One of his first dictums was to return to the original arrangements on "Back to Georgia," undoing a change I'd just made. That rubbed me the wrong way. I'd long since earned my rock 'n' roll stripes, and figured L&M could now be a real partnership, where options were discussed and compromises made.

We rehearsed for four weeks before the tour started, which was a week more than I needed to realize I couldn't take four months of this. Jimmy's old habit of stonewalling during disagreements was rearing its head again. We'd been at loggerheads about the set list for two days; Jimmy would patiently wait me out when I offered opinions, and then come back with a plan that completely ignored everything I'd said. I've been on the road since 1972, I thought, and he *still* doesn't trust me? It felt insulting. Maybe I was taking things too personally. Maybe the stress of my divorce was getting to me. Whatever it was, I realized I wouldn't be able to make it through an entire summer of this kind of power struggle. I could no longer roll over like I did back when I was still just a newbie.

As rehearsals wrapped up, Jimmy still wasn't budging, so during a lunch break I asked him and his manager, Martin Kirkup, to join me at a nearby restaurant. Our argument continued at the table, as Jimmy continued to ignore my suggestions. Finally at the end of my rope, I turned to Martin. "You'd better talk to your boy here," I said, "because if he can't begin to compromise I'm gonna head home." We were less than a week away from our first gig, and I was ready to quit. I got up and left the table, done for the day—and maybe longer.

The next day, Martin called and said he and Messina had been up all night processing the new reality, and Jimmy had come to terms with it. To Jimmy's credit, he opened up to the idea of making show decisions together, which was all I'd wanted in the first place. And yeah, I still made a few arrangement changes, like adding a churchy R&B vocal section to the vamp out of "Peace of Mind," and even a guitar solo on "Vahevala" that I played myself. I mention that solo in particular because Jimmy was always L&M's lead guitarist, and he generously yielded that space without a fuss. It was something I'd always wanted to do, but never had the confidence to try.

The most memorable moment on that tour didn't have anything to do with either Jimmy or me. In the middle of one of our first shows, at Ruth Eckerd Hall in Clearwater, Florida, von Schroeck had to sit down on a chair midstage to finish a song. As soon as the tune ended, he put down his bass, signaled for our tour manager to come over, and said he might be having a heart attack. We immediately announced a brief intermission, and Shem was hustled off to a hospital while the rest of the band gathered behind the stage curtain to discuss what to do next. Jimmy leaned toward canceling the show and doing a makeup gig later in the summer. I suggested turning it into an impromptu acoustic set. Then our virtuoso fiddle player, Gabe Witcher, piped up. "I can play the bass," he said, "and I know Shem's parts."

Jimmy and I both stared, mouths open. We had no idea Gabe played anything but fiddle, let alone knew the bass parts. Well, Gabe played bass for the rest of the show and didn't miss a freakin' note. It was amazing. We even gave him an impromptu solo in "You Need a Man," which we'd never done before, even for Shem. He was on fire, and we all knew it. It was a truly inspiring night for us all. Gabe stayed completely in the moment for two straight hours, so on the edge with every note that as soon as he came offstage he took a *huge* slug of whiskey to calm his nerves. "If I'd thought ahead at all I'd have gotten lost," he told us afterward. That guy absolutely saved the show. Best of all, Shem's issues were entirely stress-related and quickly overcome; he was back with us for our very next gig.

Even with those initial disagreements, that tour ended up being a reconciling experience for Jimmy and me, and paved the way for a second reunion tour in 2009.

Neither of those tours were the location of my defining moment with Messina, but they helped set it up. The event in question happened a few years later, during a career-retrospective *Soundstage* show I filmed in Chicago for PBS, for which Jimmy and I appeared as Loggins & Messina. (I also performed solo with David Foster, Michael McDonald, Thundercat, and my daughter Hana—the first time she'd ever appeared with me on a big stage.) It was a four-day shoot; to save on rehearsal time, I suggested

Jimmy bring his own band to back us on our L&M songs. They'd been performing them for years and already knew them inside and out.

Our first two days were spent rehearsing, with each guest receiving two hours of stage time for camera blocking and sound. As I was taking the stage with my band on the second day, I noticed Jimmy in the hallway with his guys. They'd just finished their two-hour stage rehearsal, and now they were backstage, *rehearsing some more*. This was strictly L&M's greatest hits—the same stuff they'd been playing together for a decade—yet there was so much intensity in his instruction, right there in the fucking hallway. Wow, I thought, this guy can't leave it alone. Then it hit me. Back in the day, all that rehearsal L&M was forced into had nothing to do with me or the band, and everything to do with Jimmy.

Suddenly I understood. For the first time, I felt compassion for Jimmy. What I'd taken as oppression when we were in the band together, the stuff I resented for all those years, was the same stuff that made the guy run. Jimmy needed to control his environment in order to feel safe. As I'd grown stronger and more self-assured, he simply pulled tighter and tighter on the reins until I finally had to break away. I'd taken many of our disagreements personally, but in a way, it didn't matter who was standing at the microphone next to him. In the end it was just Jimmy being Jimmy. I only wish I'd seen it sooner.

Watching him drill his musicians in that hallway in Chicago, I realized that Jimmy was just a guy. And so was I.

ONE OF THE THINGS that helped me through my separation from Julia was heavy journaling. Filling a diary had always been part of my writing process, and even through the sadness I knew the moment was rich with feelings and insights I might someday interpret into music. At the very least, that journal was an effective place to dump my blues. At first, I wrote only the painful, defeated thoughts that expressed my sadness and rage (emphasis on rage). It's like that old joke: A guy walks into a barber shop and the barber says, "Hey, Mickey, you seem kind of down. What's going on?" The guy says, "At breakfast this morning I made a Freudian slip. I meant to say, 'Honey, could you please pass the butter,' but instead I said, 'You fucking bitch, you ruined my life.'"

In a way, it was like losing my religion; when you're betrayed by your guru, God goes out the window, too. I was so angry I began buying aluminum stepladders, just to destroy them with a baseball bat in my garage as part of my Fischer-Hoffman work. I must have taken a dozen of those things apart. (I highly recommend it.)

After a few months, though, I noticed that every now and then I'd have a thought that wasn't so angry, and that even the tiniest flash of insight or forgiveness would ease the pain, if only for a moment. That was something new, so I started writing those thoughts in a different journal, which I called "The Truth Is." That was where I collected thoughts that were in any way comforting. *I will love again. She did the best she could in our time together. I own my own love.* It was there I realized Julia wasn't some kind of monster who was out to get me, but a woman keeping her wedding vow to follow her heart. I had always assumed it would lead her to me, but instead it led her away.

Did the divorce invalidate what we wrote in *The Unimaginable Life*? Not at all. The idea of telling one's entire emotional truth still resonates for me, but back then Julia and I were new at that kind of vulnerable communication. We needed more tools to be able to work with our demons when our mutual honesty revealed them to us.

The process of getting over Julia took six years—half as long as the marriage itself. One moment of clarity for me came about four years after our split, when I was talking to a guy Julia was dating. It wasn't something I sought out, but I went to the house to pick up the kids and there he was. Somehow we had a moment alone, and he confided in me that he found Julia difficult to travel with. I had to laugh, because I knew the truth of that better than anybody. Julia was so environmentally sensitive that she packed almost all of her own food, and finding a hotel room without new carpeting or fresh paint, either of which would send her into allergic fits, was always a challenge.

My first thought was, Thank God I don't work there anymore.

My second thought was, Holy crap, that's the first time I've been grateful to no longer be married. It was a sign that I was successfully moving on. Maybe I was even ready to start my next record.

I ended up taking my two very different journals to Nashville, which is the place songwriters go to cry into their beer. Country music has always honored a sad story, and I certainly had one. I spent three weeks there, and the songs I came up with turned into my *How About Now* album. I call it my divorce record.

I collaborated with seven or eight musicians down there, and it seemed like every time I told one of them about my situation we'd end up with another song—titles like "I Don't Want to Hate You Anymore" and "I'm a Free Man Now." One woman I wrote with, Beth Nielsen Chapman, had recently lost her husband to cancer, and was in the perfect emotional space to relate to the pain I'd been going through. We were writing a gospel idea I called "That's When I Find You" when I happened to tell her about my "The Truth Is" journal. Beth begged, "Oh please, let's write that song, too." That was the first time I'd ever written two songs at once; we literally wrote a line or two of one, then switched to the other, back and forth like that into the night. The opening lines of the latter song, appropriately titled "Truth Is," came directly from my journal: "Truth is, nothing lasts / We're just pretending / The truth is bound to have its way."

Another song came out of a conversation I had with songwriter (and former NFL All-Pro) Mike Reid after I casually mentioned I probably needed twelve months to let everything settle. "Okay," he said. "Let's write *that*." The resulting song, "A Year's Worth of Distance," became the album's opening track. Julia was so confronted by its first line—"All I want is the truth / I guess that's just too much to ask of you"—that she refused to play it for the kids. I don't blame her. It was intense.

One of my favorite songs on the album was written with Gary Burr, a former member of Pure Prairie League. He was the last person I wrote with before heading home to Santa Barbara, and I was feeling the strain of all the heartbreak songs I'd come up with.

"I am so fucking tired of writing songs about her," I told Gary when we met at Taco Mamacita for lunch prior to our first session. "I need to write one last goodbye song, and then I'll be done with the subject." Just like Mike Reid had done, Gary suggested we write exactly that. So we did. It's called "One Last Goodbye Song." I guess that's the Nashville way—you just kind of shoot the shit until you hit paydirt.

The other song Gary and I wrote together during that period was the album's title track, "How About Now." Strangely, I laughed my ass off all the way through writing it. Gary is one of the funniest guys I know, and even though the topic was heartbreak—again—he kept us both laughing through the pain. I figured if the guy could make me laugh while we were writing a song about the end of my marriage, he was probably good for me in more ways than one. "If I'd met you forty-five years ago we would have started a band," I told him. Gary was quick with a reply: "That wouldn't have worked. I'd have only been ten."

I wasn't kidding, though. I really did want to start a band with him.

Within a couple of years I did.

THAT CAME LATER, THOUGH. More immediately, I got a unique offer to play a corporate gig on a cruise ship in Italy. Corporate shows pay way better than regular concerts, and this was the first one I'd been offered overseas. They're a secret of the rock world; just a few of those gigs each year can pay a huge percentage of your bills. I figured that since I had transportation covered for myself and the band, why not make an actual tour out of it? I hadn't spent much time in Europe professionally, and it would be a great way to get my head out of the local sand. I tasked my manager with gauging interest, and he came back with the news that a decent-sized hall in Paris, the Théâtre Marigny, was interested in hosting me. There were some considerations, though. The money wasn't great (which is typical when you haven't spent much time building a following in a country), and I'd have to get the band there from Italy on my own dime. At that point it didn't matter. I desperately needed a change of scenery, so I told him to put together a two-week itinerary.

I went to Paris directly from my Italian gig, and was stunned by the state-of-the-art, classic French theater where I'd be playing. It was a beautiful thousand-seat room just off the Champs-Élysées, with two balconies, ornate wooden staircases, and abundant gilded design work.

We were in the middle of sound check when the promoter bounded down the aisle and hopped up onstage to ask me a question: "You're going to play your hit, aren't you?"

I didn't know what he was talking about. "I had a hit in France?" I asked.

The guy gave me an incredulous look. "What a Fool Believes," he shouted. "It was a big hit in Paris!"

Now *that* was funny. "You must be thinking of the Doobie Brothers' version," I said. "That's the song that hit No. 1."

"No, no, no," he insisted. "Their version was never a hit here. We loved *yours*."

It turned out the recording he was referring to was my duet with Michael McDonald on *Outside: From the Redwoods*. Okay, now we had to scramble. The promoter had a copy of the CD with him, so the guys and I worked it up at sound check, with me handling both vocal parts, mine and Michael's. I slotted it as the fourth song of the set, and the response was overwhelming. From the very first notes, everybody in the room stood up, and they didn't sit down again for the rest of the show. They *loved* it. Apparently, "What a Fool Believes" was *huge* in Paris and I'd had no idea. It seems my show's promoter was also the programmer of a local 1980s-format radio station, and had been responsible for bringing my music to the French masses.

The show was tremendously fun, and the audience was so into it that I ended up doing something completely new. There's a national holiday in France called *Fête de la Musique* ("Music Day"), during which musicians perform for free, outdoors, all over the city. Really, they're on every street corner. My Paris show fell on that very day, so for an encore I decided to take the audience outside for an impromptu performance. It was spontaneous; my crew was not prepared for me to do that.

I grabbed an acoustic guitar and headed for a side door with my guitarist, Chris Rodriguez. We hopped onto a nearby bus bench from which I could see the Champs, and a few of the crew guys lit us with flashlights. I sang "Footloose" again, and "Love the One You're With." The crowd ate it up, and it was just as magical for me. You can find amateur clips of it on YouTube.

That was a great start to what would be six or seven shows across almost as many countries over two weeks. We played to a full house in Sweden, maybe a thousand people, all of whom seemed to know my material by heart. We drove across Germany for a club gig that I played acoustically with just Chris and bassist Shem von Schroeck. Just like in Paris, I found out about an hour before the show that one of my old singles was popular there. This time it was "Welcome to Heartlight," which had been a moderate hit in the United States. Just like we'd done in Paris, I worked it up with the band during sound check. The song is actually quite complicated because every chorus has slightly different lyrics, but we managed to pull it off.

I guess the song wasn't *that* popular, because there were only like a hundred people in the crowd, mostly music nerds with tape recorders and notebooks. During one interview I did before the show, the reporter said to me, "Kenny Loggins, you're not just a legend, you're a myth." He meant it as a compliment . . . I think.

All of those positive vibes really helped settle the sorrow of my divorce. When I returned to the States, I decided to keep it up by filling my shows with songs that delivered peace to my heart, in the same way my fans have told me has happened for them. For the first time in my life, I let my own music minister to me.

I opened a bunch of shows with "It's About Time," a song I wrote with Michael McDonald, which begins with the lines "I shed my skin / And set aside this self-made darkness / And walk on into the light" and culminates in the chorus "If it's about joy / If it's about life / If it's about love / It's about time we get started."

Finding a place for the hits no longer mattered as much to me, although it turned out that quite a few of them were included in my set. I've always been inspired by "This Is It," and "I'm Alright" has that interlude: "Listen to your heart beating." "Footloose" was also in there, with its message of personal freedom.

Three or four songs into a show, I would invariably notice that I was completely out of pain. Dropping into each song, one word at a time, one note at a time, the sadness would temporarily recede. I'd always suspected my songs were secret messages to myself, and now I knew it was true. As I sang them, I actually began to feel happy. During one show a voice in my head said, "Someday you're going to feel like you're feeling right now, all of the time." Another voice, the one I call my Spirit, responded, "How about *now?*" I wrote that down after the show, and took the idea to Nashville to write with Gary Burr a few months later.

During a show toward the end of that tour, I was singing my opening tune, "It's About Time," pacing the stage back and forth like a southern Baptist minister, when I noticed I wasn't feeling the audience. What was missing? Reflexively, I scanned the crowd for somebody to connect with.

My old habit was to look for the prettiest girl in the first few rows—somebody I could use to build a wave of connection—but I couldn't find her. Suddenly, though, I felt a vibe from stage right. I turned, expecting to see that pretty lady, and wasn't quite ready for what I encountered. She was a girl, maybe nine years old, holding on to the lip of the stage and bouncing up and down while she grinned with joy. She was totally immersed in the music. As soon as I looked at her my heart opened. I swear her eyes sparkled at me, and just like that, more of those sparkles started showing up all around the theater. One by one, people began connecting to the song. I could feel it. "If it's about joy / If it's about life / If it's about love / It's about time we get started." As I scanned the room it felt like I was meeting everyone there, one person at a time. When the song ended, the audience jumped to their feet and gave me a standing ovation, something that almost never happens for an unknown opening number like that. It was blissful.

ABOUT FIVE YEARS after my split with Julia, and five years after I'd managed to kick my short-term benzo habit, I went in for surgery to remove a cyst from the L4 vertebrae on my back. Apparently the surgeon bruised a nerve in the process, because within two days my prostate shut down, then my bladder, then my kidneys. I was rushed to the Cottage Hospital ER, where I spent the night in intensive care. They told me later I'd been close to dying.

Doctors administered four or five drugs, one of which was, unfortunately, Xanax. Yep, another benzo. I remember waking up in the hospital one night standing on my bed and yelling, "They're trying to kill me!" I was extremely stoned on something. They'd flushed out my kidneys and I was having trouble breathing. A nurse came in and urged me to calm down, which is when I realized I was still tucked in under the covers. I'd been standing up only in my panicked head. I suspect that's the point at which Xanax became part of my protocol.

I spent a week at that hospital, and when I emerged, I was addicted all over again. It was as if I'd never stopped taking it the first time. I tried to titrate myself off of it, reducing my liquid dose to the smallest amount possible, but if I went too far it was as if I hadn't taken anything at all. Five years earlier I'd needed benzos to help me through moments of excessive stress. Now I needed them to feel calm at all. If I didn't take them, panic was guaranteed.

In the end it was my youngest daughter, Hana, then eleven years old, who motivated me to kick the habit. I hadn't realized how much those drugs were changing my personality, making me short-tempered and emotional, especially when my supply ran out. That was the situation in the car one day; I'd accidentally left my prescription at home and was screaming at traffic, desperate to get back to the house. Hana waited for me to take a breath and quietly said, "Daddy, I can't be with you when you're like this. Take me to Mama's house. I'm going to stay with her until you get help." Wow, did that wake me up. I took a breath and thanked her, promising I would seek help as soon as I could.

Before that happened, though, I had a long-since scheduled five-day rafting trip through the Grand Canyon with my friend Jeff Bouchard, the last of three such adventures we'd take. Because this one included our older kids, I didn't want to cancel it to race off to rehab. Maybe I should have reconsidered. I unthinkingly left my Xanax at the hotel, and had no choice but to go cold turkey for the duration. I found myself caught up in benzo-deprived anxiety attacks pretty much all of the time, and had to devote my concentration to just keeping things together. It was awful, but I managed to put on a brave face for the kids during the day. Nighttimes, though, got to me. It was insanely hot in the canyon, over ninety degrees long after the sun went down. Many people in our party ditched their sleeping bags entirely in favor of soaking bedsheets in the river to help find a sliver of comfort. Trying to sleep in those conditions was all but impossible, even without overnight terror, which creeped in as soon as the kids went to sleep and I could let my guard down.

Starting then, Jeff made it his goal to help me get off of the drug. "This is killing you," he told me near the end of the trip. "We have to do something about it."

He wasn't wrong, and I knew it.

Before we left the canyon we'd drawn up a plan for me to get clean. I had a limited window before my tour schedule started up again, and I decided to jump through it. If only I'd known all the rehab process entailed.

Xanax is really difficult to kick on your own, so Jeff found a hospital in Florida, the Novus Medical Detox Center, that specialized in drug dependency. He flew me down there and signed me in himself. That's where I learned that benzos present the most grueling detox on the drug spectrum, their patients suffering even more than heroin addicts. The first level, medical detox, lasts about a week. That's when they taper you down under strict supervision to make sure you won't have a stroke or heart attack. When you make it through that, the second level, psychological detox, takes much longer and is way more difficult. I'd learn about that part soon.

I stayed in a small, spartan, one-person hospital room with twenty-four-hour monitoring to safeguard against potential suicide. Yeah, that's where a number of their patients ended up. It was a two-week program, but the doctor promised I'd be medically off of Xanax within seven days. That was important, because I had a concert scheduled eight days later. They put me on an accelerated track that involved two days on Valium to help alleviate withdrawal. Valium is also a benzo, but because it lasts longer in your system than Xanax, it's easier to taper. They said my anxiety attacks might take as much as a year to dissipate entirely, and that I'd have to tough it out. A couple of my orderlies were hard-core Christians who referred to benzos as the devil, and recommended that I ask Jesus for help. I'd gone through twelve years of Catholic school, so that kind of religious psychology was familiar. I'd called on Jesus during hard times before, but I didn't think it would be necessary here. Little did I know.

On my final night in Florida, whatever religious faith I had was put to the test. I was officially off of benzos by that point, so I figured I was no longer addicted. Apart from difficulty sleeping, everything had gone smoothly. I thought I'd made it through the hardest part.

Then, at about one in the morning, I swear I saw somebody lurking in the corner shadows of my room. I jolted awake. The more I focused on it, the scarier it became. It wasn't a person, per se, but a presence—and that presence *hated* me. Was this the devil they spoke of? Shit, maybe it was. I lay in bed, too terrified even to turn on the light. There was an urgency in my chest beyond my control, and my skin started to sizzle like the world's worst sunburn. The withdrawal created its own feedback loop: anxiety, then panic, then fear about the panic, and then you're afraid of the fear about the panic. There's no end to it. You can't get away. I was locked inside my own mind, trapped in my skin. You want me to think of addiction as the devil? Well, here he is, and I'm in hell. It was without question the worst night of my life.

The next morning I couldn't have been more eager to get the hell out of there. After a thorough checkup, I was relieved when the doctors pronounced I was physically unaddicted, safe from the physical side effects of withdrawal. As I would soon learn, though, the mental aspect was the hard part. My night with the devil was only a preview of what was to come.

I had a show in Orlando the following afternoon, which I somehow got through without too much trouble. Actually, playing was easy. I'd done it all my life, and performing was second nature. It was easier for me to avoid the pain during a concert, when I was totally wrapped up in the music. It was off stage, when my mind was unoccupied, that the shaking started. I lay awake in that hotel just like I'd lain awake my last night at Novus. The devil didn't visit me again, thank goodness, but I was certain he wasn't far away. With that, I realized I was pretty fucking far from ready to go home. Luckily, I had a local ringer at the ready.

Dianne Allen was a meditation teacher in Florida, with degrees in psychology and rehabilitation counseling. Jeff had recruited her to give me somebody to talk to while I was an in-patient at Novus. Dianne had her primary office in Redington, near Tampa, so the day after my gig I called an audible and made the two-hour drive to see her. Dianne was about five feet tall, if that, and I called her Yoda. (That's a reference to her height and wisdom, not a bald head and big ears.)

Dianne really opened my eyes when she asked what I was going to do about the "generational pain." I had never heard that term before. It describes unconscious behavior that in my case moved from grandfather to father to son, played out as a matter of allegiance. I began to see my addiction to Xanax as a continuation of my father's reliance on the downer Milltown, as if I'd inherited his fear of sleep. I also thought about how my divorce from Eva had been spurred by thoughts of doing the one thing my father could never bring himself to do: leave his marriage. In that case I felt like I'd broken the chain of generational pain.

I sensed that meditation would be important to my recovery, but I didn't realize just how crucial it would become. Over the next few days, Dianne taught me to use the mantra "All is well" at every glimmer of panic. It seemed to help while I was in Florida, but I wasn't sure it would be enough once I returned home.

Before I left, I asked a couple of friends in Santa Barbara, Mary Judge and Laurie Schneider, to take turns staying at my house with me, because I felt safer when I wasn't alone. Nighttime really triggered me, and I knew I'd need some company to help me keep my head together. When I got home, I went five straight days without a moment of sleep. Five. Straight. Days.

I thought back to my sleepless nights in the Poconos after Jimmy and I recorded *Sittin' In*. What got me through back then was meditation, so that's what I did again. It wasn't a replacement for sleep, but it did help calm my nerves. On my fifth day home there was a solar eclipse. I'm not sure whether it had an effect on what happened next, but I tend to think it did. While everybody else was outside gawking at the sky, I took the opportunity to go into my bedroom, sit down in a comfortable chair, and work my mantra in the hopes that maybe, finally, I might get some sleep. Before I'd even started, my skin began to burn, just like it had at the clinic in Florida. I'd been burning off and on like that pretty much every day since. This time though, alone in my room, repeating the "All is well" mantra helped me to slow down the onslaught of anxiety, tune out the physical sensations, and move into a trance state devoid of thought. That's where I was floating when a message came into my awareness: *Think of your brain as a sick child. How would you treat your children?*

The answer was obvious. I would hold them and love them. I'd turned my brain into an addict, and that was my fault. I immediately felt deep remorse. I decided to treat it with compassion, personifying it as if it was an entirely different being. I asked it for forgiveness. In that moment, I realized this situation didn't have to be adversarial. Rather than fighting the devil, as I'd been taught, I was now parenting and comforting my hurting brain. Through love and compassion, my brain could become my ally in the healing process instead of an adversary. After all, we both wanted the same thing: to be out of pain.

It worked. Within a few minutes, the burning sensation on my skin shifted from extreme discomfort to feeling as if I was floating in a hot tub. It actually became pleasurable. Over the next month, whenever I felt anxiety coming on, I would take a few deep breaths, focus on my heartbeat, say my mantra, and send love to my brain. Soon the panic attacks ceased altogether, my fear replaced by a series of meditations on love and compassion.

ONE THING THAT really helped clear my head during that time was jogging. As an analgesic to heartache, it worked really well. Part of me knew I was running away from the pain, but I also saw how it was taking me toward a more unlimited view of my future. As long as I had my shoes and an open stretch of road, I was golden. I went on long runs every day, sometimes twice a day, along the oceanside cliffs of Santa Barbara, along the coast of the big island of Hawaii, even along the Erie Canal. My guitarist, Chris, frequently joined me on the road; we once ended up running through the courtyard of a castle in Italy where maybe fifty people were picnicking on the green.

Once that endorphin rush kicked in, I felt free. Just like that I could smell the sage and see the sky. It was ironic for me, because my brother Bob took exquisite care of his body, yet died of a heart attack while running. After that I vowed I'd never become a runner, but here I was, running for my life. I found myself talking to Bobby while I ran: "Hey, buddy. Thanks for running with me. I know that your spirit is here, kicking me in the pants and getting me on the road each morning. Thanks for sharing your love of running with me. I finally get it."

It was in the middle of a ninety-minute run along Mountain Drive in Santa Barbara that I made a decision that would impact my next several years. The idea hit me so hard that I had to stop, fish my phone from my pocket, and call Gary Burr. When he answered, I got right to the point.

"Remember when I said that if we were forty-five years younger I would start a band with you?" I said, still panting from my jog. "Well, I'm younger now, so let's start a band."

Gary was taken aback at first. "Are you stoned?" he asked. "What kind of band are you talking about?"

I had an answer ready. "An equal partnership," I said. I really should have thought through that part more. My manager would call me an idiot for structuring things that way, and he was probably right. It was my name that would set us apart from every other new country group, and removing that from consideration negated what might have been a difference-making edge. But I wanted this to be a band, not a dictatorship. I was eager to make it happen, and filled with endorphins from my run, so I told him we'd be on even footing. "We write 'em and we sing 'em, just like the old days," I said. I've always been a naïve optimist.

"Okay," said Gary. "If you're serious, I'm in."

I didn't stop there, though. I suggested that we needed a third member, a female voice. I asked Gary if he knew anybody. He did.

"Georgia Middleman would be perfect," he said, "but I don't know if she's available."

I told Gary to find out and to send me one of her demos. I wanted a strong vocal blend. When everything came back positive, my Nashville band was born. Gary would tell the story during our live shows like this: "When Kenny called, I was on a date with Georgia. Nothing moves a date along like asking, 'Do you want to be in a band with Kenny Loggins?' Then Georgia said, 'Ooooh! The Gambler?'"

Gary was the George Burns of the group, and Georgia was our Gracie. She'd put a button on the bit, saying, "When I got home, my mother told me who Kenny Loggins was, and I said, 'Oh, that's good, too.'"

Gary was a member of the Nashville Songwriters Hall of Fame (still is), and Georgia had written a few top-10 hits of her own, including Keith Urban's "I'm In," which went to No. 2 on the country charts. And, yeah, they were actually dating. I figured that with their Nashville pedigree, we might be able to get onto country radio, but it turned out that the keepers of the genre weren't so eager to let old rockers like me into their territory.

I was on the phone with Gary one day, discussing possible band names, when my new puppy ran out the open back door. I'd picked him up while visiting my old friend Jeff Bouchard in Detroit, who was getting a dog for his kids from a litter of King Charles Spaniels. I decided to get in on the action. I wanted to give my guy a Motor City kind of name, but he was too cuddly for "Marvin" or "Tammy," so I settled on Ryder, as in Mitch Ryder & the Detroit Wheels. There's that "Devil with a Blue Dress" thing again.

When I called Ryder back into the house, Gary happened to be saying, "Georgia and I were hoping for something uplifting, like 'Blue Sky.'" A lightbulb went on. "How about Blue Sky Riders?" I asked. And so it was.

A couple of factors led me to want to be in a band for the first time since the 1970s. One was that I missed the camaraderie and creative stimulation of working with regular partners. The other was loneliness. I was sick of doing Kenny Loggins alone. I wanted to throw myself into something new, challenging, exciting. My experience with Gary when making *How About Now* had been so much fun, and I wanted more of *that*. Follow the fun.

My managers, Gary Borman and Steve Moire, were less thrilled. They'd signed on with me a few years earlier, primarily because I was still a very successful touring entity, a regular cash cow that left them with a good chunk of change at the end of each itinerary. Blue Sky Riders, though, cut my solo touring in half, meaning less money for Gary and Steve, neither of whom was particularly eager to manage a start-up Nashville band, even if it was a KL production. Borman even told me I was too old to start over. "It's a grind, being in a new act," he said. "You'll be back to rental cars, cheap hotels, and stopping by radio stations at all hours in every city you visit. Please reconsider."

But my mind was made up.

I think I convinced Steve, who handled more of my day-to-day affairs, when I said, "If you don't manage us, we'll have to get an outsider and he'll argue with you about everything: conflicting gigs, recording times, everything. And God forbid we actually score a hit record. Then he's going to want me to tour with them, and you're gonna hate that. But if you manage us, we can tour together as both BSR and my solo act. We can keep it in-house. Also, it's good for my head. At the very least, we'll get some great songs out of it."

It worked. They took us on as clients.

The first song Gary, Georgia, and I wrote together, in fact, was inspired by Mr. Borman's pep talk. We called it "Too Old to Dream," but I ultimately felt like that title was a bit too negative, too on the nose, so we shortened it to "Dream." "Leave me in the rain / Send me out to sea /

Wrap me up in chains / Throw away the key / The day I ever get too old to dream."

What at first seemed like a great idea for a band became a difficult reality. For starters, Gary and Georgia lived in Tennessee, which meant we were always commuting to write together. We'd meet for a week or so at a time, at my place or theirs, then record demos of whatever we came up with. I'd take those tapes home and add my own ideas to the mix, though I learned early on not to get too attached to anything I did. We were a group of equals, and sometimes I'd get voted down. I had to be okay with that.

The arrangement was workable . . . for a while. Before too long, Gary and Georgia got married. (I sang one of Georgia's songs, "When the Right One Comes Along," which she'd written for the ABC show *Nashville*, at the wedding. I even arranged a string quartet to accompany me, as a surprise.) This created a solid two-vote coalition that pretty well enforced whatever opinions they held. It would have been better had we lived closer to each other and could hash out our ideas face to face, but that rarely happened.

When it came time to tour, Borman's prediction about how hard it would be for me to start over might even have been understated. One of our early gigs was at a twelve-hundred-seat theater outside of Philadelphia. We sold three hundred tickets. This might have been less shocking had I not been able to move almost ten times that amount as a solo act just down the street. Even when I had Blue Sky Riders open for Kenny Loggins (yeah, I opened for myself), a lot of people didn't realize it was me up there. Our BSR set often got a polite response from a quarter-filled house. Then I'd change clothes and return to the stage as the headliner to thunderous applause. It was kind of a mind-fuck for us all, including the audience.

Blue Sky Riders couldn't always be an opener, though, and our headline gigs made me choose between them or my solo act. Not only did performing alone draw much bigger crowds, but I didn't have to split the gate three ways. On top of that, I had only so much energy to pour into touring, so the decision to promote BSR on the road was often difficult for me to reconcile.

Then there was the resistance from country radio. Once again, Borman's prediction came true: We really were too old to garner serious consideration from programmers, even though much of their fan base was our same age. I pushed Gary and Georgia to write about adult themes that our audience could relate to, and we came up with some gems: "Dream," "No Fool Like an Old Fool," "I'm Feelin' Brave," and our theme song, "I'm a Rider."

On the other hand, Gary was a Beatles fanatic, and once told me he just wanted to write "She Loves You" over and over again. To him that was a perfect, simple song—catchy, fun, and not at all hung up by complex emotions. He was so against confessional lyrics that his business card read: "Gary Burr, songwriter: I make shit up." We spent our entire time together striking a pretty good balance between those respective poles.

One early promotional tour stop gave us a highlight. A *very* high light. Sleep was my nemesis at the time, so my assistant, Shannon, gave me some pot granola bars to help me out, with specific instructions: eat just a small corner at bedtime. It's probably obvious where this is going.

That night I woke up at 4 A.M., hungry. My doctor had recommended that when I found myself awake in the middle of the night, I should eat something to help balance my blood sugar. Well, I saw that granola bar on the counter, and without thinking ate the whole damn thing. Heck, I might have eaten two. I went back to bed without realizing what I'd done, but instead of falling asleep I gradually began to notice that things were getting strange. By 5 A.M. I was definitely tripping. At 5:30 A.M. my manager, Wayne, called. "Rise and shine!" he said. "We have live radio and TV all day today. Pack up—we're out the door in forty minutes."

Oh my God. I wasn't sure I could find my clothes, let alone construct a coherent sentence. There was no way I could fake my way through this. I approached the subject as delicately as possible with him. "Um . . . I can't feel my fingers," I said. "I don't know if I can play the guitar today."

"What are you talking about?" he asked. "Are you having a heart attack?" I told him I was fine, mostly, and spilled the beans about the granola bars.

"You used to play stoned all the time," he snapped. "You can do this. Now get moving." Way to overwhelm me with concern, Wayne.

He was right about having played stoned, but this was 2013 and I'd stopped using marijuana in 1971. I was completely out of practice. I was so high that I saw tracers when I moved my hands. I found myself narrating the action out loud as I got dressed, as a way to make sure I remembered what I was doing. Then, moments later, I heard my words echoing back in my ears as if on delay. "Where are my pants?" I'd say. Pause. *Where are my pants?* I'd hear. What the hell?

I freaked out a little bit and started talking to myself. "This is getting scary," I said. Then that came back, too: *This is getting scary.* My echo was validating the emotion.

It was then that I realized I could actually utilize this odd phenomenon. Maybe if I said positive stuff out loud, that echo would act like a little pep talk. "This is gonna be fun," I said. "It'll make for a great story." When those sentiments returned, it was as if they were a new idea. I know it sounds crazy, but it helped settle my nerves.

Wayne came to pick me up with Gary and Georgia already in the back of the van. Georgia was very straightlaced, not a stoner at all, so I decided not to say anything. I didn't want to worry her, or, worse, have her ask if I was okay every ten minutes.

Luckily, we had a few minutes to practice a song or two in the radio station's greenroom before we went on, and I found myself completely absorbed in the harmonies. By the end I was in a full sweat, having given it everything I had. "Holy shit," I said. "You guys are really good!"

Georgia looked at me sideways. "Are you okay?" she asked.

With that, I no longer worried about forgetting how to play our songs. In my years away from pot I'd forgotten what it was like to play high, how hypnotic becoming fully immersed in the music can be. Fielding questions, however, was another story. I wasn't even tracking my conversations with Gary and Georgia. How the hell were these interviews going to go? I went so far as to pull Gary aside and, after explaining my situation, asked that he jump in if he saw me flailing.

Once we went live, the first question was directed at me. Of course.

"Kenny, you're a great songwriter and I've always wanted to ask this question," she said. "Why do some songs seem to stand the test of time, while others just come and go overnight?"

Well, this was an unexpected philosophical turn. Aha! I thought. This I can do. "I think it's because some songs tell the truth and others don't," I answered. A smattering of applause from the engineers in the room had me feeling pretty good about my answer.

"So," the interviewer continued, "you're saying that 'Louie Louie' told the truth?"

That caught me totally by surprise. I took a breath.

"To some folks, yeah it did," I said. Checkmate. A cheer rose from the room, as if I'd won the first round. With that, it was smooth sailing. Wayne assured me that as the rock star I could be as weird as I wanted to be. Right on. So I was.

After that morning show we went to the local TV station, where we were guesting on *Good Morning Somewhere*, before shifting to a panel-discussion program. It all went pretty darn well. The challenge of staying semi-coherent was exhilarating. We caught a plane for Park City that night, and when I finally made it to bed I was still high. That's when I learned that a bit of THC actually *can* help you sleep—as long as you eat it a day before you want to go to bed. (For what it's worth, Shannon—the assistant who provided me those granola bars—proved valuable in more ways than one. She's now my personal manager.)

When we decided to make a second BSR album, instead of looking for a label deal we funded it through Kickstarter, promising perks like signed T-shirts, pre-release CDs, and even a private home concert for the right price. (A fan in Washington, DC, won that by starting his *own* Kickstarter campaign, with his patrons getting into the show. His mom made snacks for the crowd.)

The fundraising campaign was a success, but it required a hard deadline for a deliverable, which really put pressure on us to finish that album. That was when I began to skip some of our collaborative steps and make my Santa Barbara demos more complete, to the point that they sounded like a finished product. Gary and Georgia felt stuck, because there was no space left for their ideas. Without us all being in the same city, though, we just didn't have time to run everything through our three-way filter.

With that, our "just for fun" approach began to disappear. I started to see that I was taking the whole enterprise way too seriously, pushing us the way I had pushed myself thirty years earlier. When I sat down and thought about what I was really trying to prove, I came up with no satisfying answers. I was already successful. We'd done all we could to get our music heard, and it wasn't working. On top of that, I liked to experiment in the studio, an expensive style of recording that made Gary and Georgia, who were used to cutting three or four demos per session, very nervous. Meanwhile, there just wasn't any gas left in my tank for another low-paying BSR tour.

I spent the better part of six years with Blue Sky Riders, and by the end I remembered why people quit bands. It's just too much. Splitting creativity three ways involves a *lot* of compromise, especially for somebody like me, who'd been a soloist for so many years. To reach those compromises, the final version can become so watered down that it doesn't please anybody. I think we were all relieved when we hung it up.

Still, I really enjoyed writing and singing with Gary and Georgia, which kept me in a creative flow during a time when I really needed it. Our sound was fantastic, and we clicked together so well as writers it was a joy to behold.

Despite my love and respect for the two of them—which still holds, by the way—by the time I went back to being just Kenny Loggins, I appreciated my autonomy more than ever. Turns out I needed that, too.

THE LATTER PART of my career has largely been spent as a legacy act, and it's truly been fruitful. At age seventy I could sell out thousands of theater seats on a regular basis.

Yacht rock helped.

I'm pretty sure the entire genre was started as an internet video meme, but that tag helped categorize the music guys like me and Mike McDonald created naturally as an offshoot of our love for R&B.

As I understand it, the actual yacht rock phenomenon was born from an absurd, super-low-budget internet comedy series, *Yacht Rock*, in 2005 that spoofed the likes of me, McDonald, and Hall & Oates. In one episode, McDonald is crestfallen when I abandon our smooth roots and rock out on "I'm Alright." I buoy him with the line "I've got your life jacket right here—it's called the '80s, and it's gonna be around forever!" (I have to admit laughing at that.) How freakin' prophetic.

Even though they were making fun of us, the guys behind those videos really seemed to be fans. They said they never expected their brainchild to develop into an entire category of pop music, but that's exactly what happened. Michael and I weren't consciously trying to create our own genre, but don't tell them that.

So what is yacht rock, exactly? It's a specific segment of so-called blue-eyed soul. The name has something to do with nautical-themed music that rich guys listen to on their yachts. I know that I do. (Kidding.)

When Loggins & Messina released *Full Sail* in 1974, we inadvertently introduced the image of tropical sailing to rock 'n' roll. Jimmy Buffett's first lyrical nod toward Key West also came out in 1974, and Rod Stewart's "Sailing" was released a year later. Christopher Cross wouldn't hit the charts for another half decade. Jimmy and I were on the goddamn vanguard.

Then again, I've seen "What a Fool Believes" listed as the genre's definitive song, so maybe it was me and McDonald on the vanguard.

On July 12, 2019, *Houstonia* magazine's Timothy Malcolm offered what might be the most complete description of the category:

Yacht rock is music, primarily created between 1976 and '84, that can be characterized as smooth and melodic, and typically combines elements of jazz, rhythm and blues, and rock. You'll hear very little acoustic guitar (get that "Horse with No Name" out of there) but a lot of Fender Rhodes electric piano. Lyrics don't get in the way of the song's usually high musicality (some of the finest Los Angeles session players, including members of the band Toto, play on many yacht rock tunes). The lyrics may, however, speak about fools. The songs are as light and bubbly as champagne on the high seas, yet oddly complex and intellectual.

At the very least, that internet series helped introduce our music to a new generation. Since then, books have been published about yacht rock, multiple podcasts are dedicated to the category, and there are devoted genres on Spotify and Pandora, as well as a channel on Sirius XM. At yachtornyacht.com, the *Yacht Rock* intelligentsia ranked hundreds of songs by their "yachtiness," and I ended up associated with four of the top six, including the overall No. 1: which is the Doobies' version of "What a Fool Believes." Of my thirteen songs on the chart, only one is from post-1982, so I guess my yachty factor took a bit of a dive once I started cranking out soundtrack hits. Come to think of it, my departure for movie rockers is a theme they visit repeatedly throughout the *Yacht Rock* series.

In 2018, I played two sold-out nights at the Hollywood Bowl with Mike McDonald and Christopher Cross. The shows weren't billed as yacht rock, yet hundreds of fans still showed up wearing captain's hats and the occasional sailor suit. We should have taken that shit on the road. There was no doubt by that point that we were cool again.

The renewed interest has shown up in a number of ways. I played myself in *Grand Theft Auto V*, DJ'ing at an in-game radio station that plays, among other songs, "Danger Zone" and "I'm Free." The thing I really hear about, though, is the animated series *Archer* on FX. It's about a semi-competent intelligence agency with a recurring "Danger Zone" theme. Characters say intentionally expositional lines like: "Call Kenny Loggins. Because you're in the danger zone. From *Top Gun*." That started a cascade of references within ensuing episodes that culminated with me playing myself, performing a countrified version of "Danger Zone." They took to calling me "K-Log," and, oddly enough, it kind of stuck.

I also picked up the nickname "Kenny Fuckin' Loggins" from a Funny Or Die short where Paul Scheer tries to get me and the Blue Sky Riders to score different movies using tunes exactly like "Danger Zone" and "Footloose." BSR was just getting started at the time, and it seemed like a good promotional opportunity. I never really thought anything would come of it, but I realized how wrong I was when, at the wedding reception for a close friend's son, I was asked to play "Footloose." When I took the stage, the millennials in the crowd kept yelling, "Kenny Fucking Loggins!" Now *that* was funny.

CHRISTMAS HAS ALWAYS been a big deal for me. As a youngster I felt especially connected to my family during that time, which seemed to give the season a richer sense of purpose. When Eva and I first moved to Santa Barbara, I wanted to recapture that feeling by getting more involved in the community.

I started with a short show at a local club, with donated toys serving as the entry fee. Soon the idea evolved into a night of multiple sets at clubs across town, which let me collect even more toys. I actually had two bands leapfrogging from venue to venue, one setting up while the other one played. At about one-thirty in the morning, after I'd wrapped my final set at a club called Soho, a middle-aged lady came up to me in the parking lot. Her name was Barbara Tellefson, and the question she posed would affect my life for decades to come.

"Do you know where all of those toys go?" she asked. Actually, I didn't. I figured they ended up with local kids in need. Nope. "They're sent out of town," she said. "The organization doing the collecting is national, and none of the toys you gathered tonight will be given to a single kid in Santa Barbara." It turned out that Barbara managed a small organization down-town called the Council of Christmas Cheer, which also collected goods for those in need, and kept it all in Santa Barbara. They were founded in 1917 but somehow I'd never heard of them.

The next day Barbara walked me through their headquarters, a single storage container outside the Catholic Charities building on Haley Street. The place was packed floor to ceiling with items to be distributed through partnerships with organizations like Toys for Tots, the Salvation Army, the Elks Club, and various Rotary clubs. My wheels began to turn, and over the next few nights I dreamed up a plan.

"Let's take this to a bigger stage," I told Barbara. "Cooperation is what makes this so unique. Since you work with so many civic organizations, why not change your name to Christmas Unity?"

She got right on board. We planned a Christmas Unity telethon, courtesy of twenty-four hours of free airtime provided by Bob Smith at KEYT-TV. I played a set with David Foster and my band, and we were off and running.

Christmas Unity grew so quickly that within a year, Barbara had enlarged not only the headquarters but the mission statement. Now we were servicing the needy all year long, not just at Christmastime, so we shortened the name to "Unity." We maintained our annual telethons, and over the years I got the likes of David Crosby and Graham Nash to join me, along with Mike McDonald, Michael Bolton, and Marilyn Martin. With help from veteran telethon producer Joe Lake, our donations jumped from $40,000 to $700,000.

As of this writing, I've been involved with Unity for more than thirty-five years, and even though Barbara passed away a few years ago, it continues to thrive. (Brad Paisley worked with Barbara to start his own version of Unity in Nashville.)

In the winter of 2018, Santa Barbara experienced a major fire that burned more than 250,000 acres, caused more than $2 billion in damage (including one thousand homes), and forced more than a hundred thousand residents to evacuate. About a month later, the day after my seventieth birthday, in fact, we felt the aftermath: a series of mudslides that killed twenty-three people and destroyed 129 houses in town. I was proud when Unity serviced an incredible number of people in the days to follow, distributing food, clothing, and essential supplies.

Almost everyone in my Santa Barbara suburb of Montecito was touched by the disaster. Everybody seemed to know someone who'd been hurt or killed in the mud, and the grief was palpable. Weeks later, authorities were still finding bodies in the debris, assisted by a group of volunteers calling themselves the Bucket Brigade.

One day, I received a call from three teens asking whether I might headline a talent contest they were producing to raise money for survivor aid. I loved the idea of activist teenagers creating their own show, and thought the concept was compelling enough to sell tickets without me on the bill. So instead of performing with them, I helped produce their show, called "Teens Sing for Santa Barbara." I convinced them that instead of a competition, it should be a show of unity—kids singing with each other rather than against each other. Their motto, "We are stronger together," was picked up by KEYT-TV as a rallying cry for a number of significant events. They raised more than $70,000.

I chose to highlight those stories here because they illustrate how much good can be enacted by a community that cares. The stories aren't about me but about Santa Barbara, and all the people willing to devote time and effort to making it a better place. It all reinforces what a great decision it was to move to this town way back when.

I DON'T WANT to end this book without acknowledging my kids, because that's who I'm really writing it for, and whose influence I have most strongly felt over the years. Being a touring musician cost me untold time with each of them, but I always tried to make the most of what we had. I still do.

In 2006, I toured with my oldest son, Crosby, as my opening act. He was twenty-five then, and already an accomplished singer-songwriter. I'm pretty sure he didn't actually want to accompany me on the road, but I was wrestling with some demons after my second divorce, and knew that just seeing him backstage would make my heart feel lighter. I suspect he agreed to the idea mostly to keep an eye on me. He's always been sensitive like that.

Crosby knew my audience would be biased toward him. He was never sure whether a warm reception—and he got many of them—was because they actually liked his music or because it was my son up there performing with his pop. You know, "Isn't that sweet? It must be bring-your-son-to-work day in the Loggins house."

But here's the thing: Crosby was really good. He is an excellent song-writer and performer, but I always worried he might be doing it mostly to get my attention. I suspect that's the motivation behind many second-generation performers. They try to speak their parents' language to improve their chances of being heard and seen. But I *did* see Crosby—always had—although it might not always have been obvious. I under-stand now how my having to travel for a living could have been difficult for Crosby when he was a child.

He kept at it, though, and in 2008 won the MTV talent show *Rock the Cradle*, with his victory lap being a performance of his song "Good Enough." Even at a high point of his musical career, Crosby's song selection confessed ambivalence about his journey. "Can't fill the shoes that somebody else wore," he sang. "They'll never fit, they don't belong to me." I can't help but think it was written about us, though he insists it wasn't.

Either way, I saw it coming.

A year or so earlier, Croz had been in the wings at one of my shows, and came over as I walked offstage. The audience was still on its feet call-ing for an encore, and he somehow seemed upset by that. Crosby had been paying his own dues on the road, struggling as the opening act for blues guitarist Joe Bonamassa, whose harder-edged audience was not neces-sarily attuned to the more sensitive, acoustic stuff Crosby had to offer. He'd been a one-man band, driving alone in the middle of winter through the bleak, freezing landscape. I could see the wear on him. He'd clearly learned that paying dues was not as glamorous as it once had seemed.

As the applause died down, he took my hand. "Dad," he said softly, "why won't you just . . . fade away?"

I thought the fact that I was still at it well into my sixties was a good example of tenacity and perseverance. Instead, I'd inadvertently become the primary obstacle to Crosby's success, at least in his mind. He was sick of being Kenny Loggins's kid, wanting only an audience, somewhere, who wouldn't compare him to me. When you're standing in a shadow it's hard to find daylight.

Crosby quit the business just a year or two after his MTV victory. He informed me of his decision with tears in his eyes—not out of regret, but because he felt like he had somehow failed me. "Dad, I don't want to have your life," he confessed. "I'm done struggling for something I don't really want."

I was actually relieved to hear it. As far as I could tell, he'd never seemed happy as a professional musician.

"Good," I said softly. "I don't need you to have a music career for me. I'll love you no matter what you do."

Crosby is now a successful owner of his own IT business in Santa Barbara. He loves his work and seems far more comfortable in his own skin than when he was trying to wear mine.

WHEN CODY, MY SECOND CHILD with Eva, was a teenager, he came on the road with me and helped crew some of my shows. He'd stayed with Eva after the divorce, and we'd been somewhat estranged ever since. I tried to see the kids at least twice a month when I wasn't touring, but that left a lot of ground to make up, which is what made his decision to join my tour so exciting. He earned respect from the crew as a hard worker, and even traveled on the crew bus despite his six-foot-nine frame being far too big for any of the bunks. Cody insists that he loved that life. A few shows into the itinerary, he found me backstage and opened up. "Dad," he said excitedly, "I just realized you're a rock star!" It must have been like learning that your father is secretly Batman or something. All of Cody's life I'd been disguised as plain ol' Dad, the mild-mannered reporter for the *Daily Planet*. (Yeah, I mixed my Batman and Superman metaphors. Sue me.)

For years after my divorce from Eva, the loss of my relationship with Cody was a source of deep sadness for me. In an act of unforgivable stupidity, our arbitrator insisted that each of our children pick which parent they wanted to live with. It was a no-win situation for everybody involved. No matter which parent they chose, it felt like a betrayal of the other one to the kid doing the choosing.

Cody was eight years old at the time. He and Eva were very close, and it was obvious to me that he would opt to live with her. She was his stable shelter, and I was always on the road. He was angry, and it was difficult for me to get through to him during those years, especially after Eva moved to Los Angeles to start over. It wasn't long before the kids rebelled at the thought of making the ninety-minute commute between our homes each weekend. Not fully comprehending the consequences of my decision, I foolishly backed off and let them stay put, satisfying myself with bi-monthly visits instead.

I numbed the pain of our distance with work and my life in Santa Barbara with Julia. I wouldn't let myself fully acknowledge how much it hurt until about five years later, during a writing session in Chicago with Richard Marx. We'd sat together in his kitchen the night before and talked about the stuff going on in our lives. It was there that I confessed how much my distance from Cody bothered me, and openly wondered whether our rift could be repaired. By the time I made it to Richard's music room the next morning, he'd already worked up a beautiful melody on the piano. It was perfect for expressing my feelings about Cody, I thought. I rifled through my journal until I found a couple of lines I'd written about our relationship some months earlier: *Though you and I are distant, don't ever think I didn't want you, or miss you every day.*

As the song emerged, the truth of the pain I'd been trying to ignore revealed itself, and I began to cry. Every word went straight to my heart, each line confessing pain and regret. Soon Richard was crying, too. That day we wrote: "No matter where life takes you / Know that I'll still be waiting here for you / And the day that you've forgiven me, my son / The one that got away."

For months I couldn't sing that song without tears. I wasn't about to perform it without Cody's consent, so when he came out on tour with me, I called him into my rental car and played the cassette Richard and I had recorded. Talk about cathartic. Now it was Cody and me crying. He listened intently to the entire thing, then paused for some long moments. "Thank you, Dad," he finally said. I think of that as the beginning of our reconnection, our first steps toward healing the wounds of the divorce. And yeah, he gave me permission to play "The One That Got Away" in concert.

A few years later Cody moved into my guest house, and we got to know each other all over again. In the pool one day, I noticed the word "unconditional" tattooed on the inside of his forearm. I'd had no idea it was there. That's the pivotal word from "Cody's Song," which I'd written as a promise to him when he was only four years old and released on my *Leap of Faith* album. It is still my promise. Every time I see that tattoo, I feel honored. "Unconditional" is a good word to remember.

When Cody was eight, my astrologer friend Chakripani predicted that he would be our "late bloomer." Sure enough, when Cody was in his early thirties he came to me and said sadly, "Nothing excites me. All your other kids have something they're passionate about, but I have no idea. And I don't know what to do about it." He'd spent the previous decade in the hospitality industry, doing everything from waiting tables to managing restaurants. None of it was what he wanted for his life. I assured him that someday his passion would show itself. Just a couple of months later it did.

Cody's current career began when a friend dared him to take the stage during open mic night at an LA comedy club, and he killed it. It turned out that Cody had been keeping notes for years—bits and pieces of comic ideas—as a hobby. On that stage he pieced them together to great effect. That's when he knew comedy was what he wanted to do, so he and I made a plan. We decided to treat this like college. Cody would move to LA to study stand-up with Craig Shoemaker, who'd opened for me in the 1980s, and comedy writing and improv with the Groundlings and the Upright Citizens Brigade. Today he works with a comedy production team out of LA, and loves it. Cody's following his passion now, and from where I sit, he's happier than ever.

BELLA HAS ALWAYS been my hands-on-the-hips, ass-kickin' girl. Eva and I both viewed Isabella as an elegant, feminine name, and I figured I'd call her Izzy. It didn't take. Before she was five years old, our daughter told us she wanted to be called Bella, and that was that. Never one for frills, when Bella's nanny asked her to be the flower girl at her wedding, she agreed, but only if she could wear her cowgirl costume, including holstered six-guns. The pistols were a nice touch.

Like Crosby, Bella was in love with music. She graduated from Wesleyan University as a music major, though she never pursued it as an occupation. She did, however, sing on two of my children's albums. I loved her rich second alto, which blended perfectly with the alto of her younger sister, Hana.

When Bella was six, she took up the drums. (I bought her a cheap kit, with the deal that they'd live at her mother's house. Seemed fair to me.) That fit her temperament nicely. Never demure, she loved making a big noise. In middle school, Bella took to sagging her pants down below her boxer shorts and wearing either skater shoes or work boots. She always had a swagger to her style, which I often referred to as her Bella-ness. She was a skateboarder and a darn good surfer, and strove to beat her brothers at everything. Usually, she did.

She also beat them at music, in at least one way. When Bella was in the eighth grade, she, Crosby, and I went to the National Association of Music Merchants convention in LA, a showcase for the latest tech in musical instruments. As we passed by the DW Drums booth, somebody from the company chased after us shouting, "Miss, miss . . . do you play the drums?"

"Um, yes I do," Bella replied, a bit flummoxed by the sudden attention.

"We'd like you to be the poster girl for our ads," he said. He must have really liked her look.

I knew an opportunity when I saw one. "Are there drums in the deal?" I asked.

"Sure are," he said, "and cymbals and a stool!"

"I'm in," said Bella, and just like that she became the face of that year's "Hit Like a Girl" campaign. Crosby and I left NAMM that day with nothin'. Bella got an endorsement deal. Go figure.

Today Bella is in real estate development, specializing in building workforce housing. Anything she sets her mind to, she does. It's her Bella-ness.

IN 1993, LUKAS, my first child with Julia, was born at home, in the bedroom of our rented cottage on the beach in Santa Barbara. Julia's delivery team was the quintessential New Age support group: a midwife, a chiropractor, an acupuncturist, a psychic, and, of course, me. The delivery took a grueling thirty-six hours. I like to say that it was a difficult birth because our future ballplayer came out with a baseball bat in his hand and a Yankees cap on his head. I have a running joke about how the first time I threw a baseball to Crosby, he ducked, which is when I knew he was a musician. Luke, on the other hand, played catch from the time he was four years old. This kid had amazing hand-eye coordination from the get-go.

While music was central to my relationship with some of my kids, Luke and I were all about baseball (though basketball snuck in from time to time). He was my third son, just as I was a third son, and our relationship was similar to the one I had with my dad. Luke was the only member of my brood to watch *Field of Dreams* with me. Twice. There really is something magical about playing catch with your son (or "having a catch," as Kevin Costner called it in the film). I'll probably want to have a catch with Luke on my deathbed.

Whereas my other kids turned to Barney the dinosaur for comfort, baby Luke preferred watching a Betamax video of Rod Carew hitting the same pitch, over and over, on an endless loop. That was his first meditation teacher: Rod Carew. When Luke woke up crying at three in the morning it was Uncle Rod who soothed him. (Alternatively, when Crosby was a baby, Maurice White was *his* guru. When he was up at night, we'd dance to Earth Wind and Fire till the wee hours. If I dared stop, he'd start screaming all over again. It was like a scene from *They Shoot Horses, Don't They?* Dance or suffer the terrors of the undead. We were a regular zombie dance party.)

When Luke was eight, I taught him to do a full pitcher's windup, like Koufax and Drysdale, the same way I did as a teenager. We broke down each part of it like it was a dance step, from holding his hands over his head to kicking his left leg up high. During Little League tryouts, one of the managers came up to me excitedly and said, "My God, I haven't seen anyone wind up like that since Warren Spahn." Talk about a proud papa. Luke played competitively all the way through high school. On May 9, 2012, John Zant wrote in the *Santa Barbara Independent*: "Hit singles are common throughout Kenny Loggins's musical repertoire, but they are rare when his son is performing on the mound for the Dos Pueblos High baseball team." Ya gotta love that.

As a child Luke was always soft-spoken and gentle, but on the mound he was fierce. These days he has applied that fierceness to his education. Each step of the way has been guided by his belief that if you follow your joy, your spirit will lead you where you belong. He is studying environmental philosophy at Pacifica Graduate Institute, home of the Joseph Campbell Library. Campbell, of course, was the guy who coined the phrase "Follow your bliss." Perfect.

MY FIFTH CHILD, Hana Aluna, was born four years after Luke, also at home, but much more quickly, thank God. As a matter of fact, Hana damn near jumped out of the womb, all but declaring, "Here I am folks, ready or not." They (Hana is nonbinary and uses they/them pronouns) had a two-hour birth, arriving even before the midwife, who was stuck in traffic. The night before Hana was born, I had a dream that ended with the message: "She will be born into the hands of Mary." Being a Catholic school survivor, I ran out and got a statue of the BVM—Blessed Virgin Mary—to put next to Julia's Quan Yin in the bathroom.

Just before Hana arrived, we received a spontaneous visit from Julia's longtime best friend and massage therapist, Mary Sullivan. Upon hearing Julia's screams from the bedroom, Mary raced in, eyes as big as Frisbees, and said, "Oh my God, what's happening?"

"We're having a fucking baby," I answered. "What does it look like?" I was breathing in and out with Julia between contractions, holding her head, my face near hers, keeping her totally focused on the job at hand. "Have you ever caught a baby?" I asked. I was serious; Julia's friends all seemed like pioneer women to me. Mary looked as if I'd told her to drop and give me twenty. "Um, no," she stammered.

"Well, go wash your hands. You're about to."

Mary scrubbed up, and before she knew it Hana slipped 'n' slid her way right into her hands. That's the kind of person Hana is. They get right to the point.

Hana is a born singer. I first realized this when they were four years old and I was driving them around Santa Barbara. Suddenly a voice in the back seat began singing along with Beyonce on the radio, matching her lick for lick. It was my kid! In her car seat! "That's it, girl, you're a musician!" I yelped.

Hana is named after the little town on Maui that Julia and I so loved, and their middle name is taken from the female deity of the Kogis, the last pre-Columbian tribe still living in South America. Their names invoke spirituality and perseverance. They've always been a seeker, a questioner, and a challenger, and even spent a year as a born-again Christian. They may not yet fully understand this world, but they sure know why they're here.

Hana possesses all the attributes essential for somebody who is sensitive, even by singer-songwriter standards: a tender heart, tons of empathy, and a wistful melancholy that permeates every note they sing. My wise child can make "Happy Birthday" break your heart. They grew up next to me in the studio, singing background vocals on several of my records. Their voice is especially prominent on my children's albums. Our version of having a catch was to spend an hour or two doing vocal warm-ups together.

I've always believed that an important part of my role as father is to recognize each of my kids' talents, and supply tools to nurture those gifts. This is why I bought Hana a keyboard as soon as their little fingers were big enough to fit on the keys. They gobbled up lessons, and as I saw their talent emerge, I was eager to teach them everything I could about music and songwriting. Hana's sensitivity taught me to slow my approach and be gentle with my coaching, always leading with a positive comment or two before offering suggestions about how to improve. In that way, they taught me how to mentor other young artists. Artists aren't like athletes;

you don't have to work them to death in order to achieve perfection. They must be gentled like wild horses, which are quick to buck and run if you approach too impatiently. Hana taught me how to balance constructive criticism with honest praise.

When Hana was ten, we worked up the classic duet "For Good" from our favorite Broadway play, *Wicked*, to sing at their school fundraiser. When we reached the lines "Who can say if I've been changed for the better / Because I knew you, I have been changed for good," there wasn't a dry eye in the room. I'll always cherish that moment. These days, they write and record music under the name Hana Aluna. It's just another sign of their independence; Hana didn't use Loggins because they want to make sure people love their music on its merits, and not for the name.

IT WAS BACKSTAGE at a fundraiser for first responders after the big Santa Barbara fire that I met Lisa Hawkins. Lisa was the mother of Hunter, one of the many talented teens I'd been coaching. I'd seen her in town a few times, but until that afternoon she was just another mom from the teenage choir. Just before I went onstage, I happened to look up and caught her glancing back at me. I swear her eyes sparkled like a special effect in a Nicholas Sparks romance movie. A voice in my head offered clear instructions: "Ask her if she's ready to date yet." I was surprised by my own intuition, especially the word "yet." Yet? I thought to myself. Why "yet"?

I didn't know anything about Lisa other than she was Hunter's mom and single, but I decided to act. A week or two later, I saw her dropping off Hunter at rehearsal, and approached her car. Poking my head into the open passenger window, I said, "Hello again. I wonder . . . are you dating?"

"Not yet," she said. I damn near fell over. There was the word "yet" again. I took it as a sign that something was going to happen between us, whether she knew it or not. Unfortunately, Hunter was best friends with my daughter Hana, who managed to convince her that I was a womanizer (although by that point I decidedly was not). Hunter convinced Lisa, and Lisa kept on turning me down. So I waited and persisted, even as she kept ducking my approaches.

Oddly, the deciding factor came when I butt-dialed her. Lisa texted me back: "Are you trying to reach me?" I responded: "I guess my butt went around my head and committed emotional mutiny." Then I called her, and the next thing I knew we were meeting for coffee. We skipped the small-talk entirely, diving in deep from the very start. We spoke effortlessly for hours. (Lisa didn't yet know what coffee does to me.) We've been pretty much inseparable ever since.

After the drama of my split with Julia, I never thought I'd fall this deeply in love again. Then again, I've always said that my heart has a mind of its own. (Apparently, so does my butt.) Even after all I've been through in love and loss, my commitment is still to my heart—to listen and follow it when it calls. That doesn't mean it's always been easy, but thankfully Lisa is nurturing, patient, and loves family as much as I do. And hot, too. Hi, honey :)

I really appreciate how much my kids, their partners and wives, and three grandchildren (and counting, hopefully) love each other and want to be together. It might just be time for a bigger dining room table next Christmas.

IN JANUARY 2018, I turned seventy. We planned a big party at a local Santa Barbara nightclub called the Red Piano, with a guest list that included friends from nearly every stage of my life. My kids would be there, and, for the first time in the same room since my first divorce, both of my ex-wives.

I also invited many of the best musicians I'd ever played with, for what I figured would end up as an epic jam session. I usually live for that kind of thing, but as the big day approached I felt more and more anxious, even angry, though I couldn't put my finger on why. Sure, crossing seventy is a big fucking deal. Maybe that was it, but I suspected there was more to it. I still felt as young as I did at fifty, so it wasn't a mortality thing.

The night before the event I found myself storming back and forth across the house, irrational and pissed off, actually yelling out loud about how I wanted to cancel the whole damn thing. Then I started to vomit. At first I thought it was food poisoning, but by the time the sun came up I hadn't slept a wink, and wondered if it was something else. What if this was all emotional? Softened by retching and fatigue, I realized that I didn't want to go to my own party, and it was making me sick.

That's when it hit me. My real struggles were with the Kenny Loggins part of the evening. I didn't want *that* guy running the show. I didn't want him there at all. I know that sounds crazy. Let me explain.

When I was a kid, I tried to be socially acceptable by imitating my brother Danny, the cool member of the family. I set about changing all the things about me he would ridicule, which covered just about everything. I dressed like him and acted like him, adopting one affect after the other until my true self was thoroughly disguised. The older I got the better I became at it, and the deeper that little kid was buried.

As I went through high school I learned how to mask a lot of insecurities. Ears too big? Grow my hair. Chin too small? Grow a beard. When I found success with Loggins & Messina, people's rock-star impression of me carried the rest of the load. Suddenly, I was cool despite myself—and I liked it. The same girls who'd never given me the time of day were suddenly interested. Guys wanted to chat me up. I was invited to all the parties. How could I want anything else?

I hadn't had to earn people's attention for many years. They just gave it to me, or at least the person I was pretending to be. Which was precisely the problem. I was about to turn seventy and had spent virtually my entire life disowning the shy, awkward kid inside of me. That kid—the one who was never cool enough or smart enough, who I was taught to be ashamed of as a teenager—was actually the reason I made music. He was the part of me that felt everything deeply and managed to turn my childhood pain into songs. He'd written them for me. All of them. I think that's why so much of my music has been widely embraced: it's based on issues we all struggle with. We're confused. We're alone. We're afraid. We're uncool.

For most of my life I thought that kid was too embarrassing to take to a party like this. It's why I created the guy everybody knows today as Kenny Loggins. In my thirties and forties, I even convinced myself that I *was* that alter ego. Now, though, I could see that had never really been the case. It was my embarrassing self, my uncool self, my big-eared, crew-cutted self who had earned my stardom. As the sun rose on the day of my party, I finally understood that this celebration was for *him*, the guy who knew how to *feel* his life and had the courage to write about it. I was seventy fucking years old and wanted to come clean, to drop it all and just be me. The thought both excited and terrified me, and as soon as I realized it my night of nausea dissipated. For the first time in days I felt fine. I knew what I had to do.

That's how my birthday became a coming-out party for the part of myself I'd always tried to hide. I didn't want to be Kenny Loggins that night. If it meant I wasn't going to sing at my own jam session, that would have to be okay. I just wanted to be Kenny, the kid from long before Messina and McDonald and all those soundtrack hits. Not only that, I needed to acknowledge him publicly.

Which is what I did. I spent about fifteen minutes that night speaking off the cuff to the crowd about the part of me that has been in charge all along—"the feeling part of me, not the image part of me," as I put it. I talked about no longer wanting to hide my essential self, or be embarrassed by my own naiveté. I've spent my career with a mic in my hand; up until that night it was always in service to my persona. My birthday party was where I finally turned the tables.

"I didn't want to come here and be Kenny Loggins," I told my guests. "I didn't even want to come here at all. I think what's happening to me is that Kenny—the kid I was, not Kenny Loggins the rock star—is showing up more and more. When I see my life in front of me, I realize that it was Kenny who did all of this, not Kenny Loggins. I owe my music to him; I owe my friends and my family to him."

I had created Kenny Loggins to feel acceptable, even loveable. That was who the world had come to know. Now I wanted to get back to what I once had been, before I'd experienced a lick of success.

Which, starting with that speech and continuing with this book, is exactly what I've set out to do.

AFTERWORD

FOR YEARS NOW, I've been reluctant to receive lifetime achievement awards because of the clear "I'm done now" signal they send, not only to the audience, but to myself. I felt kind of the same way about writing my memoirs. For the longest time, I thought I wouldn't write my story until it was close to the end. With a belief like that, no wonder I've been putting this off.

As I approached this final segment of the book, I found myself reluctant to start writing for fear of finishing. I didn't want my story to end, because there's still so much to come. As Yogi Berra said, "It ain't over till it's over." And it ain't over yet.

Yeah, I'm getting up there in years. I tire out more quickly than I used to, and more parts of me seem to ache with each passing morning. Every time I get together with my pal (and ex-keyboard player) Steve Wood, he says, "Okay, five minutes for the organ recital." That's our allotment for complaints about our ailments, after which the topic is officially off limits for the day.

Speaking of aging, a few years back I began to notice that my vocal range seemed to decrease with practically every show. It got to the point that I could barely sing "This Is It." I was embarrassed that I no longer possessed what I once had, and was terrified by the idea of being exposed onstage.

So in 2021 I signed up for my first-ever singing lessons. My trainer, a highly respected SoCal vocal coach named Ken Stacey, informed me it was not my vocal chords that were the problem, but my technique. I'd never needed technique to sing; my voice was always strong enough to do whatever I wanted it to. When I got older, though, that lack of precision began to get in my way. Ken taught me his version of the bel canto operatic method, which coordinates breath with the muscles that control it. At first I thought the whole thing was a waste of time. My ego struggled with the idea that I was just now learning how to sing. You're Kenny Fucking Loggins, I thought. You already know how to sing.

After only a few lessons, though, I realized that Ken was right. With his direction, my voice *was* improving. With a year's worth of focused dedication, I now have higher notes than when I was forty. Take "Nobody's Fool," with its incredibly high chorus that was the peak of my range back when it came out in 1988. It was such a difficult song that I never performed it live, because I was never sure I could pull it off. Well, it's finally in my set list. Last year, after nearly every gig, people came up to me and said something along the lines of, "My God, you sound just like you did when you were thirty."

Singing is only part of it. I need to keep creating music to stay good in my head. I once read that Stephen King has to write some crazy amount of words each day or he'll get depressed. My first thought was that I don't want to be around Stephen King when he's depressed. My second thought was that the idea actually makes sense. When Columbia dropped me in 1998, I spent close to a year in a fog, trying to figure out what to do with the rest of my life. I was adrift and unhappy until Julia convinced me to get back into the studio using our savings. Just like that, my depression cleared up.

Now that I'm not making music regularly, due to a combination of the pandemic and having stepped away from the industry (and it from me), it feels like I'm playing hooky from my real life. I keep thinking about the Talking Heads lines: ". . . this is not my beautiful house / . . . this is not my beautiful wife / . . . my god, what have I done?" It all leads back to one burning question: Can I retire and stay sane?

Well, it depends on your definition of retirement. I've noticed that many of my older friends, especially men who've had some success, fear becoming irrelevant. The need to remain important seems to permeate everything, even after retirement. If I'm no longer playing the game, how do I maintain it? For me, getting off of the industry hamster wheel has actually been freeing. I no longer have to hustle to sell records—no more early-morning or late-night media hits, no crazy tour itineraries dragging my energy ever downward. I had to confront that reality with Blue Sky Riders, when my old habits consumed me to the point that Gary and Georgia called a time-out. I was running my old drill of shaking every hand I could at every station that would have us in every town we visited, never stopping to think about *why* I did it. It's just what you do to succeed, right? Well, maybe not. My partners didn't want the same version of success I was habitually chasing.

For me, the problem was that my definition of success needed updating. At this point in my life, the struggle for the kind of acclaim I knew in the '80s is a waste of energy. Commercial success is not the measure of a man—or even the measure of success, really. These days self-fulfillment is my goal, and creativity is my path to get there.

I've been at this long enough to ask a reasonable question: At age seventy-four, do I still have it? I think I got my answer a couple of years back when I wrote the theme song for the San Diego Zoo's closed-circuit TV channel, which is broadcast into hundreds of children's hospitals and Ronald McDonald Houses around the world. (I collaborated on the song with Lisa Harriton and Josh Bartholomew, who were nominated for an Academy Award for "Everything Is Awesome" from *The Lego Movie*.) While we were writing the song, I kept imagining myself as a sick child in a hospital someplace, waking up every day wondering what's next. That was my inspiration. I wanted to give those kids a positive message when they turned on the TV, and the song we came up with, "The Great

Adventure," includes the lines: "You gotta be brave like a lion / Strong like a tiger / Leave the fear far behind / Take your hand and I'll give you mine . . . / Are you ready for a great adventure?"

The zoo folks loved it, and so did I; in 2021, I added it to my set list. It always gets a great response, which is all the reassurance I need. Yeah, I can still do this. My muse still sings.

The pandemic has kept me isolated from potential co-writers, and I miss that process a lot. Collaboration has always been a key for fresh inspiration. The Grammy-winning writer-producer Trevor Horn once said that "genius is in the Rolodex," and I don't disagree. As soon as I can get back into rooms with other writers, I'll jump at the opportunity.

Ultimately, it's all a balancing act. As important as creativity is to my sense of well-being, I also don't want to make music that no one will hear. If I write something I'm proud of, getting it out into the world still feels important to me. Streaming services open up a lot of options, although tallying the number of followers a new song attracts can be the door to the abyss. Stardom comes and goes. Pop culture is a fickle lover. Let it go. The process is still more important than anything else, including the results.

Our lives are made of seasons, and this book does not spell the end. I'm just progressing to a new season of exploration. As long as I stay emotionally present and write about what I really feel, then fuck relevance.

To quote my own song: "I'm alright. Don't nobody worry 'bout me."

Kenny Loggins
Santa Barbara, January 2022

ACKNOWLEDGMENTS

For me, book writing has always been a solitary affair. Once I had the research and interviews in hand, I'd lock myself in my basement office and set to writing. Alone.

"Alone" is not how Kenny works. Loggins is a natural collaborator, a detail made obvious by the song credits on his hits: Messina, McDonald, Manchester. They're virtually all written with somebody else. Kenny realized a long time ago that harnessing the creative power of a partner can unlock your own creativity in new and unexpected ways, and that sure was the case here. Based on hundreds of hours of interviews between us, I wrote a manuscript. Then Kenny rewrote the manuscript. Then I rewrote his rewrites.

To me, the remarkable part is what came next. We read the entire book together, out loud, one line at a time, to see how it all felt. The amount of inspiration derived from effectively turning these pages into a conversation was astounding. We ended up freewheeling on a zillion topics that may or may not have been related to the subject at hand. We jarred some long-hidden memories. We came up with some really good stuff. So thanks, Kenny, for a process unlike any in which I've ever participated.

We started this project in person, but by the time our pitch sold we were in full lockdown. Every conversation since then—and there have been a *lot* of them—has been over Zoom. I spent so much time talking to Kenny over my computer that my kids took to coming home from school, poking their heads into my office and saying "Hi, Kenny," as a matter of course. Thanks to them, and to my wife, Laura, for effectively welcoming a new member of the family.

Thanks to my agent, Jud Laghi, for setting this whole thing up, and to Richard Abate at 3Arts, and to Kenny's right-hand, Shannon Trotta, for keeping everything organized on the back end. To our editor at Hachette,

Brant Rumble: Thanks, man, for laughing a lot and keeping this just as easy as it was.

J. T.

WHEN LOGGINS & MESSINA were stuck in a snowstorm back in our early days as an opening act, with an irate crowd in rural Maine growing antsy for a headliner that would not show up and rocks being thrown through our dressing-room windows, I shouted at Jim Messina: "This is fucked up, man. I didn't sign up for this!"

Jimmy calmly responded, "Yeah, this is a lousy way to make a million dollars."

I stood immediately corrected.

My version of that lesson, the one that I've tried to explain in this book, is "Follow the fun." If you love what you're doing, you'll get good at it. And if you're good at it, somebody is going to hire you. Get great at it, and somebody might pay you a bunch of money to do it for them. Bottom line: as long as you love it, whatever it is, you're going to be happy.

If you're thinking about show biz as a career, though, be warned: being a rock star is not the way out of your life, but it's a sure way into one. To survive the phoniness and sycophancy, the public scrutiny and social pressures, you must cultivate a firm sense of yourself, of your authenticity. That's not as easy as it sounds; the path to becoming an authentic person is iced over with the illusions that come with fame. If your life becomes an act, and if everyone applauds that act, it's a thousand times harder to be a real person. Realness is the opposite of show business. I have strived over the years to become more authentic on and off stage, and have found that the more real I become, the more an audience can relate to my music. In that way, my songs have become everyone's songs.

It started early. One Christmas, my folks gave me a yellow 45 rpm record by Bugs Bunny called "What's Up, Doc?" That same Christmas, my brother Danny gave me "Green Door" by rockabilly pioneer Jim Lowe. Danny had already showed me songs like "Hound Dog" by Elvis Presley, and "Blue Suede Shoes" by Carl Perkins, which even at a young age I could tell were vastly superior. But I still liked "Green Door" more than "What's Up, Doc?" that's for sure.

Thanks to Danny and my other brother, Bob, I grew up on everything from folk to rock, and even some country now and then. Little Richard opened the door to the R&B of the 1950s and early '60s. Sam Cooke to James Brown to Aretha: I loved it all. With all of that early rock and soul music as my cradle language, it was natural for me to become a moving musical target, morphing from style to style, never satisfied to be just one thing. My shape-shifting drove Columbia Records crazy. If they couldn't define me, how could they market me? But it was my ability to be a chameleon that allowed me to change with the times. It's probably why I'm still standing.

Thanks to those who took the time to speak with us: Merel Bregante, Bobby Colomby, Mac Elsensohn, Denzyl Feigelson, Don Ienner, Doug Ingoldsby, Dan Loggins, Dann Lottermoser, Melissa Manchester, Jim Messina, Terry Nelson, Johnny Palazzotto, Lee Phillips, Dean Pitchford, Adam Reader, Jimmy Recor, Guy and Jenny Thomas, and Marnie Walker. Thanks also to Shannon Trotta at Higher Vision Management, Chris Burke at Reliant Talent Agency, project manager Mark Driscoll, Michael Jensen and Ryan Romenesko at Jensen Communications, webmaster extraordinaire Alyssa Factor, Janet Rovison (my fan club president since 1997), and Melinda Williams.

It is hard to believe, but my touring days will soon be coming to a close. Instead of just disappearing, though, Lisa has encouraged me to embrace blockchain technology as a way to stay creatively connected with my fans. It would allow me to send content directly and interact in ways that enrich our connection. I've got a lifetime of stories, photos, and experiences as well as exclusive, never-released music to share. I believe Bitcoin and NFTs will be changing what is possible for the music industry, and who knows . . . you might even find me in the Metaverse.

Ultimately, this book is dedicated to my children, and to their children. You all are why I wrote it. In my many years as a "traveling salesman," rock 'n' roll has taken me far, far away, and the long way home. Just like the "hunter-gatherers" of Julia's metaphor, I've always loved coming back home to you all, where we cook the wooly mammoth and assemble for the feast.

K. L.

CREDITS

"Conviction of the Heart" written by Kenny Loggins and Guy Thomas, published by Gnossos Music and Southshore Music, courtesy of Alfred Music and Hal Leonard.

"Dream" written by Kenny Loggins, Gary Burr, and Georgina Middleman, published by Gnossos Music, Adave Music, and Slattery Songs, courtesy of Alfred Music and Do Write Music, LLC.

"Fever Dream" written by Kenny Loggins and Maurice T. Muehleisen, published by Gnossos Music, courtesy of Alfred Music.

"Footloose" written by Kenny Loggins and Dean Pitchford, published by Milk Money Music, administered by Sony/ATV Ensign Music, courtesy of Alfred Music and Hal Leonard.

"The Great Adventure" written by Kenny Loggins, Lisa Rae Harriton, and Joshua Bartholomew, published by Gnossos Music, Elle Trane Music, and Royal Rebel Music.

"I'm Alright" written by Kenny Loggins, published by Milk Money Music, courtesy of Alfred Music.

"It's About Time" written by Kenny Loggins and Michael McDonald, published by Gnossos Music and Genevieve Music/Kobalt Music, courtesy of Alfred Music and Hal Leonard.

"The One That Got Away" written by Kenny Loggins and Richard Marx, published by Gnossos Music and Chi-Boy Music, courtesy of Alfred Music and Hal Leonard.

"The Real Thing" written by Kenny Loggins and David Foster, published by Milk Money Music and Air Bear Music, courtesy of Alfred Music and Hal Leonard.

"Return to Pooh Corner" written by Kenny Loggins, published by Universal Music Corporation, courtesy of Hal Leonard.

"Sweet Reunion" written by Kenny Loggins and Steve Wood, published by Gnossos Music and Albedo Music, courtesy of Alfred Music and Albedo Music.

"Truth Is" written by Kenny Loggins and Beth Nielsen Chapman, published by Gnossos Music and Songs of Prismlight Music, courtesy of Alfred Music and Karen Schauben Publishing Administration.

"Whisky" written by Kenny Loggins, published by Universal Music Corporation, courtesy of Hal Leonard.

6/2022

$30.00